The Nature of Things

The Nature of Things

Rediscovering the Spiritual in God's Creation

EDITED BY

Graham Buxton

AND

Norman Habel

FOREWORD BY

David Rhoads

PICKWICK *Publications* · Eugene, Oregon

THE NATURE OF THINGS
Rediscovering the Spiritual in God's Creation

Pickwick Publications
An Imprint of Wipf and Stock Publishers
199 W. 8th Ave., Suite 3
Eugene, OR 97401

www.wipfandstock.com

PAPERBACK ISBN: 978-1-4982-3514-3
HARDCOVER ISBN: 978-1-4982-3516-7
EBOOK ISBN: 978-1-4982-3515-0

Cataloguing-in-Publication data:

Names: Buxton, Graham. | Habel, Norman C.

Title: The nature of things : rediscovering the spiritual in God's creation / edited by Graham Buxton and Norman Habel.

Description: Eugene, OR: Pickwick Publications, 2016 | Includes bibliographical references.

Identifiers: ISBN 978-1-4982-3514-3 (paperback) | ISBN 978-1-4982-3516-7 (hardcover) | ISBN 978-1-4982-3515-0 (ebook)

Subjects: LCSH: Human ecology—Religious aspects—Christianity. | Ecotheology.

Classification: BT695.5 N39 2016 *(print)* | BT695.5 *(ebook)*

Manufactured in the U.S.A.   11/21/16

Contents

Part 1: Presence in Creation

Part 2: Spirituality in Creation

Part 3: Suffering in Creation

Part 4: Wisdom in Creation

Part 5: Eco-Readings in Creation

Epilogue

Foreword

IT HAS BEEN INSPIRATIONAL to read this outstanding volume of timely essays and I am honored to be writing the Foreword. This is an incredibly rich collection of diverse essays that addresses the most important issue of our time. There are a number of very critical themes that weave their way through these excellent and highly stimulating essays. I would like here to reflect on a few of them.

We are in deep trouble. To realize how much, consider this: scientists and geological groups have recommended declaring a new epoch in Earth's geological history as having commenced around 1800. The word Anthropocene combines the root "anthropo-," meaning "human" with the root "-cene," standing for an epoch in geologic time. The Anthropocene defines Earth's most recent geologic time period as being profoundly human-influenced. This means that there is overwhelming global evidence that such fundamental aspects of our planet as the atmosphere, the geological make-up of Earth, the movement of ocean currents and weather systems, the well-being and survival of animal and plant life with their habitats, and other dimensions of our planet have been and are continuing to be altered significantly by human presence and activity—and not for the better. The Anthropocene follows the Holocene, the current epoch, which began approximately 11,000 years ago following the end of the last glacial period, the Pleistocene Epoch.

It is difficult to wrap our minds around the idea that collectively we humans are actually changing the direction and course of the evolution of the planet, but that is exactly what is happening. And since the industrial age, our impact has come so far that we are no longer in a prevention stage. Rather, we have moved into mitigation mode in which we hope to offset the worst impacts for life on Earth. And we are already in an adaptation posture. We cannot deny or avoid our situation. Unless we acknowledge the size of the problems, we will not grasp the extent of the efforts needed to address them. Many of us are acutely aware of this situation and living with anxiety about our future and about our children's future. To address this anxiety, there are now books, conferences, and webinars designed to foster human "resilience" in the way we cope with and address global climate change and other massive degradations of our planetary ecosystem.

We have to take responsibility for this. Human activity is having effects on a geological and global scale—heat waves, floods, droughts, famines, landslides, extreme weather of more frequent and more intense hurricanes and tornadoes, melting icecaps, rising ocean waters, dead zones in the oceans, earthquakes from fracking, respiratory illnesses from air pollution, depletion of fresh water reserves, proliferation of waste, loss of forests and degradation of soil, rapidly increasing loss of species, and more. We can no longer report these as "natural" disasters or "acts of God." They are caused or exacerbated by human activity. We are creating chaos on our planet. We are committing eco-cide. Like Alcoholics Anonymous members in crisis, we need to do a fearless moral inventory and embrace a deep repentance. And that inventory must include the ways in which our religious traditions, beliefs, and actions have contributed to the problem.

Then we need to make amends for our actions. We must become aware that every attitude or belief we have contributes to or relieves the ecological problems we face. It means that every action we take is a moral action because it has implications either for the degradation or for the well-being of Earth community. We need to stop what we are doing to destroy our natural home. We need to clean up after ourselves. And we need to engage in regenerative behavior that restores. The challenge? How do we do that as communities and as individuals entangled in a web of destructive patterns and lifestyles?

Furthermore, all of our behavior is also intimately connected with human social justice. Pope Francis has called for an "integral ecology," an ethic that addresses as one reality the justice issues for all of Earth community— human justice and justice for all living things. Clearly, the vulnerable are the most affected by the planetary crises. And they have the fewest resources to cope with the consequences. And they are invariably the individuals and societies who have contributed least to the situation in which we all find ourselves. For those of us less in harm's way, the danger is that we will hunker down and protect ourselves. However, morally and religiously, we cannot leave others behind while we scramble to survive.

The following question runs through these essays: What kind of persons must we become, individually and collectively, if we are to become the kinds of human beings we need to become in order to survive and thrive together with all of life on this planet. That is where this volume of collected essays comes to bear in crucial ways on the conditions we face. There is here the recognition that the situation in which we find ourselves is a profoundly spiritual problem in our human relationship with the rest of nature. Talk of the environment without relationship will not cut it. Talk of technological fixes without reverence for life will never be enough. Talk of behavioral change without a heart and mind change will not work. Talk of structural change without a deep love for all of Earth community will not in the end work.

In this regard, this volume deals especially with two critical issues. We will not bring renewal and restoration to our planet unless: (1) our actions and decisions are done in solidarity with our Earth community, and (2) we embrace a relationship with the spiritual depths of nature.

The one issue is this: If we are to become human beings who are prepared to live in the Anthropocene, we need to know ourselves as creatures of this Earth. Native cultures that have never lost their closeness to the land bear an important witness in this collection. The rest of us are learning from them, native cultures in Australia, New Zealand, North America, and around the world. The rest of us have become estranged from the very ground of our being. We see the world around us as a collection of things without life, commodities to be used and abused for our human purposes: land to be developed, ores to be extracted, trees to be removed, water to be squandered. We think of ourselves as living *on* Earth rather than being embedded *in* it. We think Earth belongs to us rather than us belonging to Earth. Without being aware of it, we suffer a deep human illness and sadness due to this loss of our rootedness in our natural home. We hardly know what we have been missing. Many of us are only recently discovering the healing power of nature and the transformative experience of awe in the presence of life around us.

We *are* nature. We are mammals who have evolved and emerged within the last 3.8 billion years of Earth's existence in parallel with and in relationship to millions of other species of plants and animals. We share DNA in common with all living things. We are the children of sun, air, soil, minerals, plants, and animals. And we continue to have the composition of our bodily selves formed and replaced by these elements all the time. We need a conversion to Earth in which we discover our deep and profound roots. We need to see our inextricable embeddedness in Earth. We need to see our communion with all of life. We need to recognize that we are defined by our relationships with the world around us. If we are to do this, we must develop some dramatic rituals and create some profound experiences that will result in our sense of belonging to this Earth, and a commitment of responsibility to it.

The other issue is the proper subject of this volume: we must rediscover the spiritual in God's creation as a basis for the reverence we need
to move into a new age. For 20 centuries, virtually all Christian traditions
have focused on the relationship between God and humans and between
humans and humans. In so doing, we have given scant attention to God in
relation to nature, nor our human relationship with the rest of nature, nor
our relationship with God in and through nature. This book is a powerful
witness in the effort to restore this lost dimension. Unless we experience the
sacredness in the natural world we will continue to exploit it. We need to
wake up to the world around us to see the presence of God—pouring forth
love and working for good in all things. In so doing, we will want to love the
world as God loves it. And we will see its intrinsic worth. We will reverence
the world. We will learn and grow from this mutual relationship. If we act
only to save humans, we will never do enough. Only if we love and care for
all of life for its own sake will we do what needs to be done to bring all of us
together into a new world.

It is this spirit of God in creation that is the source of our motivation
and the strength of our enduring commitment. I commend you to relish the
essays in this book, all of which are written with passion and insight urging
us to change and enrich our lives so that we will achieve a more profound
humanity as we give ourselves to the great work of our time.

David Rhoads

Professor Emeritus of New Testament
Lutheran School of Theology at Chicago

Preface

The Serafino Declaration

Rediscovering the Spiritual
in God's Creation

Context

IN MARCH 2015 APPROXIMATELY 120 delegates met in McLaren Vale, South Australia, to explore the theme of "rediscovering the spiritual in God's creation." The conference featured eight keynote addresses by well-known international scholars Paul Santmire, Denis Edwards, Bob White, Heather Eaton, Ernst Conradie, Vicky Balabanski, Norman Habel, and Celia Deane-Drummond. In addition, twenty parallel papers were presented, and conference participants appreciated three Indigenous-based experiences—a "Welcome to Country" followed by a smoking ceremony, a water ceremony expressing our connectedness to the natural world, and a visit to an important Aboriginal site on the summit of nearby Mount Barker.

The diversity of both participants and presentations was a distinctive feature of the gathering, and it was heartening to see so many people from different contexts and traditions taking time out to dialogue and listen to each other. During the last 24 hours of the conference several people—notably Ernst Conradie, Norman Habel, and Graham Buxton—were involved in crafting what we have called *The Serafino Declaration* (after the name of the conference venue) in which we outlined the perspectives and challenges arising out of the keynote addresses and shared experiences during our time together. The document was presented in the closing afternoon, and subsequently modified as the result of the table discussions that followed. This document represents both an invitation and a challenge . . . an invitation to consider deeply the insights and concerns raised during the conference, and a challenge to respond within our own particular contexts.

The Serafino Declaration

We came together at the Serafino conference center in McLaren Vale, South Australia, from 10 to 13 March 2015 to explore the theme of "rediscovering the spiritual in God's creation." We came from different geographic contexts, traditions, social locations, walks of life, age groups, and persuasions but with a common concern over various forms of ecological destruction and the intuition that this is not only a scientific, technological or economic issue but also a moral and indeed a spiritual one.

The aim of the conference was not to seek consensus, but to survey the landscape with a view to intentional responsible action. On that journey together, we were all challenged to recognize our own worldviews and to widen our horizons to encompass the enormity of the transcendence and immanence of God's presence in all creation:

- We recognized and explored the rich insights arising from the diverse perspectives on the spiritual in creation;

- We investigated the challenges arising out of these insights;

- We experienced our interconnectedness with the natural world in the distinctive Christian and Indigenous context; and

- We identified common concerns with regard to our treatment of the natural world.

Different Perspectives

We need to acknowledge that we approach the common conference theme in rather different ways:

- Some of us see "country" as embedded within the spirit world and are concerned about the destruction of ancestral land, seeing ourselves as deeply interconnected with the land, part of nature, and, where necessary, called to act as custodians of the land.

- Others of us are concerned about the destructive legacy of the Christian tradition and especially the dualisms that it has legitimized, especially between spirit and matter, soul and body, heaven and earth. We recognize that we are called to live in communion with nature, not over or above it. We then long to discern the spiritual in the material, the presence of God in every part of nature, animate and inanimate.

- Some of us treasure the rich heritage of the Christian confession of faith in the triune God and seek to explain how the presence of this God may indeed be experienced in and through nature.

- Others of us would agree but then wonder about natural disasters and examine our trust in God's sovereignty and providential care amidst and despite such disasters.

- Yet others stand in awe over the evolutionary history of the universe and of life and Earth. We wonder about the significance of the emergence of sentient life, consciousness and symbolic forms of communication. We sense that the spiritual emerges from the material and that this may help us to see ourselves as embedded in a divine milieu.

- Some of us see ourselves as standing alongside scientists, analysts, philosophers, and poets, seeking to make sense of the world around us. We look for wider horizons to interpret the world and what is wrong in the world, and find that by learning to name the world (through Christian worship) as God's beloved creation and the Earth as God's own household.

- Others of us find such household imagery attractive in speaking about the Earth as being home to trillions of creatures great and small, but are deeply concerned about the tension between human communities that seek to isolate themselves from the community of all living beings through numerous cultural prohibitions.

- Some of us observe the ways of wisdom embedded in nature, in living creatures and in the cosmic order of things—and discern in that a profound mystery, indeed God's very presence.

- Others find in such wisdom open windows to encounter the Divine Spirit at work in the world—also in the drama of the interaction between humans and other species, involving not only conflict, but also altruism and an entangled sense of justice.

We therefore adopt different points of departure in reflecting about the material and the spiritual, God and the world, church and society, religion and ecology. We seek ways of overcoming thought patterns that have trapped us in the past but we do so in different ways. We therefore organize our emerging insights in various ways and sense the need to respect each other in this regard.

Nevertheless, we have a common concern over ecological destruction and find sources of inspiration in the deepest roots of our traditions and forms of spirituality to sustain us in our efforts towards custodianship of the land / Earthkeeping / creation care. This provides us, in different locations, with a sense of joy and resilience to confront the overwhelming challenges of our times, even as we acknowledge that much good work is already happening with regard to ecological action.

Challenges

We are challenged and therefore feel free to challenge others to consider the following points summarizing a range of the diverse core insights and calls to action that emerged from participants and speakers:

- *The Healing of Earth*: mindful that humans, driven by greed and hubris, have ignored the spiritual nature of planet Earth and committed crimes against God's creation leading to abuses such as the extinction of species, the pollution of the atmosphere, and the melting of massive ice-caps, we were challenged to revive our consciousness of the sacredness of our planet and make the healing of our environment a primary mission.

- *The Narrative of Landscape*: because the Indigenous peoples of our land have long read the landscape of country as a spiritual narrative depicting the mysterious work of the Creator Spirit in forming and transforming the landscape, we were challenged to recognize the precedent of Aboriginal peoples as custodians of country with an acute sense of responsibility for maintaining its integrity.

- *The Spirituality of Country*: recognizing that the Aboriginal custodians of this land have long experienced the spirituality of this land as country and identified themselves as one with the land, we were challenged to acknowledge that the churches have undervalued this spiritual consciousness and should now work towards reconciliation.

- *God's Presence in Creation*: because God is immediately present in all creatures, through the Word, and in the Spirit, enabling all entities to exist and interact within one interrelated world, we were challenged to celebrate and experience God's presence at the heart of creation.

- *Christ in Creation*: in the light of the biblical tradition that in the cosmic Christ the whole fullness of God's redemptive presence dwells bodily in all things, reconciling, healing, and restoring all creation

(Col 2:9), we were challenged to discern the bodily presence of Christ in all communities of nature, from the nano-cosmos of our bodies to the macro-cosmos of the universe.

- *The Spirit in Creation*: given the presence of the Spirit whose work in creation has been made apparent to us in our encounters with living creatures on Earth, we were challenged to experience the Spirit guiding us to relate to fellow creatures as participants with us in a cosmic theo-drama grounded in places to which we belong.

- *Wisdom in Creation*: in learning that the scientists of the ancient Wisdom School discerned innate Wisdom to be a natural force—the primordial blueprint for all creation (Prov 8), the impulse governing the laws of nature (Job 28) and the driving character of each living thing (e.g. Prov 6:6)—we were challenged to experience innate Wisdom as a cosmic spiritual reality, as Job once did (Job 42: 2–5), by exploring the domains, laws, and forces of nature.

- *Disasters in Nature*: faced with the idea that, in a world that God pronounced good, natural disasters such as earthquakes, floods, and famines contribute to making a fertile world according to the cosmic blueprint of the universe, we were challenged to prepare for such natural disasters by enabling communities to build resilience against them and by removing unjust disparities in the use of Earth's resources.

- *The Rights of Nature*: if God's creation is a cosmos of intrinsic worth and spiritual beauty, a cosmos to respected rather than exploited, revered rather than raped, then we were challenged to respect all domains of nature and recognize their intrinsic rights as valued components of the cosmos, whether they be galaxies or gardens, coral reefs or rainforests.

- *The Consciousness of Earth Beings*: faced with the possibility that we are Earth beings emerging from planet Earth with a consciousness of an evolutionary process that contributes to an understanding of our identity, we were challenged to accept our identity as Earth beings and to celebrate Earth as our source and our home within an interconnected community of life and kin.

- *An Emerging Horizon of Hope*: invited to recognize that the world around us is God's household (*oikos*), and liturgically enabled to discern what lies beyond our immediate horizon, we were challenged to reconsider ways of looking at the world around us that legitimize current constellations of power and to express the hope that a different world is possible.

"We are alive as much as we keep the Earth alive"
—Dan George[1]

1. Chief Dan George was a famous twentieth-century Native American chief of the (Salish) Tsleil-Waututh Nation, a coastal indigenous First Nation Canadian Indian tribe located in British Columbia, North America.

Contributors

Vicky Balabanski is Senior Lecturer in New Testament at Flinders University, South Australia, and Director of Biblical Studies at the Adelaide College of Divinity and the Uniting College of Leadership and Theology. She is a writer and editor in the international *Earth Bible Project*, and is now working on an ecological commentary on Colossians, reading it in dialogue with Stoic thought.

Graham Buxton is a Senior Research Fellow at the Graeme Clark Research Institute at Tabor College of Higher Education in Adelaide, South Australia, and currently serves as a Professor of Theology at Fuller Theological Seminary in California. His most recent books are *An Uncertain Certainty* (2014) and a revised version of *Dancing in the Dark* (2016), both published by Cascade Books.

Emily Colgan has a PhD in Hebrew Bible from the University of Auckland, New Zealand. She is currently Lecturer in Theological Studies at Trinity Methodist Theological College in Auckland. Her main fields of research include work on ecological biblical interpretation, gender violence, and religion.

Ernst M. Conradie is Senior Professor in the Department of Religion and Theology at the University of the Western Cape where he teaches Systematic Theology and Ethics. His recent monographs include *Christianity and Earthkeeping: In Search of an Inspiring Vision* (Sun Press, 2011), *Saving the Earth? The Legacy of Reformed Views on "Re-creation"* (LIT Verlag, 2013), and *The Earth in God's Economy: Creation, Salvation and Consummation in Ecological Perspective* (LIT Verlag, 2015).

Celia Deane-Drummond is Professor in Theology at the University of Notre Dame and Director of the Center for Theology, Science, and Human Flourishing. She was editor of the journal *Ecotheology* for six years and has served as Chair of the European Forum for the Study of Religion and Environment from 2011 to present. Her most recent books are *Re-Imaging the Divine Image* (2014), and *Technofutures, Nature and the Sacred*, edited with Sigurd Bergmann and Bronislaw Szerszynski (2015).

Heather Eaton is Full Professor at Saint Paul University, Ottawa, Canada with a PhD in ecology, feminism, theology, and religious pluralism. Her most recent books include *The Intellectual Journey of Thomas Berry* (2014), and *Ecological Awareness: Exploring Religion, Ethics and Aesthetics*, with Sigurd Bergmann (2011). She also authors numerous academic articles on religious imagination, evolution, Earth dynamics, peace, and conflict studies on gender, ecology, religion, animal rights, and nonviolence.

Denis Edwards is a professorial fellow in theology at Australian Catholic University, Adelaide campus, and is a priest of the Catholic Archdiocese of Adelaide, and a member of both the ACU Institute for Religion and Critical Inquiry and the International Society for Science and Religion. Recent publications include *Ecology at the Heart of Faith*, *How God Acts: Creation, Redemption and Special Divine Action*, *Jesus and the Natural World*, and *Partaking of God: Trinity, Evolution and Ecology*.

Anne Elvey is an adjunct research fellow at Monash University, an honorary research associate of Trinity College Theological School, University of Divinity, Melbourne, and editor of *Colloquium: The Australian and New Zealand Theological Review*. Her scholarly publications include *Climate Change—Cultural Change: Religious Responses and Responsibilities* (2013, coedited with David Gormley O'Brien).

Patricia Fox is an Adjunct Lecturer at the Adelaide College of Divinity, Flinders University of South Australia and through Divine Word University of Madang, PNG. She has held senior leadership positions within the Institute of the Sisters of Mercy and the Archdiocese of Adelaide and worked in spiritual direction and retreats. She is the author of *God as Communion* (Liturgical Press, 2001).

Anne Gardner is an adjunct Senior Research Fellow at Monash University in Australia. She has published widely across the areas of the Hebrew Bible and Inter-Testamental Literature. In the *Earth Bible* series she contributed papers to Volumes 2 and 4, and is under contract to produce the Earth Bible Commentary on Daniel.

Norman Habel is a Professorial Fellow at Flinders University. As a biblical scholar he has been widely acclaimed for his commentary on the Book of Job and his work titled *The Land Is Mine*. He has taken the lead internationally in the field of ecological hermeneutics, specializing in ecology and the Bible, and Wisdom Literature. His writing initiatives include *The Earth Bible Series, The Season of Creation* and *Exploring Ecological Hermeneutics*.

Mark Liederbach is Professor of Theology, Ethics, and Culture at Southeastern Baptist Theological Seminary in Wake Forest, North Carolina, where he also serves as Vice President. He is Senior Fellow for the L. Russ Bush Center for Faith & Culture and a Research Fellow for the Ethics & Religious Liberty Commission. He is the joint author of *True North: Christ, the Gospel and Creation Care*.

Terence Lovat is Former Pro Vice-Chancellor and now Emeritus Professor at The University of Newcastle, Australia, and Honorary Research Fellow at Oxford University. He is editor-in-chief of *The Bonhoeffer Legacy: Australasian Journal of Bonhoeffer Studies*. His most recent book (with Robert Crotty) is *Reconciling Islam, Christianity and Judaism: Islam's Special Role in Restoring Convivencia* (Springer Press, Germany, 2015).

Mick Pope is a lecturer in meteorology and climate with the Australian Bureau of Meteorology, and is also an adjunct faculty member at Eastern College, where he teaches a unit on theology, mission and creation care. He works with Ethos: EA Centre for Christianity and Society, leading the environment think tank. His book, *A Climate of Hope: Church and Mission in a Warming World* with Claire Dawson was published by UNOH Publishing in 2015.

Dianne Rayson is a doctoral candidate and Flechtheim scholar at the University of Newcastle, Australia. She has published and presented on ecofeminism and Dietrich Bonhoeffer and serves as editorial assistant for *The Bonhoeffer Legacy: Australasian Journal of Bonhoeffer Studies*. Her previous work has spanned public health, public policy, and community and programme development in PNG and Australia's Northern Territory.

H. Paul Santmire served as Chaplain and Lecturer in Religion and Biblical Studies at Wellesley, College, Wellesley, Massachusetts, and as a pastor in academic, inner-city, and metropolitan settings. He is the author of many books, including *Brother Earth: Nature, God, and Ecology* (New York: Nelson, 1970), *The Travail of Nature: The Ambiguous Ecological Promise of Christian Theology* (Minneapolis: Fortress, 1985), and, most recently, *Before Nature: A Christian Spirituality* (Minneapolis: Fortress, 2014).

Robert (Bob) White, FRS, is Professor of Geophysics in the Department of Earth Sciences at Cambridge University and Director of the Faraday Institute for Science and Religion. His scientific work is published in over 400 papers and articles, and he has written or edited eight books on aspects of Science and Christianity. His most recent book is *Who Is to Blame? Nature, Disasters and Acts of God* (Lion-Monarch, 2014).

Mark Worthing is pastor of Immanuel Lutheran Church, North Adelaide, Australia. He has been a senior lecturer and researcher at Australian Lutheran College and Tabor College of Higher Education, both in Adelaide. He has published a number of books and articles in the area of science and faith and has an active interest in environmental issues. He lives with his family on a small farm in the Adelaide Hills.

Introduction

Norman Habel and
Graham Buxton

THE CHAPTERS IN THIS volume reflect the diversity of perspectives relating to the spiritual in God's creation that is summarized in *The Serafino Declaration*, which was crafted towards the end of the 2015 conference "Rediscovering the Spiritual in God's Creation." This declaration was provoked by its precedent, *The Adelaide Declaration,* which was the outcome of a 1997 conference on religion and ecology, also held in Adelaide.

The Serafino Declaration outlines a range of views and experiences relating to the presence of the spiritual in creation, views that are both traditional and radical, and experiences that are both subtle and substantial. The editors do not necessarily agree with each view expressed in this volume. The declaration is, in effect, a summation of the theme that was explored in a variety of ways in the conference papers, a selection of which forms the chapters in this volume.

Presence in Creation

Three of the first four chapters, which articulate the presence of God in creation, are written by keynote speakers at the 2015 conference. **Denis Edwards** poses basic questions reflected in the title of the conference: Is God, the Trinity, to be understood as really present in the natural world? If God is understood as present, is this presence of God something we can properly be said to experience? Edwards explores these two questions with the help of Athanasius of Alexandria and Karl Rahner. In dialogue with Athanasius,

Edwards explores a theology of God's presence in creatures. Building on Karl Rahner, Edwards then shows how we can truly be said to experience this presence of God. He concludes by offering three examples of the experience of God the Trinity in the natural world.

For Athanasius the eternally divine Word of God is "present in all things" via the Spirit. Each creature exists from the Source of All, the Father, through the Wisdom/Word present to each of them in the Spirit. Each creature is also a reflection of the image of divine Wisdom. Human experience of the Spirit, argues Edwards in his dialogue with Rahner, is a "mysterious and global experience, one that occurs in and through ordinary experiences of life." The everyday knowing and loving is accompanied by an experience of mystery. As well as the everyday, the Spirit is experienced through special moments of grace in our lives. Edwards' personal experiences of the Word and the Spirit take place in Brachina Gorge in the Flinders ranges, when accompanied by an Aboriginal elder in the Willunga Hills (South of Adelaide) and at Morialta when faced by the presence of a great River Red Gum.

The investigation by **Paul Santmire,** entitled "A Sublimely Natural God," develops the theme of spirituality in nature by exploring Martin Luther's paradoxical vision of Divine immanence in nature and working critically with the themes of "spirit and matter" in classical Christian thought. In Part One, Santmire discusses how Christian theology in the West has been shaped by a hierarchical spirit-matter dualism. The result of this approach has been to devalue the world of nature and to understand God as radically separate, or in the thought of St Augustine, God is spiritual and in no sense material. The image of God in humans is likewise spiritual and essentially different from nature. Santmire then asks how we deal with the current crisis, which is fundamentally material, when the theology we have inherited is fundamentally spiritual.

In Part Two, Santmire explores Luther's vision of a God who is neither distant nor separate from us, but at home in the world of nature. He discusses Luther's paradoxical language as reflected in the famous set of triple prepositions—"in, with and under"—an expression designed to reflect the concurrent transcendence and immanence of a God whose fullness can dwell in a single grain of wheat. Yet, the whole of creation is the "mask of God," a God who is powerfully present before our very eyes. Nature welcomes this Divine indwelling. In Part Three, Santmire reflects on an analogical vision of God in Godself as natural. He poses the question of how we can think of God as natural. To answer the question, he asks us to re-live his experience swimming, above the Falls, in the great Niagara River in North America, to consider the analogy of "torrential power," and to appreciate the primary analogy of God as natural rather than personal or social.

The study by **Ernst Conradie** commences with the claim that through their experience in the liturgy worshipers can see the world through new eyes, through God's eyes. In his analysis of Matt 16:13–19 he explores what he describes as "the liturgical dialectic between orientation, disorientation, and reorientation" in the imagery of that biblical passage. Conradie imagines Jesus standing on a cliff with his back to the North (the world of imperial powers) and Jerusalem to the South (where he is to be crucified). Here Jesus is leading his disciples to see the invisible, the kingdom of heaven, the realm of the future, when Peter will unlock on Earth (what lies within the current horizon) what lies in heaven (beyond the horizon).

Conradie then explores the concept of horizon, a term rarely used in the Bible, by recalling the perspectives of Hans-Georg Gadamer and Anthony Thiselton. He quotes Thiselton as saying "Every reader brings a horizon of expectation to the text . . . a text, however, can surprise, contradict, or even reverse such a horizon of expectation." For Conradie, one's current horizon is always to be understood in terms of both past and future horizons. He also explores whether a concept/experience of horizon is ecologically dangerous, working through a range of scholarly opinions and concluding that the "*horizon*-tal notion of transcendence" also has implications for an ecological understanding of the liturgy. Creation must necessarily play a crucial role in any re-orientation of the liturgy.

The final chapter in this section is by **Anne Gardner**, who has completed a close reading of 1 Kgs 18, focusing on the enigmatic expression, "a still small voice." She analyzes the wider context of this expression, especially the relationship of God with nature in the wind, storm, earthquake, and fire, as well as possible parallels in other texts.

She describes an experience of her own where she hears the "sound of silence," which she describes as a "hum" and which she suggests some scientists would associate with a form of cosmic resonance. In the Elijah narrative, however, the "faint calm sound" is associated with presence, God's presence in nature. It is only upon hearing this sound that Elijah feels safe enough to come to the entrance of the cave. (*Editorial note*: I, Norman Habel, have also heard the "sound of silence" some years ago at dusk on Kangaroo Island, a silence I associated with primordial presence).

Spirituality in Creation

The three chapters that follow explore in more detail the theme of spirituality in creation. The chapter by **Pat Fox** is a fresh examination of key sections of *The Spiritual Exercises* of St. Ignatius. Her goal is "to re-examine this sixteenth-century text through the lens of rediscovering the spiritual in God's creation." She commences by noting that the focus on God the Creator has waned in recent years, in spite of the emergence of an ecological awakening. The insights of Ignatius provide a catalyst to return to a deeper appreciation of God's presence in creation.

After reviewing Ignatius' profound experiences of God in creation, Pat Fox focuses on three of the "points" in *A Contemplation to Attain the Love of God*. These "points" are extremely relevant for gaining a "personal cosmic vision of the Creator God's incarnational and regenerating presence so that we might be drawn proactively into the work of transforming our world."

Graham Buxton begins by recognizing that a growing number of people are describing themselves as spiritual but not religious. In this chapter he seeks to address the basic connection between spirituality and ecology from a Christian perspective, assuming the presence of a God who is immanent, present in creation, as well as transcendent, other than creation. The universe, according to Buxton, may be understood as a dynamic whole whose parts are essentially related, energized and orchestrated by the Spirit, which in Stoic language is designated as *anima mundi*, the "world soul" or vital force of the universe.

For human beings, the spiritual experience is itself located in the ecological context. To pull spirituality and ecology apart is to do violence to the very fabric of creation as God's loving gift. Australian Aborigines have long functioned in a world where they experience the natural, moral and spiritual in nature. The spiritual and the natural also belong together as an expression of ultimate beauty, a beauty into which we are drawn daily as we walk with Christ in the cathedral of the great outdoors.

Mick Pope's study is concerned with a spirituality of creation within the framework of the Anthropocene, that era in which humans dominate Earth. He also explores the concepts of wildness and wilderness, and the biblical dialectic of dominion and creation, concluding with an indication of the relevance of Aboriginal spirituality for re-thinking our relationship with creation.

He discusses how five interconnected scenes of Earth plus the celestial sphere are understood in the biblical context and in the context of the current climate crisis. He links the insights of Aboriginal Rainbow Spirit Theology, where the Creator Spirit is the landowner and human beings are trustees, with the biblical commission to care for land in Gen 2:15. He cites Pat Dodson's claim that the Aboriginal Dreaming represents a beautifully worked out spirituality, "complete with a full and coherent sacramental theology." We are encouraged to learn from this spirituality in the context of the Anthropocene.

Suffering in Creation

The theme of suffering in relation to God, humanity, and the rest of creation is given explicit attention in the next three chapters. **Robert White** tackles the issue of natural disasters and their relationship with a loving God in a world where 300 million people per year are affected by such disasters. The term "natural disaster" may, however, be a misnomer. Many disasters are part of the beneficial natural process of the planet and part of the problem is how humans interact with them or deal with their predicted appearance. The common factor in all natural disasters, such as famine, is that the poor and the voiceless suffer most.

Christians need to face the truth that "nature" is not a force separate from God and that the commandment of God to "have dominion over Earth" (Gen 1:28) means humans are to keep the planet "in good order," to rule over the earth on God's behalf. White cites Job and Joseph as biblical figures who have come to terms with natural disasters. He sees hope for the future not only in God's current sovereignty over the present world, but also in the fullness of time when this creation will be renewed. While we may not make sense of God's control of the current world, the certainty of the new creation is the cornerstone of Christian hope. In the meantime, the example of Joseph anticipating and preparing for disaster provides us with a model in the current world.

Mark Worthing explores the nexus between divine, human and creational suffering, using Rom 8:15–25 as the basis of his reflection. This text raises the question of how atonement is linked to the whole of creation and in what sense creation is capable of suffering. Worthing argues that the suffering of creation means something broader than the experience of pain of sentient beings. He poses the following key questions which he claims arise from a close reading of Rom 8: Does Christ's suffering extend beyond his presence on the cross? Does God take responsibility for all the suffering in creation? Does God intend to reconcile all creation (and not only humans) through God's own suffering?

In response, Worthing argues that the pain and suffering of God are common in the Old Testament and that there is an intimate connection between the suffering of divine, human, and creational realms. Christ holds all of suffering creation together. The concept of "deep incarnation" reflects the "solidarity from the cross into the groan of creation," and "the death of Christ as the icon of God's redemptive co-suffering with all sentient life."

According to Worthing, Rom 8 opens the door to dialogue with scientists about evolutionary biology and cosmology and the idea of new life rising from suffering in the cosmos that is linked to new life emerging through the suffering of God in Christ. Ultimately, salvation/healing is for all creation through God's suffering on the cross in ways we do not yet fully comprehend.

Dianne Rayson and **Terence Lovat** explore Bonhoeffer's eco-theological ethic in what they identify as the "Gandhi Factor." In this context they seek to re-examine the concepts of stewardship and dominion. A crucial feature of Ghandi's worldview that is discerned in Bonhoeffer's eco-theology is *ahmisa* or non-violence, a concept derived from Jainism. In the last analysis humans should not harm each other or nature.

For Bonhoeffer, however, his Christology is central to any eco-theology; the work of the Suffering Christ is present throughout all of creation. Our task is to recognize the Suffering Christ in creation around us. Representing Christ in the image of God means a stewardship or dominion of care rather than domination.

Wisdom in Creation

Two chapters follow that offer a wisdom lens for interpreting the reality of the spiritual in the created world. **Norman Habel** focuses on wisdom as an often ignored dimension of the spiritual in God's creation. He explores the wisdom literature of ancient scientists who explore wisdom as a natural dimension of the cosmos. He identifies the technical terms found in the *modus operandi* of the ancient Wisdom schools. He then examines three major domains of creation where Wisdom is innate: (a) living creatures in the natural world; (b) inanimate forces and realms of nature; and (c) the cosmos as a whole.

He also cites moments when he believes he has experienced this Wisdom in nature—the migration of New Zealand godwits to Siberia to breed and nurture, the 80 thousand lightning strikes in South Australia in October 2014, and the vivid appearance of Halley's Comet in India in 1986. Habel claims that experiencing the profound mystery of Wisdom manifest in natural phenomena can arouse, in the wise, a sense of wonder, Wisdom consciousness, and spiritual awareness.

Celia Deane-Drummond seeks to discover a window to the spiritual or the Divine Spirit in the living world, with a special focus on "between species" encounters, especially between humans and other species. She identifies these encounters as an experience of the presence of wisdom or indeed the Spirit of wisdom. A number of case studies are presented to explore encounters with creaturely others. These include hyena human relations, ethno-elephantology, and macaques and ethno-primatology. In the ethno-elephantology case, for example, three principles are cited: (a) subjective agency—both humans and elephants have sentient and affective life-worlds; (b) the co-evolution of humans and elephants in mutually entangled social lifeworlds; and (c) bio-cultural methodology.

Deane-Drummond also introduces the concept of theo-drama, derived from the work of Hans Urs von Balthasar, as a way of orienting one for theology. The theo-dramatic task is a way of seeing the active presence of God in relation to humans and other creatures in terms of dynamic performance, incorporating insights from evolutionary science. The closing section of the chapter explores the issue of wild justice and fairness for all animal societies. The question is raised whether wild justice reflects the presence of God in creation. Human beings in the image of God mediate between the creaturely and the divine and thereby occupy a middle ground where they play a crucial role to act for the common good according to divine Wisdom.

Eco-readings in Creation

Readings in the biblical text which have ecological implications shape the content of the next four chapters. In contemporary society, humans have lost touch, it seems, with our interconnectedness with creation. In particular, we have failed to grasp our intimate interconnectedness with that vast creation which is not accessible to our senses—the nano-cosmos of bacteria that live in and on our bodies which we view as unclean. In this context, **Vicky Balabanski** first explores the biblical concepts of purity and contagion. She then turns to Paul's letter to the Colossians where the community of Christ's followers is grappling with what they may handle, taste and touch (Col 2:21). In that community, Paul guides believers to re-configure their relationship with "all things" in the cosmos.

Balabanski's ecological reading of Colossians is especially significant. The Colossian community seems to have adopted traditional practices about what might be handled, tasted and touched, practices that seem to be derived from their Jewish neighbors and suggest that the world around them is full of unclean people, animals, objects and food. Paul calls on the community to see that "all things" were created through Christ, whether visible or invisible, whether throne or powers (Col 1:16). Therefore "all things," if created by Christ, are clean and pure. The world is interconnected, not through purity, pollution or creation, but through Christ the Creator, because in Christ the whole fullness of deity dwells "bodily!" Our bodies mirror the presence of God in Christ.

In the context of the climate change crisis, **Emily Colgan** examines the text of Jer 31:35–37 to illustrate that a biblical text of this nature implies a world of interconnected reality, when read from an ecological perspective. The verb *nātan*, for example, is rendered "to enable," thereby implying an interactive and ongoing divine relationship with the sun, moon and stars, rather than a primordial hierarchical divine action over the material world. Likewise God "stirs" up the sea to enable her waves to continue to roar, a roar that is celebrative rather than menacing (v. 35). Colgan uses "pan-syntheism" (an expression of Ruth Page) to describe this empowering personal relationship of "God with" the material realm.

In verse 37, Colgan focuses on the claim that Earth is unexplorable and fundamentally unknowable, implying that mystery does not exclusively belong to God, but to Earth also. Colgan then proceeds to explore Earth's mysterious/unknowable character which evokes not only a sense of wonder and awe but also of "reverence and gentle receptivity" to Earth. Read from an ecological perspective, verse 36 also highlights the dependence and interdependence of entities on the divinely "fixed order" of the cosmos.

The study by **Mark Liederbach** focuses on the two key passages—Gen 2:15 and Gen 1:28—that he contends are crucial for developing a Christian ethic of creation care. Liederbach incorporates a critique of what he designates the "Eco-Evangelical Orthodoxy" translation of Gen 2:15, focusing on the Hebrew terms *'ābad* and *shāmar*. This critique involves a discussion of a range of translations by leading scholars in the field that he believes are inadequate. Liederbach recognizes that *'ābad* incorporates the idea of "serve" but that the goal or *telos* of that service is not the garden as such, but rather praise of the One who created the garden. Eden, moreover, is not merely a garden, but a place built for worship. God places Adam in the garden *to worship and obey*. The focus is not on the garden but on the Creator.

Liederbach's interpretation of the verbs *rādāh* and *kābash* in Gen 1:18 reflect a similar perspective, claiming that the traditional renderings of "rule" and "subdue" should reflect the loving God who uttered them. Humans are "unstained image-bearers whose worshipful work is to be aligned with the loving will of God." Lynn White and others who blame Gen 1:18 for our ecological problems have totally misread the text.

Anne Elvey proposes a radical eco-reading of the Magnificat which is considered appropriate for the Anthropocene Age. She begins by tracing how the Magnificat has been referenced in the press in Australia in the first half of the twentieth century focusing especially on a story by Australian writer H. Drake-Brockman that appeared in *The Australian* in 1939. Elvey argues that the Magnificat formed a kind of template among early

Australian settlers for exploring experiences of the sacred, sometimes in more-than-human frame.

In her analysis of Luke's Magnificat, Elvey explores three themes—the maternal, protest, and the cross. The body in pregnancy and the Earth share a quality of material givenness necessary for human and other forms of mammalian life. Whereas Drake-Brockman's story of a the sad fate of her child in war can be read as a protest against the failures of the God of the Magnificat, Mary's song embraces a promise of God spoken as a life-giving protest against death-dealing oppression. By locating the Magnificat in front of the cross, Elvey even sees a link between the Magnificat and our contemporary "war" on creation. Elvey concludes with a provocative and powerful version of the Magnificat for praying in the current ecological crisis.

Epilogue

The final chapter by **Heather Eaton** reflects on the overall theme of the volume. Writing from her home in Canada, she considers first how certain Christian traditions have interpreted and understood creation as a flawed and temporary reality; other traditions discerned the natural world of creation as a place of divine revelation. The concept of a dichotomy between natural and the spiritual is being challenged by an emerging eco-theology.

Eaton proposes four configurations that relate humans, nature and spirit. The first one does not consider the natural related to the sacred. A second orientation is metaphoric: nature points to "something about God." A third is to experience nature and spirit as ontologically intermingled. And a final view understands spirituality as an integral part of the cosmos. Eaton also explores the significance of evolution as more than a theory or a concept; evolution is the name of the process of nature. She then seeks to discover a spiritual vision by re-thinking the very nature of creation. She suggests that "whatever we call spirituality is essentially an active process, and an embedded dimension of all reality," as intimate and vital as breathing. She argues that we need to be present to the Earth on Earth's terms.

Eaton recognizes that a great deal is at stake in an exploration of spirituality in creation, especially in the face of ecological ruin. "We need a spiritual awakening" that will inspire us to re-awaken to the natural world as spiritual.

Part 1

Presence in Creation

1

Experience of Word and Spirit in the Natural World

Denis Edwards

Do we experience God in our encounters with birds, animals, trees, forests, mountains, deserts, and beaches? Or, to focus the question of this chapter a little more precisely, does the Christian theological tradition offer support for the idea that we can experience the triune God in the natural world? Behind this question I think there are two further questions: is God the Trinity to be understood as really present in the natural world? If God is understood as present, is this presence of God something we can properly be said to experience?

I will take up these two questions with the help of two theologians of the tradition, Athanasius of Alexandria from the fourth century and Karl Rahner from the twentieth. In the first section of the essay I will explore a theology of God's triune presence in creatures, in dialogue with Athanasius. In the second, I will seek to show that we can truly be said to experience this presence of God, building on Karl Rahner. The third section simply offers three examples of the experience of God the Trinity in the natural world.

The Presence of God in Creatures

Is God truly present in the natural world around us? When I walk on a quiet beach, can I see this beach as a place of divine presence? Can I think of a rain forest, with all its interconnected, exuberant forms of life, as filled with the presence of God? Some theologians, conscious of the costs of evolution, and the pain of many creatures, speak of the absence of God from the

13

natural world. But I remain convinced we need to think of God as radically present, even in the loss and pain evident in biological life and in the costs of evolutionary emergence.

The Christian theological tradition has long been committed to the idea that God is radically present to all creatures, conferring on them their existence and their capacity to act within a community of creation. I will illustrate this statement by reference to Athanasius, a key figure in the full articulation of the theology of the Trinity. Reading him, there is the sense of a theology that is still young and vibrant. His view of the Trinity is radically scriptural. It is never abstract, but a theology of a God engaged with creatures, a God who acts, who creates and saves. I will focus first on his view of God's presence to creatures, and then on his idea that creatures bear an imprint or image of holy Wisdom.

The Immediacy of God to Each Creature

Athanasius sees creation from the perspective of Jesus Christ and his life-giving cross. He sees the Word who is made flesh, the Word of the cross, as the very Word of creation. What John 1:3 says of the Word is foundational for all of his work: "All things came into being through him, and without him not one thing came into being." The Word through whom all entities in the universe exist is the very same Word who is made flesh (John 1:14) to bring creation to its healing and transformation. The Word of creation is the Word of salvation.

Like others in the fourth century, Athanasius sees Christ not only as the Word of God but also as the Wisdom of God. He uses these expressions interchangeably, and interprets biblical references to the Word and the Wisdom of God intertextually. Athanasius is like many others in his own time in seeing God as creating through God's Wisdom/Word. Where Athanasius differs from many of his contemporaries is in his conviction of the full divinity of both the Wisdom/Word and the Spirit. In fourth century-philosophical and theological culture, permeated as it was by Platonic thought, it was natural to suppose that there is a vast distance between finite creatures and the infinite God, and that some kind of intermediary is needed to bridge this distance. The tendency was to think of creatures as participating in an intermediary, and of the intermediary as participating in the all holy God. For the Christian community this intermediary was the Wisdom/Word. Behind this tendency there was a conviction of God's complete otherness from creatures. There was an assumption that the all-holy God is not to be contaminated or demeaned by immediate contact with creatures. In any case, finite and vulnerable creatures might not be able to withstand exposure to the fire of the divinity. Some kind of buffer was needed.[1]

It is understandable, then, that the Alexandrian priest Arius was convinced not only that the Word is an intermediary between God and creatures, but also that the Word is not to be identified with the all-holy God. In his view, there was a time when the Word was not. This means that the Word is ultimately a creature and that the true and eternal God is beyond the Word. Such a view was shared by many Christians, including influential bishop-theologians. The transcendent otherness of God seemed to rule out an immediate relationship between God and created entities.

Basing himself on his reading of the Scriptures and the Christian tradition, Athanasius completely rejects the notion of a created intermediary between God and creatures. For him there is no buffer. God is immediately present to the creatures that God creates. Athanasius shares fully in his opponents' conviction of the radical otherness of the Creator. He has a highly developed theology of creation *ex nihilo*. Creatures have in themselves no reason for their existence. They exist only because the Creator confers existence on them at every point. For Athanasius, too, there is an infinite difference, an ontological gulf, between creatures and their Creator.

How is this gulf bridged? Not, for him, by a hierarchical chain of being linking Creator and creatures; and not, for him, by a created intermediary. He insists that the gulf is bridged only by the fully divine Word coming down to be present to creatures in the fully divine Spirit. Only God can bridge the gap. For Athanasius, the eternally divine Word of God is "present in all things" and "gives life and protection to everything, everywhere, to each individually and to all together."[2] From the creaturely side, creation is an ongoing relation of participation, by which creatures exist securely only because they partake of this Word of God so profoundly present to them in the Spirit. Athanasius speaks of the Word of God as "governing," "establishing," "leading," "providing for," and "ordering" creation.[3]

Athanasius writes of divine Wisdom as enabling all the diverse creatures and the elements of the natural world to work together in balance and harmony. Like a gifted musician, divine Wisdom brings the whole universe into a beautiful interrelationship: "The Wisdom of God, holding the universe like a lyre," draws together the variety of created things, "thus producing in beauty and harmony a single world and a single order within

---

1. See Leithart, *Athanasius*, 91.
2. Athanasius, *Against the Greeks*, 41.
3. Ibid., 41.

it."[4] Because of the Wisdom/Word of God, all the elements of creation work together in kinship:

> Through him and his power fire does not fight with cold, nor the moist with the dry, but things which of themselves are opposites come together like friends and kin, animating the visible world, and becoming the principles of existence of bodies. By obedience to the Word of God things on earth receive life and things in heaven subsist. Through him all the sea and the great ocean limit their movements to their proper boundaries, and all the dry land is covered with all kinds of different plants, as I said above.[5]

It is through participating in divine Wisdom, interiorly present to all creatures, that these creatures not only exist, but are brought into productive relationships with one another. The Holy Spirit is the bond that unites creatures to Wisdom, so that it is only in the Spirit that each creature participates in divine Wisdom. For Athanasius, then, each creature exists from the Source of All, the Father, through the Wisdom/Word present to each of them in the Spirit.

The ontological gap between Creator and creatures is overcome because the triune God comes down, or "condescends," to engage with creatures on their level, in the ongoing relationship of creation.[6] God is immediately present to each entity through the Word and in the Spirit. In the act of continuous creation, the Spirit enables each creature to be open to, and to receive, the creative Word. By partaking of the Word in the Spirit individual creatures exist and interact in the community of creation. For Athanasius, both creation and new creation occur through this structure of participation of the Word in the Spirit: "The Father creates and renews all things through the Word in the Holy Spirit."[7]

The God who comes down to be with creatures is a God of humble love. God comes to be with creatures in humility out of the abundance of divine, generous and compassionate love. Athanasius scholar Khaled Anatolios points out that Athanasius radically transforms the idea of divine transcendence by means of the biblical categories of divine mercy and loving kindness. God's transcendence does not distance God from creatures. It is a transcendence of unthinkable mercy and generosity. Because of these

---

4. Ibid., 42.

5. Ibid.

6. Athanasius, *Against the Arians* 2.64.

7. Athanasius, *Letters to Serapion* 1:24.6.

biblical attributes, God can transcend God's own transcendence.[8] God can be intimately present to finite creatures.

It is precisely because the Word and Spirit are fully divine, and possess the divine capacity for mercy and loving kindness, that they can be intimately and interiorly close to creatures in the relationship of continuous creation. Because of this divine capacity no creaturely mediation is needed. The Creator is deeply present in humility and self-giving love to the creature. The character of God in creating thus accords with the kenotic character of God revealed in the incarnation.[9] In both creation and incarnation, the Word of God is a self-humbling God.[10]

So, the distinction between God and all creatures is not bridged by a created intermediary, but solely from God's side, in a loving generosity that is itself fully divine. Because Word and Spirit are one with the Father's essence, the Word's creative presence in the Spirit means, of course, that the Father, the Source of All, is also immediately present to each creature.[11] As Athanasius puts it, using again a favorite image, the one who experiences the Radiance is enlightened by the Sun itself and not by any intermediary.[12]

In Athanasius, as in other major theologians of the tradition, there is absolutely no opposition between God's transcendence and God's immediate presence to creatures.[13] On the contrary it is divine transcendence that enables God's immanence to created entities. It is a disastrous distortion of the Christian tradition to see God's transcendence as opposed to God's immanent presence. Divine transcendence enables God to be more interiorly present to creatures than they could ever be to one another. It is precisely God's transcendence, understood in terms of divine capacity for self-humbling love, that enables God to be immediately and intimately with creatures in the relationship of creation. Every creature on Earth, every whale, every kangaroo, every sparrow, exists by participation in the Father through the Word in the Spirit—"not one of them is forgotten in God's sight" (Luke 12:6).

One of the attractive elements in Athanasius's theology is that he sees the wonderful diversity and abundance of creation as springing from the absolute generativity of divine life. He brings out this generativity in the beautiful biblical images he uses for the Trinity: God is a Spring, ever pouring forth a River from which we drink in the Spirit; God is a Light with its

8. Anatolios, *Retrieving Nicaea*, 104.

9. Ibid.

10. Athanasius, *Against the Arians* 1.39; 3.52.

11. Anatolios, *Athanasius: The Coherence of His Thought*, 113.

12. Athanasius, *Against the Arians* 3.14.

13. Anatolios, *Athanasius*, 40

eternal Radiance that enlightens us in the Spirit; God is the Father, eternally begetting the Son in whom we participate by adoption as God's children in the Spirit; God is the Font of Wisdom, bringing forth the Wisdom of God, which we receive through the Spirit of Wisdom.[14]

The triune God that Athanasius defends is a God of endless life, a God who is fruitful by nature. He argues that those who reject the eternity of the Word and the Spirit are also denying the dynamic generativity of divine life. He insists that the fruitfulness of the natural world has its source in the generativity of the eternally dynamic triune God.[15] The stars of the night sky, rain forests with their uncounted life forms, this bird I can see in a nearby tree, all spring from the divine generativity of the God who is a Spring, eternally pouring forth a River of Living Water, from which all creatures drink in the Spirit.

Each Creature Bears the Imprint
of the Image of Wisdom

Athanasius sees Jesus Christ as the true Image of God. He speaks often of Christ not only as Word of God, Wisdom of God, Son of God, and Radiance of God, but also as Image of God. He sees humans as made according to the Image, who is Christ. This being made according to the Image is distorted by sin, and it is restored through the saving and deifying work of Christ, in the grace of the Holy Spirit. It is worth noting today, when Christian theology is in search of a more inclusive notion of the human in relation to other creatures, that Athanasius employs the concept of the Image of Wisdom in relation not only to humans but also to other creatures.

In his *Orations against the Arians*, after describing Wisdom as coming down to be with creatures so that they might exist and flourish, he goes on to speak of each creature as bearing the created imprint or reflection of divine Wisdom:

> But in order that creatures may not only be but also thrive in well-being, it pleased God to have his own Wisdom condescend to creatures. Therefore he placed in each and every creature and in the totality of creation a certain imprint (*typon*) and reflection of the Image of Wisdom, so that the things that come into being may prove to be works that are wise and worthy of God.[16]

14. Athanasius, *Letters to Serapion* 1.19. 1–7 .

15. Athanasius, *Against the Arians* 2.2.

16. Ibid., 2.78.

All the creatures around us, in his view, bear this reflection of the Image of Wisdom. This can only mean that, for Athanasius, all creatures are in their own way made according to the Image of Wisdom. Each of them is a creaturely reflection of uncreated Wisdom. Each of them is a created image, an icon, of the eternal Image and Wisdom of God.

In human beings, according to Athanasius, the imprint and reflection of divine Wisdom is found in their human wisdom: "the wisdom that comes to be within us is an image of his Wisdom."[17] Because humans possess this gift of wisdom, they have the capacity to recognize the image of Wisdom in other creatures—"Thus did the imprint of Wisdom come to be in created things, so that the world, as I have said, may come to know its Creator and Word, and through him, the Father."[18] The imprint of divine Wisdom in humans enables them, in their encounters with other creatures, to come to know the Wisdom who made them. And in knowing this Wisdom, they can also know the Source of All, the Father. They can come to know the triune God through the imprint of Wisdom found in the creatures around them.

In Sirach, Wisdom is said to be "poured forth" (Sir 1:9) upon on all God's works. Athanasius sees this text as referring not to Wisdom's divine being, but to Wisdom's created image poured out upon all creatures.[19] He distinguishes between divine Wisdom and her image in creatures: "For while Wisdom herself is Creator and Maker, her imprint is created in the works and is made according to the image of the Image."[20] Athanasius notes, with Paul, that in spite of God's attributes being evident in the creation since the beginning, human beings have over and over failed to recognize God and have instead worshipped false gods (Rom 1:19–21). Nevertheless, God does not abandon humanity, but out of extravagant divine generosity, sends divine Wisdom to be with us in the flesh:

> For God willed to make himself known no longer as in previous times through the image and shadow of wisdom, which is in creatures, but has made the true Wisdom herself take flesh and become a mortal human being and endure the death of the cross, so that henceforth all those who put their faith in him may be saved. But it is the same Wisdom of God, who previously manifested herself, and her Father through herself, by means of her

17 Ibid.

18. Ibid.

19. Ibid., 2.79.

20. Ibid., 2.80.

image in creatures—and thus is said to be "created"—but which
later on, being Word, became flesh (John 1:14) as John said.[21]

The Wisdom of God who is beyond all creaturely limits becomes flesh
in Jesus Christ. This same divine Wisdom is intimately present to all creatures in the act of continuous creation. They exist because they participate
in this Wisdom, and in their specific, creaturely way, they bear the created
imprint of Wisdom, and in this sense are images of the Image.

Human Experience of the Spirit

Do we human beings actually experience the Spirit of God? Do we encounter the living God in our day-to-day lives? As in an earlier discussion of this
question,[22] I will propose that the Christian answer to these questions can
only be yes, but that it is necessary to qualify this answer from the beginning in two ways. First, the experience of the Spirit is not of the same order
as the experience of particular objects in the world, such as a tree, a dog,
or a human being—the experience of the Spirit, it will be suggested, is a
far more mysterious and global experience, one that occurs in and through
these ordinary experiences of life. Second, language, culture, and psychological factors play a fundamental role in all our experiences. The fact that
all experience is mediated by language, culture, and the psychology of the
experiencer, suggests a critical and cautious approach to claims about the
experience of the Holy Spirit. Pre-existing understandings and language
always enter into experience and are necessary aspects of its interpretation.
Experience is, by necessity, filtered through the psychological history and
imaginative life of the individual subject.

Granted these fundamental cautions, I believe with Karl Rahner that
we can say that we do experience the Holy Spirit. The experience of God is
a central theme of Rahner's theological work,[23] and I find him a particularly
helpful guide on this fundamental issue. He is often thought of as a highly
philosophical thinker, but at the end of his life he insisted that all of his
theology grew from the profound conviction at the heart of St. Ignatius's
Spiritual Exercises that we really do experience the living God.[24] Rahner was

21. Ibid., 2.81.

22. Edwards, *Human Experience of God*.

23. Rahner, "Experience of the Holy Spirit," 196–97; "Reflections on the Experience of Grace," 86–90; "The Experience of God Today," 149–65; "Experience of Self and
Experience of God," 122–32; "Experience of the Spirit and Existential Commitment,"
24–51; *Foundations of Christian Faith*, 137.

24. Rahner, *Ignatius of Loyola Speaks*, 6–23; Egan, *Karl Rahner*, 28–54.

an advocate for what he called the "mysticism of everyday life:" not only the great saints, he insisted, but also ordinary Christians are called to the mystical. In the light of increasing secularization, Rahner insisted that in the future Christian faith would have to spring from an interior conviction, and that it would need to involve personal experience of God. He expressed this in his saying that the Christian of the future will be a mystic, or he or she will be nothing.[25]

Because he was convinced that ordinary people do experience the Spirit, but also that this can be an obscure and unnoticed experience, Rahner believed that the proclamation of the gospel of Jesus should begin from the place where the Spirit is already at work in a person's life, and is already experienced, at least in an obscure way.[26] He saw it as fundamental for pastoral practice to evoke such experiences of the Spirit, to bring them to consciousness. He named the pastoral process of evoking where a person or a community experiences mystery and transcendence as the practice of "mystagogy."

What insights does Rahner offer into this experience of God? I think it is helpful to see his thought on this issue as moving in three steps. The first step is his analysis of our everyday knowing and loving of other creatures, by which he seeks to show that this everyday knowing and loving is always accompanied by an experience of mystery, whether this be consciously attended to or not. By mystery he means the experience of what is boundless and incomprehensible, beyond all our everyday concepts and language. Mystery points to the inexhaustible depths of the reality that we encounter in the everyday. In our knowing of another creature we form a concept of the specific person or object, and as we focus on the specific person or object, we always do this within a wider context or horizon. Although we do not always notice it, this wider context involves all possible objects of knowledge. We situate specific objects of knowledge against an unlimited range of possible knowing. There is always an openness to more. When we ask questions, they always open us up to further questions. Our minds are never satisfied. The horizon of our everyday knowing is boundless, reaching out towards the infinite.

We experience mystery not only in our knowing, but also in our loving. Particular acts of love for another can contain an implicit invitation to a love that is unconditioned and that has no boundaries. The partial fulfillment we experience in our love and commitment to others can open out towards a love that has no limits. There is a restless yearning that is not met,

25. Rahner, "The Spirituality of the Church of the Future," 149.

26. Rahner, "Faith 1."

and which cannot be loaded onto the limited human objects of our love, without doing great damage. There is a boundless expanse to the human mind and heart, and this boundless expanse is always there as the context of ordinary knowledge and love.

Having evoked this experience of mystery that accompanies everyday knowing and loving, Rahner's second step is to appeal to Christian revelation and particularly to a Christian theology of Grace. In his theology the saving Grace of Christ is offered to all human beings of every time and place. Grace is, then, God present in self-offering love, an offer that each person is free to accept or reject. God is always present in the Spirit, offering God's self in love. Because of God's gracious presence to each person in the Spirit, the openness to mystery we experience can be understood as openness to the Spirit.[27] The dynamic openness of the human person is Spirit-filled. In the light of revelation, the experience of mystery can then be known to be experience of Grace, or experience of the Spirit, or as Rahner often says, the experience of Holy Mystery.

Rahner's third step is to propose that there are moments of special grace in our lives, where the created object we encounter may itself become a pointer to the Spirit, so that the experience of the Spirit is brought to the forefront of consciousness. Rahner offers many examples of such experiences, usually negative experiences,[28] where the limits of the everyday break down, and we are led beyond ourselves into the incomprehensible mystery of God. He speaks of someone attempting to forgive, even when there is no reward for it, and the forgiveness is taken for granted; of someone trying to love God, even when there seems no obvious response; of someone who makes a decision to follow conscience even though this cannot be explained to others.[29] In such moments, what at first seems like emptiness and darkness can be found to be the place where Love is with us, where we are held in Love.

The three examples I will offer in the next section differ from Rahner's in two ways. Following Athanasius, I will articulate the experiences in a more fully Trinitarian way, as experiences of the Word and the Spirit. And I will focus on positive experiences, particularly on those that occur in our encounters with the natural world. It is essential to keep in mind, however, the dark and painful experiences of nature, when to us human beings it can seem harsh and cold. We cannot forget the pain, loss, death, and extinction that is intrinsic to evolutionary history. We need to acknowledge,

27. Rahner, "Experience of the Holy Spirit," 198.

28. Rahner, "The Ignatian Mysticism of Joy in the World," 277–93.

29. Rahner, "Experience of the Holy Spirit," 200–203.

I believe, the real ambiguity in our experience of nature. The natural world is both unspeakably beautiful and also a place of competition and violence. In this ambiguity, I believe it is the good news of Jesus that is decisive for Christians. In Wisdom made flesh, God is revealed as Love that embraces suffering creation, transforming it from within, promising liberation and fulfillment. It is in the light of Wisdom made flesh that we may dare to think that in spite of all the violence and death, the glimpses we have of the presence of the God of love in the natural world can be trusted. It is in Christ that we can find the courage to say in spite of the ambiguity, Love is the meaning of the whole creation.

Brachina Gorge

On a recent Catholic Earthcare pilgrimage to the Flinders Ranges, a group of us were led into unforgettable experiences of Adnyamathanha country and culture. Sharpy Coultard guided us on a journey to Chambers Gorge and, walking with him up the gorge, we came to a place where it opens out into a space like a natural theater, perfectly shaped for ceremonial events, with ancient carvings on its rock walls. Sharpy shared with us his great love for this sacred place, and his feeling for it as a place of deep meaning. I had a sense of holy ground, and of quiet presence. Sharpy then led us over the low hills to a point where we could look out to Mount Chambers as he told the traditional story of its creation. On our way back we came across a large male emu, leading eight small chicks across the nearby hillside.

As we travelled the next day to Wilpena Pound, and then to a special place for me, Brachina Gorge, I reflected that while the Flinders Ranges had always been a place of spiritual connection, this sense had been heightened in me. There had been something lacking in my earlier experiences, which was no longer lacking, because of the chance to relate with Sharpy and other members of the Adnyamathanha people, and to learn from them of their culture and spirituality.

As we moved through Brachina Gorge we pondered its origins 800 million years ago, from a low-lying basin filled by the sea. We wondered at the Ediacara fossils found in and near Brachina Gorge, soft-bodied, highly developed creatures, preserved in impressions in the quartzite, creatures that lived 600 million years ago, and whose discovery gave rise to the naming of a new period of life. As we travelled through the gorge, the late-afternoon light lit up the ranges that towered above us in brilliant ochre-reds. Moving along quietly we came across dozens of shy, beautiful, yellow-footed rock wallabies come down from the hills to the creek bed.

I thought of the times I had camped in Brachina Gorge, watching the evening light on the ranges, being woken by birdsong, and finding peace, quiet joy, and inner freedom. I remembered how even on the long drive up from Adelaide, I would feel the pressures of everyday life begin to lift and something inexpressible, a sense of wholeness, begin to come to the fore. The healing and peace found in this place can be seen as the quiet, almost unspeakable, experience of the Spirit of God. And the emu with his young, the yellow-footed rock wallabies, the tree full of cockatoos, the smooth rounded rocks of the creek bed, and the brilliant colors of the cliffs above us, can all be seen as creaturely icons of Holy Wisdom.

Willunga Hills

When doing theological work, I am often sitting at the kitchen table of a little house south of Adelaide. I look out over a rolling landscape toward the Willunga Hills.[30] These hills are folded into one another in beautiful round-ed shapes that draw the eye and quieten the spirit. They run right across the horizon down to the sea on my far right. In between my window and the hills is a wide undulating plain. There are waves of late summer golden paddocks, green vineyards, olive plantations, and stands of eucalyptus.

Much closer, in the many greens of the indigenous shrubs that make up the front garden, beautiful little black and white birds with gold on their wings, New Holland Honeyeaters, flit between the branches looking for nectar, while magpies scratch around in the ground for grubs. This place leads me toward stillness. It offers liberation from the busyness of life, from the multiplicities of demands, and the noise that fills so much of contemporary existence.

There is an invitation to be quiet before the mystery it mediates. It is an invitation all too easy to resist, but to say yes, to dwell even for a short time in the mystery, is to find healing and peace. It is to be open to all that is in this place as a gift. It is to sense the presence of unspeakable Love, of the Spirit of God, at the heart of the natural world. It is to know Holy Wisdom revealed in honeyeaters, paddocks, vineyards, gum trees and the Willunga Hills.

---

30. This section is a revised version of Edwards, *Partaking of God*, 152–53.

The River Red Gum

Walking at Morialta, in the foothills near Adelaide, I have been stopped in my tracks by the sheer presence of a great River Red Gum (*Eucalyptus camaldulensis*).[31] This tree sits near a creek bed that is now often dry in summer. What arrested me first was its massive trunk, more than 4 meters in diameter. The cracked, peeling bark displays a beautiful range of muted colours: blacks, greys, browns, reds and creamy whites. The tree must be about 40 meters high. Almost lost in the blue-green leaves of its crown are flashes of the brilliant blues, greens, and oranges of dozens of rainbow lorikeets. On the ground, rosellas, orange-red with bright blue wings, forage in the undergrowth for seeds.

Older River Red Gums, like this one, drop branches, forming holes that become home for birds and many creatures. They provide shelter for insects, and some offer breeding places for fish in times of flood. Their fallen branches form habitats for many species of wildlife. River Red Gums can live for up to 700 years. The tree that I encounter was here long before Adelaide was colonized by England in 1836. It would have hosted generation after generation of indigenous Kaurna people, who in winter would move up to the foothills from the Adelaide plains for shelter, firewood, and food.

I meet this beautiful old tree in a moment of connection that takes me to stillness before its otherness. I am led into a sense of presence, to what is beyond the human and beyond words, to the uncontrollable and wild Spirit of God that "blows where it will" (John 3:8). In encountering this great tree, and all that lives in and around it, there is an experience of the Spirit as the unspeakable presence of God, as wonderfully creative fruitfulness, as the Life-Giver of the Creed, as the "dearest freshness deep down things" of Hopkins.

There is another dimension to this experience. In the Spirit, I can receive this River Red Gum as revelation, as God's self-revelation, as giving expression in its own creaturely way to that same eternal Wisdom of God that becomes flesh and has a human face in Jesus of Nazareth. In its unique, specific, and limited way, this River Red Gum is a gift and a presence of divine Wisdom in our world, a revelatory word that speaks quietly and beautifully of the eternal Word. It is the gift of the Wellspring of all creation, the generous and generative Lover, who is Origin and Source of All.

31. Revised version of Edwards, *Jesus and the Natural World*, 47, and "Sketching an Ecological Theology," 13–31.

Bibliography

Anatolios, Khaled. *Athanasius*. London: Routledge, 2004.

———. *Athanasius: The Coherence of His Thought*. New York: Routledge, 1998.

———. *Retrieving Nicaea: The Development and Meaning of Trinitarian Doctrine*. Grand Rapids: Baker, 2011.

Athanasius. *Against the Greeks*. In R.W. Thompson, ed. and trans., *Athanasius: Contra Gentes and De Incarnatione*. Oxford: Clarendon Press, 2004.

———. "Letters to Serapion." In *Works on the Spirit: Athanasius and Didymus: Athanasius's Letters to Serapion on the Holy Spirit and Didymus's On the Holy Spirit*, translated by Mark DelCogliano, et al, 51–138. New York: St Vladimir's Seminary, 2011.

———. "Selections from Against the Arians." In *Athanasius: The Coherence of his Thought*, edited by Khaled Anatolios, 87–175. New York: Routledge, 1998.

Edwards, Denis. *Human Experience of God*. New York: Paulist, 1983.

———. *Jesus and the Natural World*. Melbourne: Garratt, 2012.

———. *Partaking of God: Trinity, Evolution and Ecology*. Collegeville: Liturgical, 2014.

———. "Sketching an Ecological Theology of the Holy Spirit and the Word of God," *Concilium* 4 (2011) 13–31.

Egan, Harvey D. *Karl Rahner: Mystic of Everyday Life*. New York: Crossroad, 1998.

Leithart, Peter J. *Athanasius*. Grand Rapids: Baker, 2011.

Rahner, Karl. "The Experience of God Today." In *Theological Investigations* 11, 149–65. New York: Seabury, 1974.

———. "Experience of Self and Experience of God." In *Theological Investigations* 13, 122–32. New York: Seabury, 1975.

———. "Experience of the Holy Spirit." In *Theological Investigations* 18, 189–210. New York: Crossroad, 1983.

———. "Experience of the Spirit and Existential Commitment." In *Theological Investigations* 16, 24–51. New York: Seabury, 1979.

———. "Faith 1. The Way to Faith." In *Encyclopedia of Theology: A Concise Sacramentum Mundi*, edited by Karl Rahner, 496–500. London: Burns and Oates, 1975.

———. *Foundations of Christian Faith: An Introduction to the Idea of Christianity*. New York: Crossroad, 1978.

———. "The Ignatian Mysticism of Joy in the World," *Theological Investigations* 3, 277–93.

———. *Ignatius of Loyola Speaks*. South Bend, IN: St Augustine's Press, 2013.

———. "Reflections on the Experience of Grace." *Theological Investigations* 3, 86–90. New York: Seabury, 1974.

———. "The Spirituality of the Church of the Future." In *Theological Investigations* 20, 143–53. New York: Crossroad, 1981.

2

A Sublimely Natural God

Fragments of a Christian Spirituality of Nature

H. Paul Santmire

T HANKFULLY, IN THIS ERA of global ecological crisis, increasing des-
ecration of the poor of the earth, and deeply growing cosmic despair,
ours is the Church's first golden age of ecological theology, ecojustice
ethics, and the spirituality of nature. The rich but somewhat uneven era
of the ecotheological pioneers is over. A grand profusion of theological
works, historical, constructive, and practical, is now emerging in virtually
every corner of the earth.[1] In this chapter, I want to add a few thoughts to
these global discussions, from my own parochial setting, by identifying
some fragments of a Christian spirituality of nature,[2] with the theme of "A
Sublimely Natural God."

To develop this theme, I propose to highlight Martin Luther's rich and
paradoxical vision of the Divine immanence in nature and also share some
experiences of my own with one majestic configuration of nature, the great
Niagara River in North America. From beginning to ending, more generally, I
will be working critically with two fundamental constructs of classical Christian thought and practice, the themes of "spirit and matter."[3] For this reason,
I want to begin my discussion with some schematic historical explorations.

1. The discussion in Christian circles about ecological and cosmic questions is
now flourishing in virtually every region of the globe.

2. See Santmire, *Before Nature*.

3. Though problematic, these categories are widely taken for granted in Christian
circles and, to some extent at least, more widely in Western culture today.

Part One:
The Heritage of Spirit-Matter Dualism
in the Christian West

It is widely understood that classical Christian theology and spirituality in the West has been shaped in a significant measure by a hierarchical spirit-matter dualism. According to this way of thinking, things spiritual are good and things material are of lesser value, even, from some perspectives, such as that of Gnosticism, of profoundly negative value. The result has been a tendency at key junctures in the Christian tradition in the West to devalue the world of nature as a whole and the human body in particular, and to understand God as radically separate and thoroughly different from the material world of nature.

Many Christians today, along with an array of critics of the Christian tradition, just assume that this is how *all* Christians have thought, and do think, about the natural world. This is why my theme may sound strange to some. A sublimely natural God? Isn't such a notion contrary to the Bible itself? Doesn't the Gospel of John announce that "God is spirit" (John 4:24)? How could any reputable Christian speak of God this way? That, in fact, is a legitimate question. That the Gospel writer himself in all likelihood understood "spirit" here to mean "*the* Spirit" and, indeed, "*the* Spirit of the Creator," as that theme was attested in Gen 1:2, where we see the Spirit of the Creator hovering over the primeval waters of a creation-coming-into-being, is a critically important exegetical insight for us today.[4]

But it is also true, historically, that this Johannine text early on came to serve as a kind of pretext for a fundamental shift of meaning. The thought that God is the Spirit tended to lose its Hebraic concreteness as the Christian tradition became more and more rooted in the Greco-Roman culture of the West. After the early Christian era, it became increasingly commonplace to understand the Johannine text in terms of that hierarchical dualism of spirit over against matter that Latin culture took for granted. "God is the Spirit" tended to become "God is spiritual." Fast forward to our own time, when we can hear two professors of theology at a Catholic college in the U.S. explain, in a popular manual published by an evangelical press in 1999: "By saying God is spiritual, we mean that God is not a material being . . . God must be immaterial, that is, spiritual."[5]

---

4. For an insightful exegetical discussion of this issue, see Brown, *The Gospel According to John*, 172, 180.

5. Kreeft and Tacelli, *Handbook of Christian Apologetics*, 92.

I have traced this long and complex story, from earliest Christian times up to the modern era, in my 1985 historical study, *The Travail of Nature: the Ambiguous Ecological Promise of Christian Theology*.[6] There I identified two grand historical motifs that have shaped Christian thinking about nature: "the spiritual motif" and "the ecological motif." In this chapter, I want to distance myself from the problems of the former and claim some of the riches of the latter. But before I conclude these schematic historical considerations, I want to give one telling illustration of this problematic in the history of Christian thought, St. Augustine's reflections about the Trinity. For Augustine, we can say, God is sublimely spiritual. Augustine's thought is notoriously complex, notwithstanding its elegance. I tried to do justice to it in *The Travail of Nature*.[7] Here I want to focus only on his approach to understanding the Trinity, which is daunting enough in itself, perhaps more complex than many other themes in his thought.[8]

By the time Augustine began to throw himself into his monumental work *On the Trinity*, he himself had become critical of the hierarchical spirit-matter dualism that he had inherited from Greco-Roman culture and indeed, for some time, had himself celebrated. Early on, he had stated—a remark which was later to become enormously influential—that he wanted to know one thing and one thing only: God and the soul.[9] Notably missing from this existential statement of spiritual purpose was any substantive interest in the material world of nature. In this respect, at that early point in his theological career, he was totally under the influence of what I have called the spiritual motif. God and the soul was everything. In his later years, to be sure, he did qualify the influence of the spiritual motif in some important ways. But that motif still played a formative role, full-blown, in his mature reflections about the Trinity.

Augustine's thought about the Trinity was predicated on his understanding of the image of God (*imago Dei*) in humans.[10] And he understood that image in thoroughgoing spiritual terms. Thus, after reviewing a number of analogies from the creation in books 8–15 of *On the Trinity*, he settles on three as the most adequate statement of the divine image: memory, understanding, and will. Note that the human *imago*, thus understood, has little or nothing to do with the (material) human body. As Janet Soskice explains, "Augustine consistently privileged mind over body, sometimes

---

6. Santmire, *Travail of Nature*.

7. Ibid., chapter 4.

8. For a short introduction, see Williams, "De Trinitate."

9. Augustine, *Soliloquies*, I.

10. For this material, see Soskice, *The Kindness of God*, 131–34.

identifying the self with mind alone, and sometimes speaking of the mind as *using* the body."[11] This means that Augustine's most profound thoughts about the Divine identity are shaped by the spiritual motif. God is spiritual, for Augustine, in the sense that God's very identity is in no sense material.

No wonder, then, in the wake of such thoughts, that one major tradition in western Christian thought and practice—not only expressed, but also fomented by Augustine—bequeathed to us this problematic spiritual vision: God's relation to the material order of creation is primarily a relation of *distance* and God's own identity is *radically different* from the material order. That the same line of thinking as a matter of course held that the human creature, made in the image of God, is likewise essentially distant and different from the nature, was a set of assumptions also fraught with ominous theological, ethical, and spiritual implications.

Which puts those Christians today, who both want to take the classical Christian tradition seriously and to respond to what are the fundamentally material crises of these times, in a serious predicament. Insofar as Christian thought and practice is still under the influence of the spiritual motif, Christians are historically ill-equipped or perhaps un-equipped to respond to the nexus of crises we are now facing with human life on planet Earth in its evolutionary milieu and in the face of the unfathomable immensities and the universal destructiveness of the larger cosmos as we understand it today. This is the heritage of the tradition of hierarchical spirit-matter dualism in the Christian West. Our crisis today is fundamentally material. But the theology that many of us have inherited is fundamentally spiritual. Where does that leave us? Thankfully, not without theological and spiritual resources.

Part Two:
A Paradoxical Vision of God at Home In Nature

In *The Travail of Nature*, I identified a second approach to understanding the meaning of nature in the Christian tradition, as I have already noted: the ecological motif. I traced signs of that motif in a number of figures, among them Irenaeus in the second century, the mature Augustine, in some respects, in the early fifth century, Francis in the thirteenth century, and Luther and Calvin in the sixteenth century. Here I want to highlight Luther's theology, because of its robust rigor over against what I have called the spiritual motif and, not without importance, its conceptual accessibility.[12] Luther

11. Soskice, 133 (italics hers).

12. For both Luther and Francis, matter matters. But in Luther's case, the theological underpinnings related to nature are much more visible.

gives us, I believe, a compelling vision of a God who is neither distant nor separate from, but at home in the world of nature.

To understand Luther aright, it is necessary at the outset to identify a form of theological discourse employed by Luther which is largely out of favor in our own era, the discourse of paradox. While the word paradox itself appears now and again in theological discussions today, paradox itself is not typically employed self-consciously and consistently, as it was by Luther. Contrast the use of analogy or metaphor in theological arguments, which is frequently discussed. Sallie McFague is a prime example of this, both with respect to her reflections about the theological use of metaphor and her substantive analogical discussion of nature as the Body of God.[13] I by no means want to suggest that theological use of analogy is somehow unhelpful. Indeed, I will presently highlight one particular analogy, in order to facilitate our contemplation of the naturalness of God. Paradox, in my view, is best suited to facilitate our thinking about *how* God is present; analogy is best suited to help us to grasp *who* the God is who is present.

This is not the place to explore the discourse of paradox in detail. It was invoked, in different ways, in the modern era by thinkers as diverse as Søren Kierkegaard and Paul Tillich. I hope it will be sufficient here to note just this much. Luther was indeed a paradoxical thinker. From his earliest years as a monk, Luther's spirituality had been shaped by the paradoxical language of mystical theology, particularly as that theology had been mediated to him through German mystics such as Johannes Tauler. Thus Luther himself felt comfortable with mystical paradoxes, such as the oft-cited utterance of one Hermes Trismegistus: "God is the circle whose center is everywhere but whose circumference is nowhere."[14] Luther was at home with the experiences narrated by those mystics familiar to him, too. This is a typical utterance about what he thinks of as the *rapture* of faith: "The Christ-faith is a being-taken-away (*raptus*) and a being carried away (*translatio*) from all that is experiential inwardly or outwardly to that which is experiential neither inwardly nor outwardly, toward God, the invisible, the totally exalted, inconceivable."[15]

Luther's most favored paradoxical practice was his invocation *of many prepositions* in order to point to the Divine immanence and to the Divine transcendence.[16] Luther was by no means satisfied with the use of

13. See McFague, *The Body of God*.

14. E.g., Luther, *Werke* (Weimar Ausgabe) *Tischreden* (hereinafter referred to as *WA*), 2:1742.

15. Luther, *Luther's Works* (hereinafter referred to as *LW*), 25: 293–94.

16. On occasion, Luther was wont to employ abstract language about the Divine immanence inherited mainly from his training in the philosophy of nominalism. His

only a single preposition, such as "above" or "in," or even with the three prepositions which are most frequently associated in our time with his sacramental theology, "in, with, and under." He insists that many prepositions must be used.[17] Those familiar with these matters will recognize that this is Luther's way, highly suggestive in my view, to affirm both the transcendence and the immanence of God, the so-called apophatic and kataphatic ways.

As Luther does this, moreover, he radicalizes the idea of the Divine spatiality. Our commonsense spatial categories simply do not apply to God, he believes.[18] Thus the fullness of God can dwell in a single grain of wheat, yet be beyond all things at the same time:

> God is substantially present everywhere, in and through all creatures, in all their parts and places, so that the world is full of God and He fills all, but without His being encompassed and surrounded by it. He is at the same time outside and above all creatures. These are all exceedingly incomprehensible matters; yet they are articles of our faith and are attested clearly and mightily in Holy Scripture . . . For how can reason tolerate it that the Divine Majesty is so small that it can be substantially present in a grain, on a grain, through a grain, within and without, and that, although it is a single Majesty, it nevertheless is entirely in each grain separately, no matter how immeasurably numerous these grains may be? . . . And that the same Majesty is so large that neither this world nor a thousand worlds can encompass it and say: "Behold, there it is!" . . . His own divine essence can be in all creatures collectively and in each one individually more profoundly, more intimately, more present than the creature is in itself, yet it can be encompassed nowhere and by no one. It encompasses all things and dwells in all, but not one thing encompasses it and dwells in it.[19]

Presupposing this paradoxical vision of the presence of God, in, with, and under all things and, with that vision, the paradoxical relativization of the spatiality of God, Luther can then depict the Divine presence in nature in strikingly visual terms. Thus Luther can envision the whole creation as

---

heart, however, seems to come alive when he discourses about the presence of God using many prepositions.

17. Ibid., 37:230, quoted by Bornkamm, *Luther's World of Thought*, 190: "Faith understands that in these matters 'in' is equivalent to 'above,' 'beyond,' 'beneath,' 'through and through,' and 'everywhere.'"

18. In this respect, as others, Luther was at home with the mystical tradition, epitomized in the discourse of Meister Eckhart.

19. Luther, WA XXIII, 134–36, cited by Bornkamm, *Luther's World of Thought*, 189.

the "mask of God."[20] This means, for Luther, that God is hidden there. But it also means that God is powerfully present there, in front of your very eyes. In the same vein, Luther thinks of the Creator vividly as being "with all creatures, flowing and pouring into them, filling all things."[21] And God's activity never ceases, in Luther's view. God is "an energetic power, a continuous activity, that works and operates without ceasing. For God does not rest, but works without ceasing."[22] For Luther, therefore, God's creating is not merely some transcendental event before the beginning of time. The Divine act of creation is also now. And that Divine activity intimately and powerfully permeates the whole visible creation.

Corresponding to Luther's understanding of the whole visible creation as permeated with the presence of God is Luther's view of the fitness of the visible creation itself to accommodate the Divine presence, a view sometimes identified by the theological formula that "the finite is capable of the infinite" (*finitum capax infinitum*).[23] God can be at home in nature, according to Luther's way of thinking, because nature is a congenial place for God to dwell, not in itself some alien or even hostile setting. Nature, as it were, welcomes the Divine indwelling. This is an aspect of creation's goodness, in Luther's view.

Also corresponding to Luther's view of the creation as permeated with the Divine presence is his consistently lavish praise of the visible creation as a world of wonder and enchantment.[24] If someone would really understands a grain of wheat, Luther can say, that person would die of wonder.[25] While Luther does not generally present us with a view of the visible creation as "the theater of God's glory," as Luther's fellow Reformer, John Calvin, does, like Calvin, and indeed like numerous premodern theologians, Luther has what can be called an "omni-miraculous view" of the created world. For Luther, miracles are not supernatural. A seed is a miracle. The birth of a baby is a miracle. Indeed, Luther can say that such miracles are even greater than the Sacrament of the Altar. In one exuberant statement, Luther could even say that all creatures are sacraments.[26]

All this, the theme of *finitum capax infinitum* and the corresponding view of the world of nature as omni-miraculous, full of wonder and

---

20. Luther, *WA* XL: 1, 94.

21. Luther, *WA* X, 143.

22. Luther, *LW* XXI, 238; cited by Lohse, *Martin Luther's Theology*, 213.

23. See Hendel, "*Finitum Capax Infinitum.*"

24. For a discussion of these matters, see Santmire, *Travail of Nature*, 127–33.

25. Luther, *LW* VII, 57ff.

26. Kleckley, *Omnes Creaturae Sacramenta*, 207.

enchantment, is undergirded by Luther's theology of the creative Word of God, which Luther found attested in the Scriptures, especially in Gen 1 and many of the Psalms. For Luther, as Russell Kleckley observes: "Because of the Word, creation is filled with wonders. When miracles occur, the power of the Word working in creation is the driving force. At the same time, the usual order that creation follows . . . is neither less miraculous because we have grown accustomed to it, nor is it less dependent on the Word for its continuing existence and maintenance."[27]

All of this prompts me to observe that, for Luther, God is indeed at home in nature.[28] God is by no means far removed from nature. For Luther, the whole world of nature is charged with the presence of God.[29] A corollary of this conviction, for Luther, is that *this* is the only place to encounter God. The believer does not somehow rise above the world of nature to commune with God. This is where God is to be encountered in faith, addressed by the Word of God: in, with, and under all things. There is no other place. There is no other there.

Part Three:
An Analogical Vision of God in Godself as Natural

But which God is there? What is the identity of the God who is in, with, and under all things? To pursue my theme, "A Sublimely Natural God," I now want to move from the discourse of paradox to the discourse of analogy, in order to envision how we can think of God in Godself as natural. To this end, given the theological place in which I find myself existentially, standing within the flow of the classical Christian tradition, I will, as a matter of course, shape these reflections in Trinitarian terms. My question, then, is how can we envision the God Christians confess as "Father, Son, and Holy Spirit" as akin to nature, even as Augustine once envisioned this God as akin to spirit?

The answer is—not easily. Luther, for one, thought in Trinitarian terms, but that was not a central preoccupation of his theology. So we will probably be well advised to look elsewhere for theological guidance in this respect. Our own theological era, as is well known, has witnessed a remarkable

27. Ibid., 194.

28. It is difficult the categorize Luther's thought regarding God and the world. I propose that we think of his theology not as all things in God (panentheism) but as God (*theo*) in (*en*) all things (*panta*). Hence the term *theo-en-panism*.

29. God is not identical with nature, for Luther, by any means. His wide-ranging use of many pronouns decisively distances his thought from any pantheistic tendencies.

rebirth of Trinitarian thinking. So, in this sense, it appears that we are living in the right place at the right time. But the problems with Trinitarian thinking in our era are daunting, which also is well-known. Consider the patriarchal character of our Trinitarian inheritance. Why did my six year old daughter once ask her parents whether she could pray to the Father and to the Son and to the Holy Girl? I cannot begin to handle such questions here, if I can handle them at all. In my book *Before Nature* I try to address such matters in two respects, first, by following Jürgen Moltmann and his "new Trinitarian thinking." He envisions God in non-hierarchical, social terms and sees the first person of the Trinity, in particular, as "the motherly Father" who suffers.[30] Second, in *Before Nature*, I also recommend that we should regularly and systemically think and speak of God not just as Father, Son, and Holy Spirit, but also as Giver, Gift, and Giving. In these ways, in my view, it may be possible to demythologize patriarchal thinking and set in motion new, post-patriarchal ways of envisioning the Trinity. Here I can only announce this theological commitment and then proceed where angels may rightly fear to tread.

All Trinitarian thinking is, of course, analogical. I have already referred to Augustine's own approach to the Trinity, according to which he envisions the Trinity analogically as memory, understanding, and will. Augustine, of course, was not the first to invoke analogies to envision the Trinity. Theologians like Tertullian at the turn of the third century and Gregory of Nyssa in the late fourth century, self-consciously employed analogies in order to facilitate their discussions of the Trinity. I believe that in this, our ecological age, the time is at hand, perhaps as never before, to explore the use of *analogies from nature* in our Trinitarian reflections deliberately and intensely. Such analogies were occasionally employed in the past, but more often than not, as far as I have been able to determine, more in passing than in substance.[31]

The Analogy of Torrential Power

So come with me. I want to take you to a land far away—to a mighty river, in fact, the great Niagara River in North America, which flows between two of that continent's "Great Lakes," Erie and Ontario. And I propose to take

30. See Moltmann, "The Motherly Father," 51.

31. Analogies from nature, of course, are commonplace in popular presentations of the Christian faith in our time—water, for example, which can take three forms, as solid, liquid, and gas. But use of such analogies unreflectively may pay diminishing returns.

you there in the analogical terms of a personal narrative. Note well that this particular analogical narrative, as I choose to call it, can by no means stand alone. In *Before Nature* I give equal place to two other analogies for the Trinity that are—in terms of my discussion here—spiritual as well as natural: an analogy from a human community and an analogy of a single human self-sacrifice. But I want to highlight the analogical narrative that primarily pertains to nature here. I will call it the analogy of torrential power.

Why are we doing this? Think of the size and age of our universe, populated as it is with some 500 billion galaxies, some 13 billion years old and still expanding. Our reflection about God must be commensurate with a universe like this. Much theological and spiritual reflection these days, I have observed, is much more limited. It has a default terrestrial, if not totally anthropocentric, focus when nature is being discussed, as if God were chiefly the God of human life on earth. Such reflection often suppresses, as well, reference to gargantuan terrestrial phenomena like tsunamis, earthquakes, or volcanic eruptions. On the contrary, the triune God is a God of astounding power, in, with, and under all the cosmic immensities. To be sure, the theme of divine power is in some respects highly problematic, particularly when it is construed abstractly in terms of "omnipotence." My meanings here, however, are concrete. Divine power, in my view, means that the triune God, as the God of all things, has an all-comprehending cosmic reach.

This brings me back to the primary point I want to make here. For me, *the triune God is natural as well as personal.* God must therefore be thought of in terms of a nature analogy as well as in terms of a social analogy or a personal analogy, necessary as such analogies are. Unless nature is a primary analogy for God, as a matter of fact, nature—especially when it is understood cosmically, that is, in terms of the whole universe (or universes)—will essentially remain something distant from God or even alien to God. On the contrary, I believe, the "living God" confessed by biblical traditions is as much akin to nature and its immensities as this God is akin to communal interpersonal relationships or personal self-sacrifice. So let me show you a way now to imagine the God who discloses Godself to us.

Already as a young child, I was fascinated with the Niagara River, as its waters seemed to propel themselves from Lake Erie toward and over the magnificent thundering of Niagara Falls, and then flowed through the huge and gaping Niagara River gorge and on into Lake Ontario. Living as close to the Falls as my family did, we visited them often, both because they were such an astounding sight in themselves and because friends and family members from around the country found that our home was a convenient station on *their* way to visit the Falls. When I was a teenager, too, in the midst of the sometimes oppressive summer heat, my friends and I would on occasion jump into someone's car and head for the Niagara River. Our destination was only halfway between Lake Erie and the Falls, but we thought of the Falls intensely as we plunged into the surging river waters far above the Falls to see if we could make any headway swimming upstream. We couldn't. Obviously, we were horrified by the thought of being carried too far downstream. Images of helpless human bodies, being swept along by the torrents and then over the Falls, filled our minds. But it was safe enough for us, all accomplished swimmers, as we flailed our arms at the height of our powers against the currents, only to remain stationary. In retrospect, I think that that swimming was a kind of (safe) adolescent dancing with death.

Who can describe Niagara Falls, this icon of the historic American consciousness? Many writers and countless painters have tried. I will only tell what little I know. The Falls were formed at the end of the last ice age. Waters from three of the bodies we now call the Great Lakes carved out these Falls, leaving the gigantic river gorge before them, as those waters made their way forward, eventually, toward the Atlantic Ocean and as they relentlessly chiseled away at the bedrock underneath, inching the Falls ever closer back toward Lake Erie.

Today, over the two separate branches of the Falls, the American and the Canadian, more than 6 million cubic feet of water fall every minute. They plunge over heights that reach as high as 170 feet, and they extend more than a half mile wide. *Thundering* is indeed a good word to describe the impression they make when you stand on the observation platform, feet away from the apex of the Falls. My brother remembers feeling the ground tremble under his feet at that point, on the Canadian side, when he stood there as a boy. Sometimes, looking down from that point, he and I would watch a little ship, far below in the gorge, often obscured by the mist—it was called the "Maid of the Mist" in those days—making its way toward the Falls, with yellow-coated tourists packed on its decks, and then turning around, just in time it seemed to me. Often, when my family had visitors and we motored down to see the Falls, after we had come home I would go to bed at night astounded. I would lie there thinking: never mind whether *I* am awake or asleep, *those tons and tons of water* keep flowing over the Falls and keep carving out the gorge in front of them without ceasing! It was truly an awe-inspiring memory for me as I lay there in the solitude of my bed.

Once, as a young man, Paul Tillich—who, after he emigrated to the United States, was to become one of the nation's leading theologians during the middle of the twentieth century—visited a steel mill in his native Prussia. It was my privilege to study six years with Tillich as an undergraduate. The visit to the steel mill was a story he told more than once in my hearing, although I am not sure whether he ever wrote about it. With youthful passion and spiritual abandon, he recounted, he looked at the flowing molten steel and said, "That is God." Tillich would later qualify such statements carefully. But I know what he had meant. Had I had the same kind of inspiration in my own youth, I could have easily looked at the Falls and the gorge and the turbulent waters below and said, "That is God."

The Niagara Falls and the Trinity

If we consider the mysterious majesty of the Trinity, such exuberant statements can, indeed, readily emerge from the mind and heart. Consider the Falls themselves, ever overflowing, throwing down immense cascades of water every second of the day. *God the Father* is like that, always and ever overflowing with goodness and creativity, however alien to us that goodness and creativity might sometimes be, always and ever, indeed eternally, being *the Giver*. Whether we humans sleep or not, whether we notice it or not, the Father is constantly the Giver, pouring forth power, from alpha to omega of the whole creation and, indeed, in the eternal being and becoming of God in Godself.

Notice, further, that those waters that pour over the Falls are thereafter channeled for a number of miles. The cliffs lining the river below the Falls keep those waters moving in a single direction rather than chaotically flooding everywhere. The cliffs give a kind of good order to the waters below. The cliffs, as it were, channel the overflowing divine goodness and creativity in a specific direction and give them a certain kind of form as these move toward the vast basin of Lake Ontario. Early on in the Christian tradition, the "word" (*logos*) referred to in the first chapter of John, where the Son of God was being envisioned as co-creator with the Father, was interpreted in the metaphysical categories of the day as the logos of the creation, that ontological structure which "holds all things together" (see Col. 1:17). The *Son of the Father*, called the logos of God, was understood to be the divine agency that gives form and good order to all things and sustains them in their being. Thus I imagine the cliffs of the Niagara River gorge, on either side of the river below, as a gift in a certain sense: a gift of order and direction.

So we have this image thus far. The eternally overflowing creative goodness of the Father is akin to the waters cascading over the Falls. The shaping and directing function of the cliffs downriver from the Falls are akin to the workings of the eternal Son or *logos*, holding all things together, shaping and directing all things toward their future consummation in the eternal kingdom of God, as the river flows on into the vast reaches of Lake Ontario.

But do not overlook the turbulence of the waters, especially at the base of the Falls, as they cascade down into virtually immeasurable currents and eddies and countercurrents and countereddies. Contemplate that turbulence. That apparently chaotic churning appears to be what moves those waters downstream and works to carve out ever new ways for the pulsating river to rush on toward its resting place in Lake Ontario. That turbulence, we may think, is like the work of the *Spirit*, the "lifegiver" announced in the New Testament and in traditional images. That, in turn, is akin to the vision of the chaotic "tongues of fire" that fell down on humans and drove ordinary men and women to become saints and martyrs. It suggests to me also the impulsive life force of God that draws the evolutionary history of our cosmos forward toward its eternal resting place in God. It recalls, likewise, the image of the breath or spirit of God "hovering" creatively—giving birth is what the text suggests—over the primeval waters of the first days of creation depicted in Gen 1. Christian interpreters of that Genesis text by the second century already understood that "breath" or "spirit" of God to be the Spirit of the triune God.

Sometimes, when I was a young boy and had just returned from a visit to the Falls, I would spend an inordinate amount of time in my bath just before going to bed. I would use all the force available to my boyish arms to swirl those waters in what I imagined to be a hundred different directions. As I did, I would contemplate all the currents and eddies, insofar as I could see them. And, in doing so, I would recall the turbulence of the Niagara River at the base of the Falls and beyond, and I would marvel at its complexity and power and mystery. I now believe that the Spirit of God once worked, in many times and in many ways, on the soul of that young boy as he contemplated the overflowing waters—ever flowing, it seemed, in his mind and heart—and the work of the river walls below that captured and channeled that overflowing, even as those currents were astoundingly turbulent, moving in ways that no mortal mind could predict or understand. So I thought in those days—and so I still think.

Isn't it in reach of at least a few mortal souls to think of God not only in spiritual terms, such as joy and love, but also as one who is, at once, resplendent with the glory of eternally overflowing creative goodness, however alien it may be to us, a God of immeasurable and indeed inconceivable power, holding and shaping every creature and all creatures at once in being, for countless millennia, channeling all creatures wondrously toward the end for which they were first created, in their becoming, and at the same time moving them forward by the turbulence of this process to their final fulfillment, on the day when God will be all in all?

Bibliography

Augustine. *The Soliloquies of Saint Augustine.* Translated by Thomas F. Gilligan and Robert P. Russell. New York: Cosmopolitan Science and Art, 1943.

Bornkamm, Heinrich. *Luther's World of Thought.* Translated by Martin H. Bertram. St. Louis: Concordia, 1958.

Brown, Raymond E. *The Gospel according to John.* Anchor Bible 29A. Garden City, NY: Doubleday, 1970.

Hendel, Kurt, K. "*Finitum Capax Infinitum*: Luther's Radical Incarnational Perspective." *Seminary Ridge Review* 10.2 (2008) 20–35.

Kleckley, Russell C. *Omnes Creaturae Sacramenta: Creation, Nature and World View in Luther's Theology of the Lord's Supper.* Dissertation théologie München. Columbia: privately published, 1990.

Kreeft, Peter, and Ronald K. Tacelli. *Handbook of Christian Apologetics: Hundreds of Answers to Crucial Questions.* Downers Grove, IL: InterVarsity, 1994.

Lohse, Bernhard. *Martin Luther's Theology: Its Historical and Systematic Development.* Translated by Roy A. Harrisville. Minneapolis: Fortress, 1999.

Luther, Martin. *Luther's Works.* Edited by Jaroslav Pelikan. St. Louis: Concordia, 1972.

———. *Werke* (Weimar Ausgabe) *Tischreden.* Weimar: Böhlaus, 2000.

McFague, Sallie, *The Body of God: An Ecological Theology.* Minneapolis: Fortress, 1993.

Moltmann, Jürgen. "The Motherly Father: Is Trinitarian Patripassianism Replacing Theological Patriarchalism?" *Concilium* 143 (1981) 51.

Santmire, H. Paul. *Before Nature: A Christian Spirituality.* Minneapolis: Fortress, 2014.

———. *The Travail of Nature: The Ambiguous Ecological Promise of Christian Theology.* Minneapolis: Fortress, 1985.

Soskice, Janet M. *The Kindness of God: Metaphor, Gender, and Religious Language.* New York: Oxford University Press, 2007.

Williams, Rowan. "De Trinitate." In *Augustine through the Ages: An Encyclopedia*, edited by Allan D. Fitzgerald et al., 845–51. Grand Rapids: Eerdmans, 1999.

3

An Emerging Horizon

Learning to See the World in a Different Light through the Liturgy

Ernst M. Conradie

ONE MAY OBSERVE THAT there is a certain dialectic at work in the Christian liturgy: Worshipers are led to come before God (*coram Deo*), to focus on God alone in order to experience the triune God's presence in the world, to seek God's face, to see the invisible, to see God (*visio Dei*). This very experience helps worshipers to see the world in a new light, in the light of the Light of the world, namely as God's beloved creation, as something worth dying for and as God's own sanctified home through the permeating presence of God's Spirit. This vision emerges at best through the celebration of the liturgy in which God's counter-intuitive presence in the world is recognized, most notably in the cross of Jesus Christ.[1]

When Christians (as a people on the way) depart from the liturgy with God's blessing, they look at the world through new eyes, having been trained to see it through God's eyes, with what Desmond Tutu calls the eyes of the heart, with delight, grief, and compassion—and therefore with a sense of justice, as something so valuable that it is worth dying for (John 3:16). They return to the world and their daily lives seeing the world as God's world. Thus, as Christoph Blumhardt once remarked, one is converted twice: first from the world to God and then from God back to the world through an awakening of one's vocation in the world. Such a liturgical vision therefore

---

1. Conradie, *The Earth in God's Economy*, 51–59.

suggests the need for a dual epistemological movement from the world to God and from God to the world.

In *The Earth in God's Economy* (2015) I suggest that Christians are enabled through such an emerging liturgical vision to see the world as the whole household of God and the history of the universe as God's economy (or house-holding). This moral vision (seeing as) counters the dominant images of the world in liberal romanticism, late-industrial capitalism, social Darwinism and nature mysticism alike. It has far reaching implications for a distinct ethos, praxis and spirituality (being as) amidst economic inequalities and ecological destruction.

In this contribution I will first illustrate the liturgical dialectic between orientation, disorientation and reorientation with imagery found in Matt 16:13–19. I will then explore the question how the liturgical experience in which God and the world are held together in a common vision becomes possible in the first place. After all, we can see neither God nor the world as such. How does one detect God's presence in the world and the world's participation in God? I will investigate the strengths and limitations of the concept of an "emerging horizon" that becomes possible through a hermeneutic "fusion of horizons."[2] Does this enable one to see further from within a specific (liturgical) location and to surmise what lies beyond the horizon, where land and sky, earth and heaven meet? I will suggest that creation theology accounts for such liturgical reorientation by locating any particular place within a wider context, within what lies beyond an always shifting horizon.

The Cosmic Width of the Rock
in Matthew 16:13–19

The local and the cosmic are connected in the language of the biblical witnesses with remarkable ease. One may say that cosmic reflection is enabled by particular experiences in a particular locality. Every place may serve as the center of the cosmos. In terms of contemporary cosmology every galaxy is the center of the universe. Instead of offering a generalized survey of the use of cosmic language in the biblical texts (which would be impossible), I will focus on only one example.

According to Matthew's version of the gospel, the furthest that Jesus travelled northwards was to the area around the town of Caesarea Philippi, 40 km north of the Sea of Galilee. The city was previously known as Banias, an Arabic pronunciation of Panias. This name honoured the Greek god

2. See Gadamer, *Truth and Method*.

Pan—a half-man, half-goat deity often depicted playing a flute—who was worshiped in a famous grotto there. During the time of Jesus' ministry the area was ruled by Herod the Great's son Philip, who had renamed the city Caesarea. To distinguish it from the coastal Caesarea Maritima, it became known as Caesarea Philippi. This was as pagan a territory as could be found in Israel at that time. Most inhabitants were either Greek or Syriac.[3] The city had been built near the Banias spring, which gushes from a rock face and flows into one of the streams that feed the Jordan River. It lies at the southern slope of the massive Mount Hermon (16 km north of Caesarea Philippi), rising 2,814 meters above sea level on the border between Syria and Lebanon.

According to the tourist guides for visiting the Holy Land,[4] it is easy to visualize Jesus standing by the steep cliff of the Banias spring and telling Peter, using the local imagery, that he would become the rock on which the church will be built. Moreover, the event of the Transfiguration took place 6 days later on a "high mountain" (Matt 17:1). Although Christian tradition places this event on Mount Tabor near Nazareth (575m), some believe Mount Hermon to be a more likely site.

The scene could not be more dramatic. Imagine Jesus standing on the cliff with his back to the north (the world of imperial powers) looking beyond the horizon in the direction of Jerusalem (around 200 km to the south) where he rightly anticipated that he would be killed by the collusion of imperial and religious powers. In between lies Galilee, the breeding ground for political resistance against Roman occupation, anxiously awaiting the coming Messiah who would liberate them from imperial oppression. Further to the south lies Samaria with its complex history of religious compromise and resistance against foreign influence and Jerusalem rule. In this context Jesus asked his disciples: Who do you think I am? Peter's response is an intimidating one: You are the Christ, the expected Messiah. No wonder Jesus instructed his disciples (including Simon the Zealot—Matt 10:4) not to spread the word.

Given this constellation of powers, how are the disciples supposed to make sense of the world in which they lived? Although Peter is called "blessed" (*makarios*), it would have been hard to make sense of that given the situation beyond the temporary retreat of the current location. What lies beyond the horizon? What is required here is to see the invisible, a notion that is still widely recognized in indigenous spiritualities. It therefore comes as no surprise that Jesus used cosmic language to help the disciples

3. Keener, *Matthew*, 424.

4. See http://www.seetheholyland.net/caesarea-philippi/.

to reorientate themselves in this world. The gospel according to Matthew uses the term "heaven" four times in the space of three verses to locate the rock on which they were presumably standing in a wider cosmic context. Jesus suggests that it is his Father in heaven who revealed his true identity to Peter. Peter will receive the keys (symbolizing authority) to the kingdom of heaven so that what Peter locks on earth will be locked in heaven and what he unlocks on earth will be unlocked in heaven.

Clearly, the realm of the invisible is crucial here, but where would this kingdom be located and would this be of any earthly (not to mention ecological) use? Reflection on this kingdom may be understood as a matter of inclusion and exclusion in persecuted Christian communities (surely faced with issues of security and betrayal), but the cosmic terminology should not be domesticated. The imagery here is of a temple as the center of the cosmos, built upon a firm rock above the primordial waters, with secure gates separating the underworld from the reign of the Father. Eduard Schweizer reports that "Israel pictured the earth as a hollow mountain towering above the primordial sea, and later as the capstone introduced into the structure of the cosmos by God to keep the floods of the primordial ocean contained."[5] He adds that "the rock on which the temple was built was thought of as sealing the gateway to the underworld with the rest of the world extending around it; as such it is also termed the gate of heaven." The keys are therefore not merely an indication of administrative responsibility for storerooms or entrance to living quarters but of maintaining cosmic order, of distinguishing between the world of the living and the world of the dead. The persecuted church built on this rock is being threatened but will not be overcome.

My sense is that it would help to translate the Greek *gēs* here as "land." If so, "heaven" indicates not so much a vertical axis (looking up into the night sky) but what lies beyond the distant horizon. It is the realm of the future, of expectation, of something that is already present but not yet visible from the current location (even if standing on a cliff). The connection between what happens (what Peter will unlock or lock) on earth (what lies within the current horizon) and in heaven (what lies beyond that horizon) should be noted. The key here is of course the reality of the church (at the time when Matthew wrote the gospel). The church is built on a rock that transcends imperial power. It will not be overwhelmed by the forces of death and destruction, symbolized by the Gates of Hades (is there an allusion to the Banias spring here?), the threshold leading to the shady underworld, the realm of the dead (Sheol, not to be confused with hell).

---

5. Schweizer, *Matthew,* 341–42.

Whether that rock is a symbol for the Petrine office (as Catholic interpreters are inclined to stress) or the apostolic witness to Jesus Christ (as Protestants may wish to insist) or Jesus' own words is rather immaterial.[6] What is important is to see (with the eyes of hope), beyond the present constellation of powers, how the resurrection of the crucified Messiah will unlock a new dispensation, the coming reign of God, the establishment of the household of God which Jesus will build (*oikodomē*—verse 18) through the church on this rock (Peter).

The Hermeneutical Function of Emerging Horizons

I need to acknowledge up front that the word "horizon" is scarcely found in the biblical roots of the Christian tradition. In some translations it is used in Job 26:10: "He marks out the horizon on the face of the waters for a boundary between light and darkness" (NIV), but it is hardly used anywhere else. Norman Habel suggests that Gen 1:1 may be translated as "land" (instead of earth) and "sky" (instead of heaven): "In the Beginning, when God created the sky and the land, the land was unformed and empty; darkness was upon the face of the deep, and the Spirit of God glided over the face of the waters."[7] Land and sky are thus held together by gazing at the horizon. However, the concept horizon has played no substantive role in theological reflection on God's creation.

In Christian ecotheology the term horizon has been used in titles such as *Ethics for a Small Planet: New Horizons on Population, Consumption and Ecology* (1998) and in *Christian Faith and the Earth: Current Paths and Emerging Horizons in Ecotheology* (2015).[8] However, it plays no substantive role in these volumes in terms of theological content. A more substantive use of the term horizon may be found in philosophical hermeneutics, usually

6. The wordplay with Peter (Aramaic: Cephas) and rock (Greek: petra) is obviously deliberate but the allusion to Simon-bar-Jonah is trickier. Is this simply an abbreviation for "John" or a reference to the prophet Jonah (who, like Peter was reluctant to preach the gospel to the gentiles) and thus to the sign of Jonah (Matt 12:38–42). If the latter, it could allude to the subsequent martyrdom of Peter and the hope for the resurrection of the dead and the day of judgement (also of imperial powers). Or is Simon ("whom God has heard") Peter (the rock) contrasted here with Simon the zealous / Zealot? One may also recall another Simon-bar-Kohba, the leader of a revolt against the Roman Empire in 132 who established an independent state for three years. On this, see Gundry, *Matthew*, 328.

7. Habel and Corowa, *Rainbow Spirit*, 10.

8. Maguire and Rasmussen, *Ethics for a Small Planet*; Conradie, et al., *Christian Faith and the Earth*.

with reference to Martin Heidegger's description of temporality as the given horizon of meaning within which our everyday understanding is situated and in the light of which we see something *as* something. Heidegger speaks of the interpretation of time as the possible horizon for any understanding of Being. The point is that we are always standing within a horizon and cannot view it as it were from the outside. The horizon both enables and limits one's ability to see and thus understand something against a particular background. The use of the term horizon (a more graphic rendering of the notion of preunderstanding) is taken further in Hans-Georg Gadamer's description of the process through which an interpreter encounters another world. A horizon is for Gadamer not something static or a rigid frontier, but something that shifts with one and invites one to advance forward.[9] This implies two dimensions of the notion of "horizon:" First, "it represents a standpoint that limits the possibility of vision . . . The horizon is the range of vision that includes everything that may be seen from a particular vantage point."[10] At the same time, this narrowness of a horizon allows the possibility of an expansion of horizon and the opening up of new, emerging horizons. Within a limited horizon where one cannot see far enough, one tends to overvalue what is near, while one can assess the relative significance of things if one can see beyond such a narrow horizon.[11] The expansion of one's horizons is possible given a sense of historicity. Gadamer explains: "The historical movement of human life consists in the fact that it is never utterly bound to one standpoint, and hence can never have a truly closed horizon. The horizon is, rather, something into which we move and that moves with us. Horizons change for a person who is moving. Thus the horizon of the past out of which all human life lives and which exists in the form of a tradition is always in motion."[12]

For Gadamer, the encounter with another's horizon is similar to the understanding that takes place in a conversation when one discovers the standpoint and horizon of another person without necessarily having to agree with that person, but in the process also gains clarity on the distinctiveness of one's own standpoint and horizons.[13] This implies the awareness of a tension between two "worlds" that requires a willingness not to cover up this tension between a classic text and the present through naïve assimilation within the horizon of a pre-existing tradition. That would imply

9. Gadamer, *Truth and Method*, 217.

10. Ibid., 269

11. Ibid.

12. Ibid., 271.

13. Ibid., 270.

premature closure. At the same time (and this may appear to be contradictory), interpretation also involves what Gadamer calls a "fusion of horizons." Interpretation entails an appropriation of the meaning of (for example) a text, but then in such a way that the distance, the otherness of the text is maintained and respected and consciously highlighted.[14]

The term horizon has been imported into theological discourse especially by Anthony Thiselton, whose books include *The Two Horizons* (1980) and *New Horizons in Hermeneutics* (1992). A Festschrift in Thiselton's honour is aptly titled *Horizons in Hermeneutics*. Porter and Malcomb (the editors) note that the title utilizes one of the dominant metaphors in hermeneutics to capture Thiselton's own contribution to hermeneutics as "the attempt to illuminate the transforming engagement of the horizon of the interpreter with the horizon of the biblical text."[15] They add that such an engagement must begin with the acknowledgement that the text to be interpreted is genuinely other. Thiselton's earlier work explored the nature of such an engagement (given the historical situatedness of both the classic text and the contemporary interpreter. His later work focused on the transformative dimension of such engagement. Here he draws on the reception theory of Hans Robert Jauss to describe the "horizon of expectation" that a reader brings to a text. Such a horizon of expectation includes a network of provisional assumptions which are open to revision. The interpreter may not be conscious of all that a horizon of expectation sets in motion, makes possible or excludes.[16]

Thiselton explains: "Every reader brings a horizon of expectation to the text. This is a mind-set, or system of references, which characterizes the reader's finite viewpoint amidst his or her situatedness in time and history. Patterns of habituation in the reader's attitudes, experiences, reading-practices, and life, define and strengthen his or her horizon of expectation. A text, however, can surprise, contradict, or even reverse such a horizon of expectation."[17] For Thiselton, this transforming engagement does not imply that the two horizons are merely "fused." The present horizon of the interpreter can only be understood by situating that within some larger frame.[18] A description of "objective" (e.g., sociological or psychological) data derived from present experience is never value-neutral. Reading the signs of the time requires discernment. Likewise, the biblical texts (or other classic

---

14. Ibid., 273.

15. Porter and Malcolm, *Horizons in Hermeneutics*, x.

16. Thiselton, *New Horizons*, 44.

17. Ibid., 34.

18. Ibid., 608.

sources) are resituated in contemporary contexts that enlarge the scope of their influence. This implies a double shifting of horizons. What does the "fusion" of horizons then entail? Both the text and the contemporary context are situated within the larger frame of an eschatological horizon that incorporates past and present as moments in history.[19] History is thus the most comprehensive horizon of Christian theology.[20] This provides the hint that a fusion of horizons does not merely entail an expanded vision but also a sense of being situated within a more encompassing historical framework.

If so, there is a dual movement in which one incorporates new encounters (including the reading of classic texts, but also liturgical experiences) into one's current horizon—which therefore simultaneously expands one's horizon (as when climbing a hill). However, such new encounters also remind one of the need to situate one's present position within a larger frame, namely of that which lies beyond the immediate horizon. Given the temporal positioning within such a horizon, the present moment is thus situated in terms of the legacy of the past and whatever tomorrow may bring. Of course, one does not know what lies beyond the horizon. Nevertheless one may gather a glimpse of what that may entail on the basis of previous experiences of shifting horizons. This accounts for the possibility of experiences of transcendence.[21] Intimations of emerging horizons are governed by a sense of anticipation but also of anxiety and surprise. That is a common experience in climbing towards a ridge or a mountain peak.

The Horizon as an Ecologically Dangerous Metaphor?

It may be noted that the term horizon is used in philosophical hermeneutics in a clearly metaphorical sense and scarcely with any reference to any particular landscape or horizon. Thiselton does note (following Heidegger) that the term "world" has hermeneutical significance in providing and sustaining a given "horizon of meaning." A mountain for example, is not merely an object at hand, but has a distinctly different meaning from the standpoint of a climber, a cartographer and an artist.[22] The value of the term horizon is that it captures the network of revisable expectations and assumptions that a reader brings to a text. It "calls attention to the fact that our finite situatedness in time, history and culture defines the present

19. Ibid.

20. Ibid., 332.

21. For a discussion, see Conradie, "A Semiotic Notion of Transcendence."

22. Thiselton, *The Two Horizons*, 30–31.

(though always expanding) limits of our 'world,' or more strictly the limits of what we can 'see.'"[23]

By contrast, in the context of cultural anthropology and cultural geography the use of the term horizon as a function of the description of a landscape is problematized. This may be illustrated with reference to Tim Ingold's work on the perception of the environment. Although his approach is deeply influenced by the work of Merleau-Ponty on perception and Heidegger on phenomenology, he offers a sustained critique of the distancing that visual metaphors such as "horizon" seem to imply. Ingold suggests that we do not see the sky. It is not so much what we see as what we see in the sky. Likewise, seeing requires light; we see something in the light. We do not see the light. The sky is not illuminated; it is luminosity itself.[24] Ingold emphasizes the tactile engagement with the immediate environment instead of seeing landscape as a visual representation.[25] For Ingold, perception is about movement. Seeing is not the achievement of a mind in a body, but of the whole organism as it moves about in its environment. What is perceived is not a thing as such but paths that may intersect with the organism's own movement.[26] Indeed, for Ingold, movement *is* knowing.[27] Here the tactile senses have a certain priority over visual perception. It is sensing the movement that invites vision and discernment in order to make sense of what has been experienced.

Ingold explains that the "scape" in the word "landscape" is derived from the Old English *sceppan* or *skyppan* (see the Afrikaans *skepping*, "creation") and not from the Greek *skopos* (the mark towards which the bowman aims, from the verb *skopein*, "to look"). In other words, the landscape is being shaped through inhabitation; it is not the distanced object of gazing, at a landscape painting, for example. Landscape is a verb not a noun, a process and not an object or an image.[28] This suggests an interplay between the haptic and the optical. Ingold argues that haptic engagement is close ranged and hands on, while an optic relation between mind and world is founded

23. Ibid., 46.

24. Ingold, *Being Alive*, 129.

25. Ingold seems to avoid the term horizon deliberately. "Horizon" does not appear in the index of Ingold's major books such as *The Perception of the Environment* (2000) or *Being Alive* (2011).

26. Ingold, *Being Alive*, 11.

27. Ibid., 160.

28. John Wylie captures Ingold's position: "The definition of landscape as a way of seeing perpetuates a duality of culture and nature, and erases first order issues of materiality, agency and embodied performance by locating landscape within a disembodied realm of cultural discourse and signification." In Wiley, "Landscape," 410.

on distance and detachment. Landscape as cartographic and optical projection is tainted by an objectifying bias.[29] Ingold thus challenges the Western privileging of sight over the other senses as a source of objective knowledge. Accordingly, hearing binds people together in community, while seeing isolates the individual from the world. With the ascendency of vision in the West, religion gave way to science.[30] In Marxist analyses, though, landscape is viewed in terms of process of economic production and cultural consumption. The optic gaze over the landscape towards a distant horizon is then one of exploration and exploitation.

From this perspective (sic!) the term horizon is hardly attractive for an environmental ethos. As John Wylie observes, "The conceptual shift from landscape-as-image to landscape-as-dwelling correlates with a substantive shift from horizon to earth. In general the proliferation of research on the body and embodied experience turns landscape from a distant object or spectacle to be visually surveyed to an up-close, intimate and proximate material milieu of engagement and practice."[31] Whereas dwelling suggests an ecological motif of being embedded in the land, the term horizon seems to suggest a distancing, less embodied Cartesian gaze.

The philosopher Edward Casey has a somewhat different view. He describes a horizon as a primary feature of landscape. He defines the horizon as "an arc within which a given landscape comes to an end—an end of visibility, of presence, of availability. A place as such has no horizon, only an enclosure or perimeter. Only when places are concatenated in a landscape is there anything like a horizon, which is the undelimited limit—or, better, the boundary—for the landscape as a whole."[32] A horizon constitutes the boundary of the landscape as a whole but this sense of boundary does not act as a barrier: "As a boundary, the horizon does not merely close off the landscape; it opens it up for further exploration, that is, for bodily ingression and exploration."[33] The self is then resituated within this landscape, within a sense of place, and is not merely defined in terms of self-consciousness.

Horizon and Our Infinite Longing

Such a more affirmative use of the term horizon, without losing the emphasis on an embodied sense of place, is also adopted by Didier Maleuvre in his

29. Ingold, *Being Alive*, 133.

30. Ingold, *The Perception of the Environment*, 155, 248.

31. Wylie, *Landscape*, 166–67.

32. Casey, "Between Geography and Philosophy," 690.

33. Ibid.

work *The Horizon: A History of Our Infinite Longing* (2011). He argues that the fascination with the outer reaches of life and knowledge is indeed the engine of Western civilization. In what follows I will draw rather extensively from the introductory and concluding chapters in Maleuvre's book and then return to the significance of the concept of horizon for an ecological understanding of the Christian liturgy.

Maleuvre does not shy away from the visual dimension of the horizon, nor from the obvious connotations of finitude and transcendence. This is how he describes the horizon:

> The horizon holds an image of human finitude, our limitedness in time, space and comprehension. The horizon isn't an objective boundary; it isn't really the place where earth and sky weld shut. It marks not the factual edge of the world, but the shifting line where perception trails off. A reflective phenomenon, a horizon bespeaks a beholder—the who, where, and when of its sighting. The "where" in particular: inasmuch as it limits perception, any horizon assumes the presence of a perceiver dwelling within, rather than above, the landscape. The horizon entails a ground-level immanent viewpoint on reality. It forbids the all-knowing proverbial eye in the sky. Not that the sky and what it symbolizes (the beyond, the unseen, the transcendent) is absent. On the contrary: the horizon arises from the action of casting an internal perspective on the faraway. Speaking theologically, it is a groundling's view of a world rife with transcendental openness.[34]

For Maleuvre, the horizon is an epistemological frontier:

> Insubstantial yet insuperable, the horizon symbolizes the shifting frontline between knowledge and reality. It is an image of the elusive, slippery, onward character of human finitude, of our limitedness in time, space, and understanding. Like the end of existence or the outer edge of knowledge, the horizon at the far end of earth and sky does not draw an objective limit; there, earth and sky do not come lip to lip. Drawing not the empirical boundary of the world but the soft edge where perception fades off, the "offing" is really a trick of vision. Where it glimmers, sight beholds its own vanishing. This vanishing—the trace of human vision seeing itself out—is indeed what we mean by horizon . . . Horizon highlights the subjective, makeshift nature of perceived reality . . . To perceive oneself perceiving is, inevitably, to look inward; it is to become conscious of the reach of

34. Maleuvre, *The Horizon*, xiii.

human experience. Images of the horizon crystallize perennial preoccupations within the overlapping limits of knowledge and existence.[35]

Maleuvre also recognizes the link between a horizon and both a secular and a religious notion of transcendence as a critique of a closed worldview (which he finds in Edward Casey's position[36]). He observes that, cosmologically, modernity is a journey from a closed world to an infinite universe, but that, at the moral and aesthetic level, "modernity takes the reverse trip from infinity to finity, and from transcendence to immanence."[37] Instead, he argues that immanence without transcendence is a prison and a conceptual contradiction. He holds that "It is from the horizon—from an absolute and unanswerable objection to immanence—that we derive a sense of place."[38] He explains: "The horizon is the child of curiosity—it is the inquiring, expectant, far-looking mind that beholds a horizon. To this extent, the horizon is wedded to the concept of transcendence, a concept that is not inherently high-flown or mystical but underpins everyday human knowledge. Outside religion, transcendence designates the second-guessing nature of human consciousness, the fact that, self-limiting as it is, knowledge is moved to wonder about the space beyond its perimeter."[39]

He adds:

> A world without . . . transcendence would be oppressively hidebound. Transcendence is the mental experience that consists in regarding the plane of known reality as open-ended. Now, the horizon beckons toward transcendence but does not fulfill it. A gateway it isn't. It points to finality but leaves the élan in midstride. In philosophical terms, we may say that the horizon is the creation of a diligently immanent observer possessed by an unrequited longing for the unseen . . . Put otherwise, the horizon arises from a religious longing that chooses not to avail itself of the available answers—those by which the satisfied longing hardens into dogma . . . Art, like religion, is moved by transcendence; it is human expression probing the limits of the

35. Ibid., 2.

36. Maleuvre comments on the difference between his and Casey's approaches: "Casey's notion of world tends to be self-contained and spiritually parochial. His central tenet is that we are placed inside an unsurpassable phenomenological horizon; my approach is to take seriously the image of horizon to show that, as horizon, this boundary is turned outward rather than inward." Ibid., xix.

37. Ibid., xvii–xviii.

38. Ibid., xix.

39. Ibid., 3.

utterable, but it is a form of expression passionately committed to the human immanent plane. To the convinced religionist, the horizon holds majesty but no mystery; to the materialist, it holds mystery (one can always travel farther and gain more) but no majesty. It is to the poet-philosopher, the hoping skeptic, that the horizon really and beautifully shimmers.[40]

A sense of epistemological finitude and ecological embeddedness does not preclude a sense of wonder and longing. However, Maleuvre also grounds this lure of transcendence in an ecological immanence that avoids any sense of escapism. He insists that we need to inhabit the reality we ache to transcend.[41] He rejects the possibility of seeing ourselves through God's eyes, as if we can abandon our finite horizons, but also suggests that immanence does not imply materialism any more than transcendence implies an infatuation with the supernatural. He says: "This is where the horizon proves its creative cure. Although undeniably aglow with religious feeling, the horizon disappoints this radiant promise. No one can logically or practically travel through the horizon. An optical dream of transcendence, it actually plants us deep in immanence. The horizon holds in tension the antinomy of transcendence and immanence and gives a spatial image of their exquisite union *and* separation. Let either transcendence or immanence tip the balance to its own camp and the horizon vanishes. The horizon is just the forever-suspended eventuality that one may dominate the other."[42]

Maleuvre concludes that "it is only by facing the horizon . . . in sight of a beyond we never reach, [that] we raise ourselves from the prosaic to the poetic, from occurrence to significance."[43] This does imply a sense of infinite longing but not an escapist spirituality. He explains:

> We live before a horizon; we are creatures of the horizon. Our here is never just here, and we never quite settle for it; on the other hand, we are not irrefutably known to have ever gone beyond it either. There is no contradiction in singing the glory of earthly life (humanism) and concurrently looking to the end of life (religious otherworldliness): exclusive focus on the latter turns man into a ghost who plays dead so as never to fear death; exclusive attention to the former turns us into brutes. It is the delicate equipoise of this-worldliness and otherworldliness that produced the horizon. One fails to live if death is not the

40. Ibid., 3–5.
41. Ibid., 325.
42. Ibid., 3.
43. Ibid., 327.

destination; but one also fails to live if the destination eclipses the way. We are beings-toward-death, not beings-in-death. This towardness rests on a delicate balance. Tipping too far toward immanence or too far toward transcendence breaks the symmetry and causes the horizon to drop. And without this horizon, human existence loses its poetic unfolding before a terrible and magnificent background. Without the horizon of life, we are a race of beasts or gods—inured to awe and art and prayer.[44]

I can only affirm and appreciate Maleuvre's eloquent intuitions: to expand one's horizons, to anticipate emerging horizons is not to deny an embedded sense of place but to be able to make sense of one's current location within a wider framework, to situate this moment in a historical context, to read the signs of the time, to discern the movement of the Spirit. Such a *horizon*tal notion of transcendence also has implications for an ecological understanding of the Christian liturgy.

The Role of Creation Theology in Liturgical Reorientation

I suggest that this metaphorical use of the term horizon may be appropriate for understanding the tangible dimensions of a liturgical sense of place. The liturgy enables one to experience an emerging horizon, to see what may lie beyond the horizon, to see the world around us, in all its grandeur and misery, its ironies and ambiguities, its delights and its distress, its panache and its pain, its inadequacies and injustices, as God's beloved household.

This way of seeing the world is admittedly deeply counter-intuitive. The problem is not only that the meaning of the metaphor is stretched so that it begins to break down (as any metaphor does). The problem is also not merely one of making sense of transcendence, i.e. that the house is ascribed to God, or that it is ascribed to this particular triune God (the God of the helpless). The deeper problem is that the "house" of God does not really seem to provide a safe space, a sense of belonging, a home or a hearth.[45] The problem is not merely the Darwinian logic of "eat or be eaten," but that of exclusion and the deliberate destruction of habitat. Given experiences of pain, suffering, injustice, and evil, the household of God does not provide a home to all creatures.[46] Among human creatures there are environmental refugees, homeless street children and victims who have been raped by

44. Ibid., 326–27.

45. See Oduyoye, *Introducing African Women's Theology.*

46. See Bouma-Prediger and Walsh, *Beyond Homelessness.*

family members in their own "homes." A sense of home therefore does not describe experiences of belonging but the content of an attractive vision, of an eschatological longing.[47]

One may argue that Christian theologies of creation also have the function to provide a sense of orientation that is cosmic in scope. The purpose of any such orientation is to locate oneself within a system of co-ordinates that requires in infancy little more than one's mother's breasts, voice and smell. This system of coordinates is not static but continues to expand and retract. It constitutes something like a navigation system for uncharted terrain that is adapted along the journey of life.[48] While some of the immediate landscape may be quite familiar, one also needs a few points of reference for navigating through uncharted terrain with little more than a basic sense of direction. One may argue that the creation theology found in Gen 1 responded to a sense of disorientation amongst the Babylonian exiles who had lost their dynasty, their temple, their city, and a trust in their God. Accordingly, creation theology is aimed at liturgical reorientation, as an ongoing, weekly discipline.[49] It is best understood when it responds to experiences of displacement, landlessness,[50] and alienation from the means of production and one's own labor. Creation theology itself becomes radically distorted when it serves to legitimize the social order that reinforces the sense of orientation of the powerful (which is all too often the case). In an illuminating essay, Vitor Westhelle seeks to explain the apparent absence of creation theology in Latin American liberation theology. He suggests that creation faith presupposes a sense of belonging that is absent from the experiences of displaced and landless peasants. I would suggest that the priestly narrative in Gen 1 responds precisely to the displacement of the exiles. If so, creation theology at best addresses contemporary forms of disorientation on the basis of a "dangerous recollection" of some former orientation and with a view to future reorientation.[51]

Such reorientation is only possible on the basis of a prior sense of orientation that now needs to be expanded in order to address the problem of disorientation. In that case, creation theology may well need to revise its system of coordinates in terms of salvation theology (i.e. in terms the

47. This is the argument that I developed in *An Ecological Christian Anthropology*.

48. See the metaphor employed in Conradie, "The Journey of Doing Christian Ecotheology."

49. On such a need for orientation and liturgical reorientation, see Lathrop, *Holy Ground,* 51–67.

50. For a description of this dialectic between landlessness and landedness, see Brueggemann, *The Land*.

51. See Westhelle, "Creation Motifs."

Orient, Jerusalem, Calvary). However, such a new set of coordinates cannot be found unless it replaces a previous set now discarded as inadequate because it leads to disorientation. Any such sense of orientation cannot be merely based on a sense of place. It requires a form of navigation in the journey of life and of evolutionary, planetary, and indeed cosmic history.

Bibliography

Bouma-Prediger, Steven, and Brian J. Walsh. *Beyond Homelessness: Christian Faith in a Culture of Displacement.* Grand Rapids: Eerdmans, 2008.

Brueggemann, Walter. *The Land: Place as Gift, Promise and Challenge in Biblical Faith.* 2nd ed. Overtures to Biblical Theology. Minneapolis: Fortress, 2002.

Casey, Edward S. "Between Geography and Philosophy: What Does It Mean to Be in the Place-World?" *Annals of the Association of American Geographers* 91 (2001) 683–93.

Conradie, Ernst M. *The Earth in God's Economy: Creation, Salvation and Consummation in Ecological Perspective.* Berlin: LIT Verlag, 2015.

———. *An Ecological Christian Anthropology: At Home on Earth?* Aldershot, UK: Ashgate, 2005.

———. "The Journey of Doing Christian Ecotheology: A Collective Mapping of the Terrain." *Theology* 116 (2013) 4–17.

———. "A Semiotic Notion of Transcendence." *Studia Historiae Ecclesiasticae* 39 (Supp.) (2013) 39–54.

Conradie, Ernst M., et al., eds. *Christian Faith and the Earth: Current Paths and Emerging Horizons in Ecotheology.* London: T. & T. Clark, 2014.

Gadamer, Hans-Georg. *Truth and Method.* Translation edited by Garrett Barden and John Cumming. London: Sheed & Ward, 1975.

Gundry, Robert H. *Matthew: A Commentary on his Handbook for a Mixed Church under Persecution.* 2nd ed. Grand Rapids: Eerdmans, 1994.

Habel, Norman C. and John Corowa. *The Rainbow Spirit in Creation: A Reading of Genesis 1.* Collegeville, MN: Liturgical, 2000.

Heidegger, Martin. *Being and Time.* Translated by John Macquarrie and Edward Robinson. Oxford: Blackwell, 1962.

Ingold, Tim. *Being Alive: Essays on Movement, Knowledge and Description.* London: Routledge, 2011.

———. *The Perception of the Environment: Essays in Livelihood, Dwelling and Skill.* London: Routledge, 2000.

Keener, Craig S. *The Gospel according to Matthew: A Socio-Rhetorical Commentary.* Grand Rapids: Eerdmans, 2009.

Lathrop, Gordon W. *Holy Ground: A Liturgical Cosmology.* Minneapolis: Fortress, 2003.

Maguire, Daniel C., and Larry L. Rasmussen. *Ethics for a Small Planet: New Horizons on Population, Consumption and Ecology.* Albany: State University of New York Press, 1998.

Maleuvre, Didier. *The Horizon: A History of Our Infinite Longing.* Berkeley: University of California Press, 2011.

Moltmann, Jürgen. *God in Creation: An Ecological Doctrine of Creation.* The Gifford Lectures 1984–1985. Translated by Margaret Kohl. London: SCM, 1985.

Oduyoye, Mercy Amba. *Introducing African Women's Theology.* Introductions to Feminist Theology 6. Cleveland: Pilgrim, 2001.

Porter, Stanley C., and Matthew Malcolm, eds. *Horizons in Hermeneutics: A Festschrift in Honor of Anthony C. Thiselton.* Grand Rapids: Eerdmans, 2013.

Santmire, H. Paul. *Ritualizing Nature: Renewing Christian Liturgy in a Time of Crisis.* Minneapolis: Fortress, 2008.

Schweizer, Eduard. *The Good News according to Matthew.* Translated by David Green. London: SPCK, 1975.

Thiselton, Anthony C. *New Horizons in Hermeneutics: The Theory and Practice of Transforming Biblical Reading.* Grand Rapids: Zondervan, 1992.

———. *The Two Horizons: New Testament Hermeneutics and Philosophical Description with Specific Reference to Heidegger, Bultmann, Gadamer and Wittgenstein.* Grand Rapids: Eerdmans, 1980.

Westhelle, Vitor. "Creation Motifs in the Search for a Vital Space: A Latin American Perspective." In *Lift Every Voice: Constructing Christian Theologies from the Underside,* edited by Susan Brooks Thistlethwaite and Mary Engel Potter, 146–58. Maryknoll, NY: Orbis, 1998.

Wiley, John. *Landscape.* London: Routledge, 2007.

———. "Landscape." In *Dictionary of Human Geography.* 5th ed. Malden, MA: Wiley-Blackwell, 2009.

4

The Still Small Voice of Nature

Anne E. Gardner

FIRST KGS 19, THE chapter where Elijah hears the "still small voice" is part of a group of stories (1 Kgs 17–19) that focus upon Elijah and his relationship with his God. In 1 Kgs 17, Elijah and God are in constant communication but less so in 1 Kgs 18 and not at all at the beginning of 1 Kgs 19, although an angel appears to help him. In the key passage for the present chapter, 1 Kgs 19:11–13, nature reflects God's past deeds at Horeb as well as those of 1 Kgs 18. Then it manifests a gentle sound that draws Elijah back into the world around him and into communion with God and to furthering God's plan once more.

1 Kings 19

In 1 Kgs 19:2 Jezebel sends a messenger to Elijah on account of Elijah's slaughter of the prophets of Baal (1 Kgs 18:40) saying, "Thus may the gods do to me and more also, if by this time tomorrow I do (not) make your life (*nephesh*) as the life (*nephesh*) of one of them." As the reader will find out, Jezebel is courting trouble. Her predicted end (1 Kgs 21:23–24) and her actual end (2 Kgs 9:30–37) will indeed be worse than that experienced by the prophets of Baal. Elijah, however, does not know this. He flees into Judah and thus beyond Jezebel's jurisdiction, leaves his servant in Beer-Sheba and travels one day into the wilderness where he sits under a juniper tree and asks God that he might die. Instead, during his sleep, an angel touches him and tells him to arise and eat (1 Kgs 19:5), whereupon Elijah finds a cake baked on hot stones as well as water. He partakes of them then lies down again. The angel, specified to be "an angel of Yahweh" the second time he appears, touches him again and urges him to eat and drink again for the journey will be long (1 Kgs 19:7).

The reader is then told that Elijah went to Horeb, the mountain of God, on the strength of the food for forty days and forty nights. That the angel warns Elijah that the journey will be long implies that Elijah had changed his mind, or had his mind changed for him, about wanting to die at that point in time. When Elijah reaches Horeb and takes up residence in a cave, Yahweh speaks to him, asking what he is doing there (1 Kgs 19:9). This reinforces the ambiguity of whether God via his angel had directed Elijah to Horeb, like the angel who led Moses to his meeting with Yahweh (Exod 3:2), or whether Elijah had decided to go there of his own volition. Elijah's reply to God's inquiry is an oblique one. It makes a strong allusion to the Mosaic covenant, for Elijah protests, "I have been very zealous (*qannō qinnē'thî*) for Yahweh God of Hosts for the children of Israel have forsaken the covenant, thrown down your altars and killed your prophets with the sword and I alone am left and they seek my life to take it away" (1 Kgs 19:10).

Elijah is then told to "Go out and stand on the mount before Yahweh." It is at this point that one of the most famous passages in the Hebrew Bible appears:

> Behold Yahweh passed by and a great and strong wind (*rûach*) tore the mountains and shattered the rocks before Yahweh but Yahweh was not in the wind and, after the wind, an earthquake (*ra'ash*) but Yahweh was not in the earthquake and after the earthquake a fire (*'ēsh*), but Yahweh was not in the fire and after the fire a still small voice/sound (*qôl demāmāh daqqāh*). Upon hearing (it) Elijah wrapped his face in his cloak and went out and stood at the entrance of the cave and behold a voice (*qôl*) came to him and it said why are you here Elijah? (1 Kgs 19:1 1–1 3)

Elijah replies by repeating his earlier answer, "I have been very zealous (*qannō qinnē'thî*) for Yahweh God of Hosts for the children of Israel have forsaken the covenant, thrown down your altars and killed your prophets with the sword and I alone am left they seek my life (*nephesh*) to take it away" (1 Kgs 19:14). Commentators have been puzzled as to why Elijah was so afraid in 1 Kgs 19. After all, in the previous two chapters when he was in dangerous situations he was not overcome by them. In order to understand what is transpiring here it is necessary to analyze Elijah's experience and thus to see the importance of the still small voice and its meaning.

Horeb/Sinai

Horeb, also known as Sinai, is Elijah's destination and it is there that his experience on the mountain takes place. The importance of Horeb/Sinai in the narrative is reinforced by the framing of the encounter with Yahweh by Elijah's allusion to the first commandment. He declares that he has been very zealous (*qannō qinnē'thî*), thus explicitly linking himself with Yahweh who had announced in Exod 20:5 and Deut 5:9 that he was a zealous/jealous (*qannā'*) God. Indeed, in the previous chapter, 1 Kgs 18, where Elijah displayed his zeal by killing the prophets of Baal, there are a number of allusions to the Mosaic covenant and the forefathers of Israel.

When Elijah meets Ahab, the latter says to him, "'Is it you, you troubler of Israel?'" And he answered and said, "'I have not troubled Israel; but you and your father's house in that you have forsaken the commandments of Yahweh and you have followed the Baalim'" (1 Kgs 18:17–18). Here the commandments of Yahweh and obedience or disobedience to them are paramount. The contest between the prophets of Baal and Elijah, the prophet of Yahweh, ensues to see whose God is able to ignite the sacrifice. The prophets of Baal are unable to rouse their deity to action and this is underlined when it is said twice when they entreated him, "There was no voice (*qôl*), no answer ('*ōneh*)" (1 Kgs 18:26, 29), with 1 Kgs 18:29 adding "no drawing near" (*qāsheb*). This stands in contrast to Yahweh's actions as will be seen later. When it was Elijah's turn to entreat his God, the narrator says, "Elijah took twelve stones according to the number of the tribes of the sons of Jacob, unto whom the word of Yahweh came, saying, Israel shall be your name" (1 Kgs 18:31),[1] thus focusing on Israel as an entity in relationship to Yahweh. After preparing the altar and making a trench around it, Elijah ordered that four barrels of water be poured on the offering and on the wood, and this was repeated twice more and the trench filled with water (1 Kgs 19:32–35). Elijah then pleads with Yahweh, "O Yahweh, the God of Abraham, Isaac, and Israel, let it be known this day that you are God (*'elōhîm*) in Israel and I am your servant and that I have done all these things at your word. Answer me ('*anēnî*), Yahweh, answer me ('*anēnî*) that this people may know that you, Yahweh, are the God and you have turned their hearts back again" (1 Kgs 18:36–37).

Here the forefathers are highlighted again, as is Israel in relationship to Yahweh. The latter sends fire to ignite the sacrifice (1 Kgs 18:38), demonstrating that unlike Baal he does answer, that he is Lord over nature and that his power is great for his fire is able to overcome the thrice poured

---

1. The twelve altar stones are an allusion to the altar of Moses at Sinai in Exod 24:4, as noted by Carlson, "Élie à l'Horeb," 427.

water. The watching people fall on their faces and acknowledge him saying, "Yahweh is the God, Yahweh is the God" (1 Kgs 18:39). It is at this point that Elijah instructs the people to seize the prophets of Baal. He takes them to the Wadi Kishon and kills them there (1 Kgs 18:40).[2]

A further reference to Horeb/Sinai and the Mosaic covenant may be present in 1 Kgs 19 in that a great and strong wind, earthquake, and fire appear on the mountain. DeVries says these are "the familiar symbols of the theophanic presence (cf. Exod 19:16–19),"[3] but on checking that passage it is clear that the allusions are not exact:

- Wind is not mentioned there;

- The fire is prior to the mountains quaking in Exod 19:18 whereas in 1 Kgs 19:11 it is the other way round,

- In Exod 19:18 it is said that Yahweh descended upon the mountain in fire but that is explicitly denied in 1 Kgs 19:12.

In other words, in addition to a harking back to the setting for the giving of the commandments, something else is being highlighted by the appearance of wind, earthquake, and fire in 1 Kgs 19. Mordechai Cogan says that it is "The startled and frightened reaction of nature to the appearance of YAHWEH (and that this) is a standard image in early poetry (Judg 5:4–5; Hab 3:3–6; taken up in Ps 18:8–10; 68:9) and prose (Exod 19:16, 18; 20:18)."[4] There is no suggestion though in 1 Kgs 19:11–12 that nature is frightened. Rather the natural elements are portrayed as extremely powerful and potentially very destructive. Elijah cowers in his cave instead of standing on the mount as God instructed (1 Kgs 19:11) while the elements make their presence felt: the wind is great and strong and shatters rocks before Yahweh, but he is not in the wind nor in the earthquake nor in the fire. On a surface reading of the narrative, the most that can be said about these elements is that they precede Yahweh. Was this of their volition or of his?

2. Elijah then tells Ahab to eat and drink while he himself ascended Mount Carmel with his servant. When he sees the first rain cloud he sends his servant to warn Ahab that there will be a deluge and to move from where he is. Ahab goes by chariot to Jezreel and "the hand of Yahweh was on Elijah . . . and he ran before Ahab to the entrance of Jezreel" (1 Kgs 18:46).

3. DeVries, 1 Kings, 236.

4. Cogan, 1 Kings, 453.

Yahweh Working with Nature

In 1 Kgs 17–19 it is shown on multiple occasions that Yahweh works with nature. He sends ravens to feed Elijah when he is in hiding (1 Kgs 17:3–4); gives the widow of Zarephath a supply of oil and flour that will not fail until the end of the drought (1 Kgs 17:13–14) and restores the *nephesh* to her son when he dies. In 1 Kgs 18 Yahweh sends fire to ignite the sacrifice despite it having been soaked with water and he brings the rain that breaks the drought. Indeed the rain would become a storm, for the narrator tells us that "the heaven grew black with clouds and wind and there was great rain" (1 Kgs 18:45). In 1 Kgs 19 an angel, said to be of Yahweh in verse 7, provides food and water for Elijah. All these incidents serve to demonstrate Yahweh's ability to work with nature. Accordingly, the wind, earthquake and fire that precede the "still small voice/sound," and which to some extent reflect the events of the previous chapter are, contra Hauser,[5] likely to have been in his service also. Indeed, a perusal of the passages where these elements appear elsewhere in the Hebrew Bible shows that to be the case.

Wind

As far as wind is concerned, it is said in Gen 8:1 that the flood waters were calmed when "God made a wind (*rûach*) to pass over the earth" and in Num 11:31 that "there went forth a wind (*rûach*) from Yahweh and brought quail from the sea" in order to feed the people traveling with Moses through the wilderness. Clearly then, God can press the wind into his service for whatever task he wishes to accomplish. A particularly apposite passage appears in Ps 135 for, in keeping with 1 Kgs 18–19, it highlights Yahweh's greatness, his choice of Jacob/Israel as well as his control over wind amongst other natural elements. The Psalmist declares,

> For Yahweh chose Jacob for himself,
>   Israel for his treasure.
> I know great is Yahweh
>   and our lord out of all gods
> All that Yahweh desires he does,
>   in the heavens and in the earth
>   in the seas and all deeps

---

5. Hauser, "Yahweh Versus Death," 70, thinks that Yahweh had no part in the extreme weather conditions.

Causing vapours to rise up from the ends of the earth
He makes lightning for rain
Causing wind (*rûach*) to go out from his treasuries. (Ps 135:4–7)

In Ps 147 also, Yahweh's control over nature is highlighted and verse 18 states, "He causes his wind (*rûach*) to blow." His giving of statutes and judgments to Israel is mentioned as well (v. 19), as is his greatness and might (v. 5). A further element appears: the kind of people he supports, and those he does not, for it is said in verse 6,

Yahweh upholds the meek;
He brings the wicked down to the ground.

This asserts God's awareness of the acts of individual people and his ability to give recompense. Psalm 107:25 also points out God's control over the wind but as the Psalm is one of the few instances where *demāmāh* (still) appears, it will be considered in more depth later.

Earthquake and Fire

Ra'ash (earthquake) appears as a noun in 1 Kgs 19:12. It appears as a noun also in Isa 29:6 where, in company with thunder, whirlwind, tempest, and fire, it is part of a visitation of Yahweh upon Jerusalem. As in Isa 29:6, *ra'ash* is associated with fire and with God's anger in Ps 18:8–9 [7–8],[6] although there it is in verbal form. Then in the words of the Psalmist,

He delivered me from my strong enemy
and from them that hated me,
for they were too mighty for me. (Ps 18:18[17])

The deliverance happened because the Psalmist was righteous and kept God's statutes (Ps 18:21–25 [20–24]). Earthquake, fire, and God's anger then function as a triad. They work against the wrong-doer but deliver those deserving of deliverance.

The Extreme Weather Conditions and Their Implications for 1 Kings 19:11

The above examples of earthquake and fire, along with the other manifestations of extreme weather conditions, help to illuminate 1 Kgs 19:11. It is clear from what is said two verses later (1 Kgs 19:13) when Elijah went to

---

6. God's anger and the shaking of the earth also appear in Ps 60:3–4 [1–2].

the mouth of the cave upon hearing a "still small voice/sound," that he had disobeyed God's instruction in 1 Kgs 19:11 where he had been told to go and stand [upon the mount][7] before Yahweh. Instead he must have cowered inside the cave. Now we understand why. He believed that God was angry with him. Why would that be so? It is clear that he suspected that God was wrathful with him even before the appearance of the extreme weather conditions, for he had tried to justify himself in the previous verse when he said, "I have been very zealous (*qannō qinnē'thî*) for Yahweh the God of Hosts for the children of Israel have forsaken the covenant, thrown down your altars and killed your prophets with the sword and I alone am left and they seek my life to take it away."

In addition to justifying himself, Elijah's statement implies that God had not acted quickly enough to prevent the deaths of his other prophets, nor had he dealt with Elijah's enemies, perhaps because he thought that Elijah was not worth saving. The extreme weather conditions are part of God's response: they say that he is powerful, that he can harness the natural world to destroy when he so wishes. That Elijah was not harmed by them indicates that God had no wish to bring about his death. After the passing of the storm, comes the "still small voice/sound" and it represents the second part of God's response for it encourages Elijah to go to the mouth of the cave.

The Still Small Voice/Sound

What was the "still small voice/sound"? The *qôl demāmāh daqqāh*? This has been much discussed by scholars. The usual translation of "still small voice" comes from the KJV, AV and RSV, but it is rendered as "the sound of sheer silence" by the NRSV. *Qôl*—"voice/sound"—however, implies something audible and this is reinforced by its description as *daqah* translated as "small," as will be seen later. Provan renders the whole phrase as "a gentle whisper,"[8] perhaps under the influence of the LXX, but this is to anthropomorphize it. Indeed, if the "still small voice" follows the pattern of the previous elements, then it should be part of the natural world. Stamm recognizes this when he posits that the phrase should be understood as indicating "a gentle little breeze"[9] and Carlson, who follows Stamm, thinks it may involve the rustling

7. "Upon the Mount" appears only in the MT, Vaticanus, and Proto-Lucianic. It strengthens the contrast between being inside the cave and outside it.

8. Provan, *1 and 2 Kings*, 146.

9. Stamm, "Elia am Horeb," 327–34. The NASB implicitly adopts Stamm's understanding when it renders the phrase as "a sound of a gentle blowing." In a note it refers the reader to Job 4:16 (discussed in this chapter) and Zech 4:6. Zech 4:6 does not

of the leaves on trees.[10] However, if correct, one would have expected the mention of trees being uprooted when the strong wind was blowing but instead it was rocks that shattered, indicating a barren landscape. Further, if a breeze was involved surely the word meaning "wind" (*rûach*) would have featured in the phrase *qôl demāmāh daqqāh* rather than the more generic *qôl* meaning "sound." It seems then that further exploration is required. *demāmāh* usually translated as "still," appears elsewhere in the Hebrew Bible only in Ps 107:29 and Job 4:16. The former has some similarity to 1 Kgs 19 in that Yahweh brings a storm prior to the *demāmāh*, but it is a storm at sea so the context is different. Ps 107:29 does not enlighten us either as to the sound (*qôl*) of the calm (*demāmāh*) in the passage in Kings. Job 4:16, which is often referred to by commentators, has *demāmāh* and *qôl* but *demāmāh* does not describe *qôl*. Rather *demāmāh* calm/stillness precedes *qôl* and the whole phrase reads, "Stillness/calm, and a voice I heard."

From what follows in Job 4:16, it is clear that the voice, the *qôl*, is of God. Here it should be remembered that in 1 Kgs 19:13 one verse after the "still small sound" *qôl demāmāh daqqāh* a *qôl*, a voice, clearly that of God, comes to Elijah (Job 4:16). Unfortunately, though, it does not help us to interpret the "still small sound" of 1 Kgs 19:11.

One last word from the phrase *qôl demāmāh daqqāh* remains to be investigated. This is *daqqāh*, the feminine adjective meaning "small" or "slight" that describes *qôl* (sound). Elsewhere in the Hebrew Bible it describes the "thin" cattle and "thin" ears of corn in Gen 41; a "thin" hair in Lev 13:30; "small" dust in Isa 29:5; incense beaten "small" and in Lev 16:12 a "small" flake, "small" as the hoarfrost on the ground. Nowhere, apart from in 1 Kgs 19:12, does it describe a sound; but, as its other occurrences inform us, it indicates something slight. Accordingly, when *daqqāh* is used in conjunction with *qôl* a "faint sound" would be appropriate as a translation. The whole puzzling phrase, *qôl demāmāh daqqāh*, then means "a faint calm sound."[11]

In my own experience, I encountered a phenomenon that instantly reminded me of the *qôl demāmāh daqqāh* and allowed me to gain an insight into its meaning. My husband and I were considering a property that was

---

include any of the words of the phrase under discussion and so is irrelevant here. The Jerusalem Bible renders the phrase as "the sound of a gentle breeze" and in a footnote says "The whisper of a light breeze signifies that God is spirit." While not denying that God is spirit, there is no indication that "breeze" was intended—see the following arguments in the main body of this chapter.

10. Carlson, "Élie à l'Horeb," 435.

11. The NEB has "a low murmuring sound" which is similar, although it provides a quality to *qôl demāmāh daqqāh*, which is not necessarily present when it asserts that it is to be translated as "murmuring."

for sale. The house was primitive but we could see its possibilities although my husband was quailing at the amount of work to be done. On our second visit the lady owner offered to watch our two then very young children while my husband and I walked around the land (17.5 acres). When we did so, I, a townie, heard something that I had never heard before—the sound of silence. Except it was not quite silent, for there was a faint hum.

What Was the Hum?

Whatever the hum was, it came from nature. There were no overhead power lines in the vicinity, yet the closest I can get to a description of the hum in everyday terms is that it sounded like a faint electronic emission. It may be that my hearing is particularly acute for I can hear the sound made by an electronic device designed to keep rats and mice at bay although that sound is supposedly inaudible to human ears, apart from those of very young children. A search for "hum" on the Internet brought me to a site[12] which defines the Sanskrit term "Pranava." It means "Cosmic Sound" and the site says it is the hum of the universe. The site also indicates that those who have heard it say that "the verbalization "Om" comes the closest of all sounds to . . . this hum." Certainly "Om" with the "m" as a continuous sound represents very well what I heard. I went in search of a modern scientific explanation although readily admit to a lack of expertise in the area. A friend had suggested to me that what I had heard was the faint echo of the Big Bang at the beginning of the universe. The Big Bang, apparently "more like a deep hum than a bang, according to an analysis of the radiation left over from the cataclysm,"[13] still resonates today. However, John Cramer of the University of Washington who produced a CD of the sound made by the Big Bang had to boost the frequencies of its cosmic radiation by a factor of 1026 to make it audible to the human ear. It seems unlikely then that that is what I had heard! Scientists, however, continue to advance our understanding of the environment in which we live and of our relationship to it. It is now known that the "Pulse of the Earth" (the Schumann Resonance or Wave) and alphawaves in the human brain have a frequency of 7.83Hz and that that particular frequency is likely to be connected not only to the beginning of life but also to the continuation of life as we know it.[14] Perhaps

12. http://www.pranava.com/pranava_whatis.html.

13. According to Chown, "Big Bang Sounded like a Deep Hum."

14. For those of us without expertise in the scientific realm, these advances in knowledge are explained in Russell and Webster's documentary film *Resonance: Beings of Frequency.*

an accepted scientific explanation for the hum I heard will emerge in time. Meanwhile, back to my experience and how it illuminates that of Elijah.

My Experience and that of Elijah

When I heard the hum I had the sense that I was in a very safe, very secure place and my husband had a similar feeling, although he did not hear the hum. This matches to some extent Elijah's experience for when he heard the "faint calm sound" he went to the entrance of the cave, so felt safe enough to face the world once more. That it was his expectation to meet God out there is indicated by him wrapping his face in his cloak for, according to Exod 33:20, one cannot meet God face to face and live.[15]

Why Had Elijah Been Afraid?

In 1 Kgs 17, it is noteworthy that Elijah and God are in close contact. Elijah announces to King Ahab in the name of Yahweh that there will be a prolonged drought. He is then told by Yahweh to hide by the Wadi Cherith whose waters he is to drink and where ravens will feed him (1 Kgs 17:3–4). When the wadi dries up (1 Kgs 17:6), Elijah is not left to die; rather Yahweh tells him to go to Zarephath which belongs to Sidon and stay with a widow who will sustain him (1 Kgs 17:8–9). When the widow's son dies, Elijah takes the child and prays to Yahweh to return his *nephesh* to him. Yahweh listens and does as Elijah asks (1 Kgs 17:19–22). Communication then between Yahweh and Elijah is constant;[16] there is no hint that Elijah is afraid.

In 1 Kgs 18, Yahweh responds to Elijah's pleas to ignite the sacrifice, but the only directive in the whole chapter that Yahweh is said to issue occurs in 1 Kgs 18:1. There Elijah is told by Yahweh, "Go show yourself to Ahab and I will send rain upon the earth." It seems then that Elijah acted on his own initiative when he set up the competition to see whose God was the most powerful and when he subsequently killed the four hundred and fifty prophets of Baal.[17] Indeed, it is noteworthy that Elijah's latter action mirrors

---

15. Fritz also thinks it indicates that God was present (*1 and 2 Kings*, 198). However, Provan interprets Elijah's wrapping of his cloak about his face as indicative of "not seeing" like Jezebel in 1 Kgs 19:1–2 (*1 and 2 Kings*, 146).

16. "Word of Yahweh" appears in 17:2, 5, 8, 16, 24, and Elijah called unto Yahweh in 17:20, 21.

17. After the rain came, it is said that he was able to run to Jezreel quicker than Ahab who was riding in his chariot, because the "hand of Yahweh" (1 Kgs 18:46) was upon him, Elijah.

that of Jezebel, for she slew the prophets of Yahweh (1 Kgs 18:4), as did the apostate people of Israel (1 Kgs 19:10, 14).

In 1 Kings 19, there is no direct contact between Yahweh and Elijah until the latter arrives at Horeb. Could this be because he went beyond what God had required of him and broke the commandment not to kill? This would fit with Elijah's request to die, "It is enough now; take away my life for I am not better than my fathers," (1 Kgs 19:4) which indicates guilt on Elijah's part. Nevertheless, he tries to justify himself for he protests that he has been very zealous for Yahweh and he complains that he alone is left, for all the other prophets of Yahweh have been killed.[18] Indeed the same protestation and complaint are made both before the storm at Horeb and again after the appearance of the "faint calm sound," the *qôl demāmāh daqqāh*, when he and God communicate once more. The message that God has for him is simple: Elijah is not alone, for there are 7,000 in Israel who have not worshipped Baal; and he, Yahweh, has already planned how to dispose of Elijah's (and his own) enemies. Elijah has a part to play, for he is to anoint the future leaders of Israel and Syria who in wars between them will kill all the apostates and he is to anoint his successor as prophet. Elijah then has been put firmly in his place and reminded that God, not he, is the arbiter of all life. At the same time Elijah is told there is a place for him in God's world which includes the whole created order which works in harmony with him and spans an eternity. Indeed it was the created order—however the "faint calm sound," the *qôl demāmāh daqqāh* should be defined in scientific terms—that invited Elijah back into God's presence.

Bibliography

Carlson, R. A. "Élie à l'Horeb." *VT* 19 (1969) 416–39.

Chown, Marcus. "Big Bang Sounded Like a Deep Hum." *New Scientist,* 30 October 2003.

Cogan, Mordechai. *1 Kings. A New Translation with Introduction and Commentary.* Anchor Bible 10. New York: Doubleday, 2001.

DeVries, Simon. J. *1 Kings.* Word Biblical Commentary 12. Nashville: Nelson, 2003.

Fritz, Volkmar. *1 and 2 Kings.* Translated by Anselm Hagendorn. Continental Commentaries. Minneapolis: Fortress, 2003.

Gray, John. *I & II Kings.* 2nd ed. Old Testament Library. London: SCM, 1970.

Hauser, Alan J. "Yahweh versus Death—The Real Struggle in 1 Kings 17–19." In Alan J. Hauser and Russell Gregory, *From Carmel to Horeb: Elijah in Crisis,* 9–89. JSOT Supplement Series 85. Sheffield: Almond, 1990.

18. In 1 Kgs 18:4 the narrator informs the reader that Obadiah "who feared Yahweh greatly" had hidden a hundred prophets of Yahweh and given them sustenance. On this apparent contradiction see Gray, *I & II Kings,* 383–86.

Olerich, G. "What Is Pranava?" http://www.pranava.com/pranava_whatis.html.

Provan, Iain. *1 and 2 Kings*. New International Bible Commentary: Old Testament Series. Peabody, MA: Hendrickson, 1995.

Stamm, H. J. "Elia am Horeb." In *Studia Biblica et Semitica: Theodoro Christiano Vriezen qui munere professoris theologiae per XXV annos functus est, ab amicis, collegis, discipulus dedicate*, 327–34. Wageningen: Veenman, 1961.

Russell, James, and John K. Webster. *Resonance: Beings of Frequency* (DVD). Borehamwood: Patient Zero Productions, 2012.

Part 2

Spirituality in Creation

5

Reclaiming Creation

The Spiritual Exercises of Ignatius of Loyola

Patricia Fox

THE ECOLOGICAL CRISIS CONFRONTING our planet has challenged both scholars and practitioners of many faith traditions to re-examine sacred texts, rituals, and ethical norms through the lens of this destructive global reality. Substantive critical studies from within the Christian corpus have yielded liberating fresh insights not only from biblical and liturgical sources but also from spiritual texts and practices. In recent decades the *Spiritual Exercises* of Ignatius of Loyola (1491–1556) has assisted people from various Christian traditions to embrace a form of contemplation that enables a person to find God in all things in a way that leads to transformative action. For this reason I have chosen to re-examine this sixteenth-century text through the lens of rediscovering the spiritual in God's creation. To begin, I will frame this exploration by reflecting briefly on the critical significance of the doctrine of Creation and Christian belief in the relationship of the Creator with the creature. I will then trace some key sources and elements relevant to this issue from Ignatius of Loyola's personal journey that provide the basis of his *Spiritual Exercises*. Finally, I will explore briefly the relationship of the Creator with the creature within the *Exercises*, finishing with a focus on the *Contemplation to Attain the Love of God*, which Ignatius places at the apex of his spiritual classic.

Doctrine of Creation

In a recent article in *Theological Studies,* Thomas Hughson SJ identifies the Christian understanding of Creation as an "ecumenical problem." His concern is that despite the emergence of a developing ecological awakening, for many Christians nature, humanity and the cosmos are "no longer experienced or recognized primarily as 'creation' and dependent on the Creator."[1] He also suggests that this growing phenomenon, which he describes as an "inaccessible sense of creatureliness,"[2] saps both faith and justice. He claims that "at stake is the monotheistic and Christian sense of the cosmos as creation and of human persons as creatures."[3]

Hughson suggests that this shift has occurred because Christianity has stopped paying attention to its own participation in the Creator-creature relationship and to the experience of primordial faith.[4] He believes however, that the emerging "green experience" offers the churches an opportunity. He notes that a rising ecological concern is being accompanied by a return to a deep appreciation of nature and suggests that this opens up a path for Christians towards a renewed reception of the key doctrine of Creation. Further, Hughson claims that a contemporary experience of the *Spiritual Exercises* can enable a powerful engagement with the Creator God in both a cosmic and deeply personal mode of the Creator's presence as one "who creates and superintends the randomness in a cosmos more than 90 billion light years across with at least 125 billion galaxies, each containing billions of stars." He claims that the opportunity for such a personal encounter with God "enlightens primordial faith so that it becomes belief in God as Creator of an ever evolving universe and recognition of all reality other than God as creation."[5]

As someone who has both participated in and directed the *Spiritual Exercises,* Hughson's claim rings very true to me. The structure of the *Exercises* consists of four weeks of biblically based prayer that invites each person into a personal encounter with the Trinitarian God through an active participation in the unfolding stories of Creation and Redemption. This is done in a way that is both grounded in a heightened awareness of the materiality of place and consistently engages all the senses, as well as the mind, emotions, and imagination. Since this prayer form emerged directly from

---

1. Hughson, "Creation as an Ecumenical Problem," 823.
2. Ibid., 825.
3. Ibid., 837
4. See ibid., 836.
5. Ibid., 841–42.

Ignatius' own personal experience of God the Creator, a glimpse into some of these encounters in his early life can provide an entry into the significance of creation within the text of the *Exercises*.

Ignatius' Personal Journey

Throughout a brief autobiography which towards the end of his life he reluctantly dictated to a confrere, Ignatius of Loyola describes himself as a pilgrim.[6] He begins his pilgrim story with an account of a Damascus-like event that led to profound interior transformation and spiritual growth. This inner event occurred after both his legs were seriously wounded in battle in northern Spain in 1521. His conversion experience occurred during a lengthy convalescence in the family castle at Loyola in the Basque country. Ignatius describes his late twenties' self as a courtier turned soldier, and as "a man given over to worldly vanities and having a vain and overpowering desire to gain renown."[7] The only reading available for this impatient young caballero during his convalescence was a *Life of Christ* and the lives of the saints.[8] Reading this material while immobilized in a place of enforced solitary space became life changing for Ignatius. Gradually, he discovered within himself a capacity for spiritual reflection and self-knowledge that became transformative for him and subsequently, for literally countless other people ever since. His autobiography describes something of the impact of his attraction to the person of Jesus and to the saints who in their different heroic ways left all to follow him. More significantly, for our purposes, Ignatius also describes the unfolding of an inner process which yielded a series of key insights which formed the basis of his rules for the discernment of spirits. These rules remain at the heart of the *Spiritual Exercises* and of Ignatian spirituality today.

Ignatius describes the core experience of this growing capacity to discern the authentic movements of God as a "consolation." One such experience occurred during lengthy periods of his contemplating the night skies at Loyola. Speaking of himself in the third person, he remembers it this way: "The greatest consolation he received at this time was from gazing at the sky and the stars, and this he often did for quite a long time. The result of all this was that he felt within himself a very strong impulse to serve Our

6. See Tylenda, *The Autobiography*. Ignatius refers to himself throughout this text as a pilgrim.

7. Ibid., 37.

8. The *Life of Christ* by Ludolph of Saxony, and *The Golden Legend* by Jacopo ds Voragine, both translated into Castilian.

Lord. He spent much time reflecting on his resolution and wished to be fully recovered so he could set out on his journey."[9] For an interpreter of the Exercises today, this brief description of Ignatius' conversion is laden with meaning.[10] These are the words of the sixty-two year old Ignatius, founder and elected leader of the Society of Jesus which by then already had over a thousand vowed members proclaiming the gospel in many different parts of the world. This primary experience which he describes as "consolation" had provided him with a profound and particular awareness of God's direct action in his life. It enabled him to distinguish good spirits from bad. The experience became a touchstone for his capacity to discern God's will throughout his life, through very many complex and creative years of faith-filled discipleship and leadership. Hence these sparse sentences offer a key to the spiritual wisdom of the Exercises and merit some further attention.

Ignatius' gazing at the sky and the stars, "often and for quite a long time," was an experience of powerful consolation because as a result "he felt within himself a very great desire to serve Our Lord."[11] He experienced this as a profound awakening and as a call to a radical following and service of Jesus exemplified in the lives of saints such as Dominic and Francis, whose stories he had recently read. He realized, by contrast, that the lure of battle and courtly love that had previously so entranced him, now held no pull at all. This acute shift, facilitated by his returning to look at the sky and the stars, left a permanent imprint within his being. It functioned like an internal compass that provided him with a capacity for discerning "true north"—God's direction—for the rest of his pilgrim life. It enabled him to discern ways within himself as creature that were congruent with those of a Creator God and which were therefore creative of new life. This capacity also enabled him to recognize other inner impulses that were not of God and were to be avoided.

When Ignatius was able to walk again, albeit with a limp, he took the long road from Loyola to the monastery at Monserrat in Catalonia where he cast off his identity as courtier and soldier and set out on foot in the simple dress of a pilgrim. He intended to proceed on his way to Jerusalem but went first to nearby Manresa to absorb the significance of the recent events in his life. There he found a cave in which to pray and do penance and there he experienced much peace and joy. He established a pattern of working in the hospital where he lived, participating in services in the local church,

9. Tylenda, The Autobiography, 50–51.

10. John English SJ, noted interpreter of the Exercises, in a lecture at the Institute of Practical Asceticism, Guelph Ontario, May 1973 claimed that: "Ignatius was not a poet but his language was always accurate."

11. Tylenda, The Autobiography, 51.

praying for hours a day, and begging for his daily food. It was a time when he had to learn to deal with physical and spiritual darkness and his limits. He stayed there for eleven months and according to his own description, "God was dealing with him in the same way a schoolteacher deals child while he instructing him."[12]

In Manresa he also experienced some seminal moments of encounter with God. One was when "his understanding was raised on high, so as to see the Most Holy Trinity under the aspect of three keys on a musical instrument," thus signifying a musical chord whereby three distinct notes produce a single harmony.[13] This was a profoundly affective experience and provides a glimpse of God's revelation within Ignatius in a deeply incarnational mode, one that continued throughout his life to shape his unfolding relationship with God as Trinity. A further very formative event took place not long after this on the banks of the river Cardoner:

> The road followed the path of the river, and he was taken up with his devotions; he sat down for a while facing the river flowing far below him. As he sat there the eyes of his understanding were opened and though he saw no vision, he understood and perceived many things, numerous spiritual things as well as matters touching on faith and learning, and this with an elucidation so bright that all these things seemed new to him . . . if he were to gather all the helps he received from God and everything he knew, and add them together, he does not think they would add up to as much as he received at that one occasion.[14]

This profound experience of God's presence while he was sitting on the banks of the Cardoner facing the river flowing far below him, further deepened his capacity for the discernment of good and bad spirits. It became a touchstone for his whole life.

God as "Creator" in *The Exercises*

Later, it was in a cave near the river Cardoner that Ignatius wrote the *Spiritual Exercises*. It is thus perhaps not surprising that he refers to God as "Creator" very frequently in this document[15] and that he constantly situates his understanding of self in relationship with all creatures of God's creation. For

12. Ibid., 74.
13. Ibid., 75.
14. Ibid. 78–79.
15. 27 times.

example, early in the first week of the *Exercises* during which the retreatant is invited to discover her or himself before God as a loved sinner, the fifth point of the Exercise reads: "This is a cry of wonder accompanied by surging emotion as I pass in review all creatures. How is it that they have permitted me to live and sustained me in my life! . . . the heavens, sun, moon, stars, and the elements; the fruits, birds, fishes, and other animals—why have they all been at my service! How is it that the earth did not swallow me up . . . ?"[16]

The various *Exercises* are based on Ignatius' own experience of his Creator and Lord engaging him directly and lovingly as a "creature." Further, his naming the "devout soul" a "creature" also provides an insight into his anthropology. For him, a human person is understood as a creature among and in relation to all other creatures with and in whom the Creator God engages with love. Ignatius' *Rules for the Discernment of Spirits* also use the language of Creator and creature to develop a deeper understanding of the meaning and significance of consolation within the *Exercises* and within the spiritual life as a whole: "I call it consolation when an interior movement is aroused in the soul, by which it is inflamed with the love of its Creator and Lord, and as a consequence, can love no creature on the face of the earth for its own sake, but only in the Creator of them all."[17] Further, in the "Introductory Observations" Ignatius also inscribes this advice for a director of these *Exercises*: "[I]t is more suitable and much better that the Creator and Lord in person communicate Himself to the devout soul in quest of the divine will, that He inflame it with His love and praise, and dispose it for the way in which it could better serve God in the future. Therefore the director of the Exercises . . . should permit the Creator to deal directly with the creature and the creature directly with his Creator and Lord."[18] This authoritative advice can be read as a direct commentary on his own profound experience. At both Loyola and Manresa, Ignatius experienced the immediate action of God in his life in a way which became a fundamental premise of the *Spiritual Exercises*.[19] One can assume that it is advice that he lived out again and again on his pilgrim journey with his companions and with many other people—all kinds of people—whom he directed along the way. The message is clear: Do not get in the way of the Creator and Lord communicating directly with this person created by God. For an interpreter of the *Exercises* today the same advice still holds. Every creature on the face

---

16. Puhl, *The Spiritual Exercises of St Ignatius*, #60, 30. The number reference # denotes the number of the Exercise used in all translations and publications.

17. Ibid., #316.3, 142.

18. Ibid., #15, 6.

19. O'Malley, *The First Jesuits*, 43.

of the earth—friend or foe, sibling or parent, colleague, dearest friend, butterfly, wombat, red back spider, mountain range, running creek, wild wind, soaring bird—can be the means whereby the human person is drawn into the immanent presence of the one who is Creator and friend and who is also the transcendent One and utterly other.

Three Significant "Points"

A Contemplation to Attain the Love of God is in some sense both the bottom line and the summit of the *Spiritual Exercises* of Ignatius of Loyola. It is structured in a similar manner to the other *Exercises* with notes and opening preludes and points. Considerable emphasis in this final exercise is normally given to the *first point* which is a powerful invitation to "call to mind all the blessings of creation and redemption, and the special favors I have received" throughout the whole of life and specifically the thirty days of the *Exercises*. This is followed by a further invitation to pray in total trust and surrender to the God who creates and redeems: "Give me Thy love and thy grace, for this is sufficient for me." It is the three points that follow, however, that hold particular significance for this present discussion.

For a person of Christian faith living in the twenty-first century, called to ecological conversion, these words can focus the deepened relationship of the Creator with the creature in a vivid, intimate and uniquely engaging way:

> *Second point*: This is to reflect how God dwells in creatures: in the elements giving them existence, in the plants giving them life, in the animals, conferring on them sensation, on man bestowing understanding. So [God][20] dwells in me, gives me being, life, sensation, intelligence; and makes a temple of me since I am created in the likeness and the image of the Divine Majesty.

Here is an invitation to enter affectively, imaginatively, and cognitively into an awareness of God's personal presence deep within the materiality of all creation—from the complexity and variety of micro-organisms, into plants and all kinds of living creatures, evolving into the wondrous variety of human beings—made in the image of God's very self.

> *Third point*: This is to consider how God works and labors for me in all creatures on the face of the earth, [God] conducts [Godself] as one who labors. Thus, in the heavens, the elements,

---

20. The modification of the translation in this section to avoid the use of an exclusive personal pronoun for God is mine.

the plants, the fruits, the cattle etc., [God] gives being, conserves them, confers life and sensation, etc.[21]

Here the invitation is to enter into an even deeper, more multi-dimensional awareness still—of a loving God's actively re-creative and redemptive Spirit at work within me and within the tiniest particles of matter reaching to the outer regions and dynamic immensity of the entire cosmos . . .

> *Fourth point:* This is to consider all blessings and gifts descending from above. Thus, my limited power comes from the supreme and infinite power above, and so too justice, goodness, mercy, etc., descend from above as the rays of light come from the sun and the waters flow from their fountains etc.[22]

And here finally, we are left with a consoling glimpse of the sheer tenderness and beauty of the manner in which this Creator God engages with and within us and all creation—with "justice, goodness, mercy," descending upon us like rays of light from the sun and water flowing from a fountain . . . This last "word" of the *Exercises* offers an enduring encouragement to embrace a profoundly personal cosmic vision of the Creator God's incarnational and regenerating presence so that we might be drawn proactively into the work of transforming our world.[23]

Bibliography

Hughson, Thomas, SJ. "Creation as an Ecumenical Problem: Renewed Belief through Green Experience." *Theological Studies* 75 (2014) 847–62.

O'Malley, John W. *The First Jesuits.* Cambridge: Harvard University Press, 1993.

Puhl, Louis J., SJ. *The Spiritual Exercises of St Ignatius: Based on Studies in the Language of the Autograph.* Chicago: Loyola University Press, 1953.

Tylenda, Joseph N., SJ, ed. and trans. *A Pilgrim's Journey: The Autobiography of Ignatius of Loyola.* Rev. ed. San Francisco: Ignatius, 2001.

---

21. The use of "etc." conveys Ignatius' intent for the person making the *Exercises* and the one directing them to add other more apt examples that come to mind.

22. *Spiritual Exercises* #235–37.

23. Col 1:15–20.

6

The Animating Spirit of Life

A Pneumatological Perspective on Ecological Spirituality

Graham Buxton

Nature-Deficit Disorder

W E LIVE IN A complex and uncertain world, characterized by increasing urbanization, fragmentation, dislocation, and alienation. Young people especially, seeking their place in such a world, need fixed points to anchor their deepest longings for identity, belonging, and fulfillment. Recent research in Australia (recapitulated elsewhere in the Western world) suggests that there is a growing number of people who may be described as SBNRs—"spiritual but not religious"—amongst whom are many young people.[1] The American theologian Philip Clayton suggests that the rise of SBNRs is not a sign of spiritual decline but rather a new kind of spiritual awakening.[2]

In this chapter, I argue that one important dimension of this spiritual awakening is a growing concern for the environment and for the ecological health of the planet. Amongst many people, however, notably the young—notwithstanding the eclectic blend of inputs into their spirituality-mix that includes a concern for the ecological health of the planet—there are increasingly strong cultural pressures leading them away from a spirituality that

1. McCrindle Research, *Australian Communities Report.*
2. Clayton, "Letting Doubters in the Door."

connects vitally with nature. The child advocacy expert Richard Louv refers to what he calls "nature-deficit disorder" to describe the disturbing trend amongst today's "wired generation" to plug in to a culture of "connected cocooning" rather than seek a more holistic life-enhancing connection with the natural world.[3] This chapter addresses this elemental connection between spirituality and ecology from the perspective of the Christian faith, and locates it in the Christian doctrine of the Holy Spirit.

Community of Creation

On a recent visit to Assisi in Italy I bought a parchment on which is recorded St Francis of Assisi's well-known canticle, the Canticle of the Creatures—otherwise known as the Canticle of Brother Sun and Sister Moon. Born in 1181, St Francis is revered as the patron saint of ecologists. Perhaps one of the most famous incidents in Francis' life is his *Sermon to the Birds*, celebrated in a painting by the Italian Renaissance artist Giotto, which can be found in the magnificent Basilica of St Francesco d'Assisi. Francis had a great love for all God's creatures, and taught about our responsibility and privilege to care for the environment as those who are creatures ourselves. Travelling with some of his companions, he asked them to "wait for me while I go to preach to my sisters the birds." Legend has it that the birds surrounded him, drawn by the attraction of his voice. On one occasion when I was at San Damiano, I took a photo of a statue of St Francis, and at first I thought that the bird was part of the sculpture! Passing it again on my way back, I was sure that the bird had changed position . . . and so it had! The bird was real—so even today St Francis has not lost his magnetism and charisma!

In 1966, Lynn White, a professor of medieval history in the United States, delivered a famous and oft-quoted lecture tracing the roots of the present ecological crisis, laying the blame not only at the door of secular progress in the form of the industrial revolution but also at the door of Judeo-Christian theology. For White, Christianity was an anthropocentric religion, serving the needs of human beings at the expense of nature, arising out of and contributing to dualistic thinking about the relationship between human beings and the natural world. In his unbending critique of Christianity, White nonetheless makes reference to St Francis as "the greatest spiritual revolutionary in Western history" because, in his words, he "tried to depose man from his monarchy over creation and set up a democracy of all God's creatures. With him the ant is no longer simply a homily for the

---

3. Louv, *Last Child in the Woods.*

lazy, flames a sign of the thrust of the soul toward union with God; now they are Brother Ant and Sister Fire, praising the Creator in their own ways as Brother Man does in his."[4]

St Francis of Assisi exemplifies most completely a conviction that is becoming increasingly recognized today that we are called to live *in communion with nature*, not over and above it. God is present in his creation in a profound way, and, more deeply than we realize, we ourselves are part of what Jürgen Moltmann calls God's "creation-community," a community of both creatures and environments contributing to a "web of life on earth." The English mystic, Evelyn Underhill, writing at the beginning of the twentieth century, described many Christians as "deaf people at a concert." "They study the program carefully, believe every statement in it, speak respectfully of the quality of the music, but only really hear a phrase now and again. So they have no notion at all of the mighty symphony which fills the universe, to which our lives are destined to make their tiny contribution, and which is the self-expression of the Eternal God."[5] The "mighty symphony" to which Underhill alludes may be interpreted as the symphony of a creation that is replete with biological diversity and fecundity, a creation that may be described as the self-expression of the divine Trinity.

Whenever we consider approaches to the natural world that depend upon a dualistic separation between God and his creation, we are denying the Trinitarian nature of the God who has made space for the world within himself, and who loves this world with a passion that ultimately led to the incarnation and the cross. That is why we cannot endorse dualism if we truly believe in God as Trinity. God is not a deistic being, separate and remote from his creation, keeping things going "from a distance;" nor is he in dualistic opposition to it. He is intimately involved in all that he has made—he is immanent, present within his creation, as well as transcendent, other than his creation. But in what way might we describe God's presence in creation? It is here that the Christian doctrine of the Holy Spirit—pneumatology—has much to offer in our search for a Christian theology of nature.

Interconnected Reality

Fritjof Capra, an Austrian-born American physicist whose insights into science and faith have been shaped by a strongly Taoist and Buddhist view of reality, may not be the most immediately obvious person to quote in a

4. White, "Historical Roots," 1607.

5. From the first of four broadcast talks by the English mystic Evelyn Underhill, subsequently published under the title *The Spiritual Life*.

Christian theology of the natural world in which we live and move and have our being. However, his commitment to promoting a worldview that emphasizes the interconnectedness of all things in a holistic system of reality challenges the strong reductionist worldview of the so-called New Atheists that, in the words of the philosopher Thomas Nagel, "owes some of the passion displayed by its adherents precisely to the fact that it is thought to liberate us from religion."[6] Whilst we might well need to be liberated from *religion* in our desire to live truly human lives, we most certainly cannot be liberated from *spirituality*—however hard we might try—because the spiritual dimension is an essential aspect of our humanity.

Whilst caution needs to be exercised in interpreting Capra's ideas in terms of his speculative links between physics and oriental spirituality, his systems approach—drawing together key themes in contemporary physics, such as quantum mechanics, chaos and complexity, emergence and self-organization—alerts us to the value of interpreting the physical universe as an integrated, holistic and interconnected reality. His ideas are helpful as "stepping-stones" in understanding, from a Christian perspective, the relationship between the real world which science describes and the God who has brought that world into being and who sustains it by his Spirit.

The Spirit is the eschatological power of God at work in all creation, enabling all that exists—personal and non-personal—to fully and finally become itself in the freedom of divine love.[7] There is an identity between the regenerating, redeeming Spirit of Christ and the creative, life-giving ecological Spirit of God: the Spirit, who, in the language of Augustine, is the love that flows between Father and Son, and who draws human beings to God, is the same Spirit "who is present in every flower, bird, and human being, in every quasar and in every atomic particle, closer to them than they are themselves, enabling them to be and to become."[8] Contemporary physics—especially quantum physics—reminds us that all of creation may be interpreted within a holistic frame of reference. Translating this into a Christian perspective, the universe may be understood as a dynamic whole whose parts are essentially related, energized and orchestrated by the Spirit, manifesting God's "loving entanglement" with the world.[9] However, the Spirit has often been confined to personal piety and ecclesial activity, with

6. Nagel, *Mind and Cosmos*, 12.

7. On this, see Buxton, *Trinity, Creation*, 238–45, and Denis Edwards' chapter in this volume.

8. Edwards, "For Your Immortal Spirit Is in All Things," 56.

9. The language of entanglement, drawn from quantum physics, should be qualified here, as it runs the risk of blurring the radical distinction between God and the world, between infinite and finite.

little attention being given to his role in creation. Whilst there are only a few biblical texts that demonstrate the link between the Spirit and creation, their scarcity should not undermine their vital connection. Clark Pinnock traces the scriptural evidence, concluding that the "Spirit is present and active in creation—in its inception, continuation and perfection." He goes on to say that the Spirit "indwells creation and works on the inside of it by means of subtle operations."[10]

Anima Mundi and *Imago Dei*

In the sixteenth-century the Dominican monk and philosopher Giordano Bruno was condemned to death by the Catholic authorities. Amongst other things, he was accused of heresy by identifying the Spirit with the *anima mundi*, or "world soul," a pure universal spirit regarded by ancient philosophers as the divine essence that enfolds and energizes all life in the universe: the Stoic philosophers believed the *anima mundi* to be the only vital force in the universe. In fact, the Greek philosopher Plato was the first to suggest that the notion of "world soul" held the same relation to the physical creation as the human soul did to the body in anthropology. Of course, the term "world soul" could be misleading as an expression of the life force of the universe because of its appropriation in Asian philosophical thinking and in Hindu religion, where it assumes a pantheistic significance. However, if the Spirit of God, *distinct* from creation, is understood to be the organizing, orchestrating energy of the world, then it is logically possible to retain the idea of the Spirit as the divine *anima mundi* without dissolving God in the world or losing sight of his transcendence.

Bruno was burnt at the stake in 1600, in spite of his defense that his ideas were those of a philosopher rather than a theologian. However, his advocacy of the Spirit as *anima mundi*—or "soul-ecology," in the words of Thomas Moore[11]—lives on in contemporary theological thinking. Jürgen Moltmann describes the Creator Spirit as a divine artist who pours his whole soul into his creation.[12] Sallie McFague is similarly inspired, referring to the Spirit as "a sensibility that sees other people, animals, mountains, and even city buildings as presenting themselves to us vividly, each in its own particularity, independence, and subjectivity."[13] Elizabeth Johnson declares that "the Spirit is in the highest sky, the deepest hole, the darkest night,

---

10. Pinnock, *Flame of Love*, 66.

11. Moore, *Care of the Soul*, 268.

12. Moltmann, "From the Closed World to the Infinite Universe," 169.

13. McFague, *Super, Natural Christians*, 112.

farther east than the sunrise, over every next horizon."[14] In his new book, *Before Nature: A Christian Spirituality*, the American ecological theologian Paul Santmire, alluding to Ps 104, describes the Spirit as the Lifegiving One who is also "the *rejuvenating* energy that renews the face of the earth."[15]

These insights, therefore, are not foreign to the biblical narrative: in fact, they are embedded in the text. Whilst Ps 104 presents us with a picture of God delighting in his creation (culminating in v. 31: "May the Lord rejoice in his works"), Ps 148 may be described even more remarkably as a "cosmic choir" or orchestra, with each created being contributing in their own particular and distinctive way to a symphony of praise to God simply by being themselves and fulfilling their divinely-ordained role in creation. As human beings who have been created to live in communion with the natural order of things, we need to learn how to join with all creation in worshipping God, for only then can we truly experience transformation as we discover afresh our basic humanity in solidarity with God's created order. Planet Earth is our home and we have been summoned by God to care for it precisely because it has integrity in itself as the creation of God. Furthermore, Christians are not those who have somehow been "caught up" by the Spirit, and transported out of this world and into some mystical, spiritual reality that has no bearing on the created order. We are grounded, landed creatures, created to live in this good earth.

Here the integrating concept of *imago Dei* is highly significant because to be disconnected from the world of nature is to violate our identity as human beings created in God's image. Not only do we—as created beings—live and move and have our being within the world of nature, but spiritual experience is itself located within the ecological context. To pull spirituality and ecology apart is to do violence to the very fabric of creation as God's gift of self-communicating love. Spirituality and ecology are intimately connected within a worldview that invites us to embrace—or *be embraced by*?—the physical creation as an expression of our God-given humanity.

Aboriginal Spirituality

Whilst this insight may be foreign to many Westerners, especially those who espouse a radically secular and reductionist philosophy of life, it is prevalent amongst those religious belief systems, such as in the Aboriginal world, where people live in a sacred universe where there is no sharp dichotomy between the physical and the spiritual. In this regard, we need to steer clear

14. Johnson, *Women, Earth and Creator Spirit*, 42.

15. Santmire, *Before Nature*, 175.

of the cultural myopia of those who view Aboriginal spirituality through white, Western glasses. Indigenous perspectives on what it means to be a human being often collide with Western ontologies: we have much to learn from our Indigenous brothers and sisters, whose spirituality—and indeed essential personhood—is linked deeply to the land.

Mick Dodson, the former Aboriginal and Torres Strait Islander Justice Commissioner, has spoken powerfully of the connection that Aboriginal peoples feel to their land:

> To understand our law, our culture and our relationship to the physical and spiritual world, you must begin with land. Everything about aboriginal society is inextricably woven with, and connected to, land. Culture is the land, the land and spirituality of aboriginal people, our cultural beliefs or reason for existence is the land. You take that away and you take away our reason for existence. We have grown that land up. We are dancing, singing, and painting for the land. We are celebrating the land. Removed from our lands, we are literally removed from ourselves.[16]

The Dreaming is a term used by some Aboriginal peoples to describe the relations and balance between the spiritual, natural and moral elements of the world. Silas Roberts, first Chairman of the Northern Land Council, has put it this way:

> Aboriginals see themselves as part of nature. We see all things natural as part of us. All the things on Earth we see as part human. This is told through the ideas of dreaming. By dreaming we mean the belief that long ago, these creatures started human society. These creatures, these great creatures are just as much alive today as they were in the beginning. They are everlasting and will never die. They are always part of the land and nature as we are. *Our connection to all things natural is spiritual.*[17]

As they walk through their country, Aboriginal peoples are continually reminded of the presence of these great ancestral beings that are celebrated in paintings and songs and sacred ceremonies. In essence, the Dreaming is the spirituality of the Aboriginal people, and it is a spirituality that is inseparable from the land, reflected today in virtually all Aboriginal paintings. As those who have lived lives disconnected from the land, we have much to learn from this deep relationship to land that is at the heart of Aboriginal spirituality. To live responsibly as human beings within the created order is

16. Cited in *Art, Land and the Dreaming.*
17. Cited in *Dreaming and the Dreamtime.*

to move beyond a purely utilitarian ethic and to embrace a spirituality that acknowledges the wonder and mystery of creation as "sacred reality." For too long the Christian church has failed to demonstrate respect for and concerned involvement in nature, a neglect over the years that has prompted Sallie McFague to insert what she calls a "deeply subversive" comma between "super" and "natural." Her writings express a passionate desire to see Christians live not just "supernatural" lives, but "super, natural" lives, living "*in* the earth, and *for* the earth . . . understanding ourselves as excessively, superlatively concerned with nature and its well-being."[18]

Imaginative Naturalism

In his remarkable first book entitled *The Immense Journey*, the American scholar and scientist Loren Eiseley writes with reverence and lyricism about the wonders of the universe, imagining himself at different stages and in different places in the unfolding journey of the universe through time and space. The book is a remarkable narrative of life unfolding through time, a delightfully imaginative and sensuous voyage through history in which the storyteller invites the reader into a rich tapestry of experiences and events that reflect Eiseley's own sense of awe at the mystery and wonder of creation. One incident that he recounts has come to be known as "the judgment of the birds." In a sunlit glade a sleek black raven gulps down a squirming nestling, indifferent to the helpless outrage of the little bird's parents. Then into the glade flutter a few other birds, then many others, until in the hush the crystal note of a song sparrow is picked up. Soon the whole glade is filled with the joyous sound of birdsong. In Eiseley's account, they sang "because life is sweet and sunlight beautiful. They sang under the brooding shadow of the raven. In simple truth they had forgotten the raven, for they were the singers of life, and not of death."[19] Commenting on this poignant incident, Douglas John Hall observes that "human spirituality is cheapened when it fastens on the divine in such a way as to exclude nature and even history from the realm of transcendent wonder."[20] John Muir, the pioneer conservationist and "Father of the National Parks" in America, once said, "I only went out for a walk and finally concluded to stay out till sundown, for going out, I found, was really going in."[21]

18. McFague, *Super, Natural Christians*, 5–6.

19. Eiseley, *The Immense Journey*, 175.

20. Hall, *Imaging God*, 138.

21. Muir and Wolfe, *John of the Mountains*, 427.

The life of Henry Thoreau, another "imaginative naturalist," was infused with a rich and profound sense of wonder. He was a "complete human being" who had discovered how to live fully *imago Dei* with his fellow beings and with nature. The following is an example of Thoreau's prose in *Walden: The Pond in Winter* (which describes the simple life he led at Walden Pond for over two years):

> Standing on the snow-covered plain, as if in a pasture amid the hills, I cut my way first through a foot of snow, and then a foot of ice, and open a window under my feet, where, kneeling to drink, I look down into the quiet parlor of the fishes, pervaded by a softened light as through a window of ground glass, with its bright sanded floor the same as in summer; there a perennial waveless serenity reigns as in the amber twilight sky, corresponding to the cool and even temperament of the inhabitants. Heaven is under our feet as well as over our heads.[22]

There is no doubt that, like many today who seek to relate to nature, Thoreau's understanding of God was eclectic, with discernible traces of nature mysticism, but this should not discourage us from seeing in his life an example of a person who was convinced of the interconnectedness between all things in creation. In particular, he insisted that human beings have a responsibility to care for creation in order to allow the natural world to be free to express itself in all its beauty and wonder . . . and, at times, untamed brutality, or what he calls "meanness." He writes in *Walden*: "I wanted to live deep and suck out all the marrow of life, to live so sturdily and Spartan-like as to put to rout all that was not life, to cut a broad swath and shave close, to drive life into a corner, and reduce it to its lowest terms, and, if it proved to be mean, why then to get the whole and genuine meanness of it, and publish its meanness to the world; or if it were sublime, to know it by experience, and be able to give a true account of it in my next excursion."[23]

Ultimate Beauty

When we live on this planet imbued with a desire to care for it and do what we can to live in an ethical and sustainable way, caring for *all* of God's creation—other people, all animals, birds and fish, and the inanimate world of plants and land and water—then we will discover a new freedom to live "super, natural" lives. And when this begins to happen in our lives, we will find

22. Thoreau, *Walden*, 275.

23. Ibid., 87.

ourselves following the Spirit of God, who, in Elizabeth Johnson's evocative words, "dances on ahead" of us, preparing us for that day when the promise of a restored humanity, as foreseen in Isa 35:5-6, is framed by the promise of a restored world, in which the desert will rejoice as it blossoms like the crocus, the burning sand will become a pool and the thirsty ground bubbling springs: then will the blind see and the deaf hear. These two eschatological promises are inextricably linked and are not to be pulled apart: as it will be in God's new creation, so is it now in the genius and goodness of God's lush creation . . . and so can human beings experience it today.

The spiritual and the natural belong together as an expression of ultimate beauty, a beauty into which we are being drawn daily as we walk with Christ, in whom resides true beauty. For all who are seeking to make sense of their lives in a world of swirling change and unsettling insecurity, the ecological spirituality presented here challenges the disturbing pervasiveness of "nature-deficit disorder" by promising a healing participation in all that God is doing through his Spirit to make all things new in Christ. Drawing deeply from the wells of both Christian tradition and the "material-vital" world of God's good creation, we are all invited—young and old alike—to embrace this bifocal Christian spirituality, "where the cathedral of the great outdoors and the cathedral of historic Christianity are one world."[24]

Bibliography

Art, Land and the Dreaming (2000). No pages. http://www.aboriginalartonline.com/culture/land.php.

Buxton, Graham. *The Trinity, Creation and Pastoral Ministry: Imaging the Perichoretic God*. Milton Keynes, UK: Paternoster, 2005.

Clayton, Philip. "Letting Doubters in the Door." *Los Angeles Times*, March 25, 2012.

Dreaming and the Dreamtime (2000). No pages. http://www.aboriginalartonline.com/culture/dreaming.php.

Edwards, Denis. "For Your Immortal Spirit is in all Things: The Role of the Spirit in Creation." In *Earth Revealing—Earth Healing: Ecology and Christian Theology*, edited by Denis Edwards, 45–66. Collegeville, MN: Liturgical, 2001.

Eiseley, Loren. *The Immense Journey: An Imaginative Naturalist Explores the Mysteries of Man and Nature*. New York: Vintage, 1957.

Hall, Douglas John. *Imaging God: Dominion as Stewardship*. Grand Rapids: Eerdmans, 1986.

Johnson, Elizabeth A. *Women, Earth, and Creator Spirit*. Madeleva Lecture in Spirituality 1993. New York: Paulist, 1993.

Louv, Richard. *Last Child in the Woods: Saving Our Children from Nature-Deficit Disorder*. Chapel Hill, NC: Algonquin, 2005.

24. Santmire, *Before Nature*, xvii.

McCrindle Research. *Australian Communities Report: Spirituality and Christianity in Australia Today* (2011). See http://olivetreemedia.com.au/News.aspx?id=9.

McFague, Sallie. *Super, Natural Christians: How We Should Love Nature.* Minneapolis: Fortress, 1997.

McGrath, Alister E. *The Re-Enchantment of Nature: Science, Religion and the Human Sense of Wonder.* London: Hodder & Stoughton, 2003.

Moltmann, Jürgen. "From the Closed World to the Infinite Universe." In *Science and Wisdom*, 158–71. Minneapolis: Fortress, 2003.

Moore, Thomas. *Care of the Soul: A Guide for Cultivating Depth and Sacredness in Everyday Life.* New York: HarperCollins, 1992.

Muir, John, and Linnie M. Wolfe. *John of the Mountains: The Unpublished Journals of John Muir.* Boston: Houghton Mifflin, 1938.

Nagel, Thomas. *Mind and Cosmos: Why the Materialist Neo-Darwinian Conception of Nature Is Almost Certainly False.* Oxford: Oxford University Press, 2012.

Pinnock, Clark H. *Flame of Love: A Theology of the Holy Spirit.* Downers Grove, IL: InterVarsity, 1996.

Santmire, H. Paul. *Before Nature: A Christian Spirituality.* Minneapolis: Fortress, 2014.

Spirituality (2009). No pages. http://australianmuseum.net.au/Indigenous-Australia-Spirituality.

Thoreau, Henry. D. *Walden: An Annotated Edition.* Boston: Houghton Mifflin, 1995.

Underhill, Evelyn. *The Spiritual Life.* Harrisburg, PA: Morehouse, 1997.

White, Lynn. "The Historical Roots of Our Ecologic Crisis." *Science* 155 (1967) 1203–7.

7

Rediscovering a Spirituality of Creation for the Anthropocene

Mick Pope

WILDERNESS HAS BEEN DEFINED as areas "untrammeled by man, where man himself is a visitor who does not remain."[1] Such places often "provide a common ground for shared experience of what some people call the revelation of God in creation."[2] In "The Earth is Full of Your Creatures," I examined the fact that there is no longer any genuine undisturbed wilderness, instead advancing the idea that it was the presence of wild creatures that made wilderness wild.[3] The doxological nature of creation is in its variety, sheer abundance, and danger.

This present chapter seeks to advance that work in three ways. Firstly, it places a spirituality of creation within the framework of the Anthropocene, the domination of the Earth by humanity. Secondly, it extends the discussion of wildness to include other aspect of the Earth, including land, atmosphere, and oceans. Thirdly, it examines the biblical dialectic of dominion and creation care versus divine providence and care for creation. This is contextualized to examine the myth of *terra nullius*, and the need to learn from Aboriginal theology.

---

1. Wilderness Act, *Public Law 88–577*.
2. Stanley, *Forest Church*, 20.
3. Pope, "The Earth Is Full of Your Creatures."

Life in the Anthropocene

Human influence on the Earth system has been so profound, a new geological epoch has been suggested; the Anthropocene.[4] The precise beginnings of the Anthropocene are still debated, but candidates include: the adoption of agriculture, the invasion of the Americas by Europeans, the beginning of the industrial revolution, nuclear weapon detonation, or the introduction of persistent industrial chemicals.[5] Of particular interest is the "Great Acceleration" which captures the massive and widespread changes in the socio-economic and biophysical spheres of the Earth system that have occurred since the 1950s.[6] The Anthropocene is characterized by the threatened or actual breaching of the nine planetary boundaries which represent a safe operating space for humanity: climate change, ocean acidification, species loss, stratospheric ozone depletion, disruption of natural chemical cycles, land-system changes, fresh water use, atmospheric aerosols, and the introduction of novel chemicals.[7]

The implication of this framework is that there is no wilderness as defined as regions unaffected directly by human presence or indirectly by human activity. Such an understanding is critical in considering a spirituality of creation.

Christian Spirituality and the Six Spheres

The Earth is composed of five interconnected spheres or components: the biosphere or sum total of living matter, the geosphere or solid earth, the atmosphere, the hydrosphere or water cycle including oceans, rivers and rainfall, and the cryosphere or frozen water. Theologically, creation is viewed as a temple. Walton describes the Gen 1 account as the dedication of the cosmos-temple, with humans as God's image or idol.[8] Although there is a biblical trajectory of God's particular presence in the tabernacle (Exod 26), temple (1 Kgs 6), and then church (1 Cor 3), there is both the recognition that no human temple can contain God (1 Kgs 8:27) and the eschatological filling of all, as the city of God contains no temple (Rev 21:22). In developing a spirituality of creation for the Anthropocene, it is important to understand

4. Crutzen, *Geology of Mankind*, 23.

5. Lewis and Maslin, *Defining the Anthropocene*.

6. Steffen et al., *The Trajectory of the Anthropocene*.

7. Steffen et al., *Planetary Boundaries*.

8. Walton, *The Lost World of Genesis One*, 68.

each of these five terrestrial spheres, plus the celestial sphere or night sky as part of this temple-cosmos.

Biosphere

The biosphere represents the sum total of all organic entities and their interrelationships. The diversity of creatures and their sheer numbers is a testament to the creative activity of God. In Gen 1, God creates every kind of creature on the dry land (vv. 24–25), while the waters swarm with living creatures (vv. 20–21). Creatures are to be fruitful and multiply (v. 22), fulfilling their temple function. Likewise, the doxological crescendo of Ps 104 is a reflection on the manifold nature of God's works in variety, size, and plentitude (vv. 24–25). MacKinnon has argued that much thinking about nature is overly sentimental.[9] However, the biblical witness to the divine provision for lions (Ps 104:20–22) and Leviathan (Ps 104:26–27) suggests that doxology comes with danger. Leviathan is undomesticable by humans, but not by God (Job 41:1–34). What makes wilderness doxological is that it is dangerous and untamed, a testament to both divine power and human impotence.

The death and suffering that is observed in nature is seen as a problem for theodicy, i.e. how can God permit a process that necessarily involves such disvalues? Does such suffering make evolutionary process less doxological? Rolston doesn't think so, noting that the transfer of value from one component of an ecosystem to another (e.g., in predation) results both in the creativity of the process and the very aesthetic values we admire in both predator and prey.[10] What is more pertinent for humans to address is our own impact on the doxological value of creation due to species loss, to the extent that the present age is characterized as the sixth mass extinction.[11]

Geosphere

In the Ancient Near East (ANE), the Earth was thought of as a flat disk.[12] In some instances, there was a cosmic mountain at the center. The Old Testament attests to both of these ideas (Isa 40:22 and Mic 4:1–2 respectively). The geological processes that produce continents, mountains and valleys

---

9. MacKinnon, *False Idyll.*

10. Rolston, *Disvalues in Nature*, 270.

11. Colbert, *The Sixth Extinction.*

12. Walton, *Ancient Near Eastern Thought and the Old Testament*, 171–72.

result in earthquakes in the Middle East, due to fault lines originating in the Pleistocene.[13] Earthquakes sometimes accompany theophanies (Pss 18:7; 29:6; Exod 19:18). Earthquakes and volcanoes are "natural disasters" and remind humans of their finitude and lack of control over the earth. However, Rolston sees the randomness of geological processes in the larger context of its creative power to create aesthetically pleasing scenery.[14]

Many theophanies have occurred on mountain tops, including the burning bush (Exod 3), the giving of Torah (Exod 19–20) and the transfiguration (Mark 9). Likewise, as Santmire notes, "Saints and mystics, throughout the Christian ages . . . have frequently imagined themselves to be on a spiritual pilgrimage, indeed, climbing up to mount Zion or to some other great mountain, in search of a beatific vision."[15] Furthermore, the divine creativity is manifest in that the mountains are fit habitation for wild creatures quite apart from human wants or needs (Ps 104:18).

While geological processes create and destroy mountains in God's time, human beings can now destroy mountains. In the Appalachian Mountains in the United States, coal companies "bulldoze the forest, decapitate the peaks with explosives, push the shattered rubble into adjacent valleys, and destroy the ecologically crucial headwater streams that had been there before."[16]

Atmosphere

The atmosphere is wilderness not in its remoteness but in its wildness and extremes. One of the marks of the Holocene or recent past 12 millennia is that the climate has been relatively steady.[17] Prior to this, large swings in climate played a role in the adoption of agriculture in the Levant.[18] Even so, decadal long drought has helped shape the fates of civilizations such as the Akkadian in Mesopotamia, and the Mayan in Mesoamerica.[19] In ANE thought, the atmosphere is the middle heavens between the Earth and the firmament.[20] It is across this dome that the birds fly (Gen 1:20). The weather does not originate from the sky, but from storehouses above the firmament.

13. Baly, *The Geography of the Bible*, 22.

14. Rolston, *Disvalues in Nature*, 265.

15. Santmire, *Before Nature*, 133.

16. Butler, *Plundering Appalachia*.

17. Lewis and Maslin, *Defining the Anthropocene*, Figure 2.

18. Bar-Yosef, *Climatic Fluctuations and Early Farming in West and East Asia*.

19. deMenocal, *Cultural Reponses to Climate Change*.

20. Walton, *The Lost World of Genesis One*, 30.

God is the father, of the rain who holds hail and snow in storehouses, and who makes a way for rain and lightning (Job 38:22–28). Such provision is not just for humans, but all creation (Job 38:26–27; Ps 104:13).

Sometimes rainfall is linked to divine judgment as in the Flood (Gen 6:5–7) or Elijah's drought (1 Kgs 17:1). At other times, climate variability is a means for God to achieve some greater end (e.g. Gen 41). The weather is meant to keep us in humble dependence upon God. While there is wisdom in sheltering from the weather, or the provision of forecasts and warnings, humanity has attempted to usurp divine control. Climate disruption by the burning of fossil fuels has been followed by hubristic dreams of climate engineering.[21]

Hydrosphere

For the Hebrews, the ocean was a source of chaos and danger. In Gen 1 God brings form to the amorphous chaos of the *tohu wabohu*. This chaos is separated behind the firmament (Gen 1:6–8), which is our "hedge against chaos."[22] God's power is shown in his control of this chaos (Ps 104:5–9). The sea itself is called upon to praise God and to look forward to his coming (Ps 98:7–9). Jesus' control over the wind and the waves is meant to drive the reader to consider Jesus' divine identity (Mark 4:41). Yet this chaos can be released by human sin (Gen 6–9).

Sea level has risen and fallen over millennia as the climate has warmed and cooled. Tropical cyclones produce storm surges and earthquakes generate tsunamis. The power of the oceans reminds us of our smallness and, at times, helplessness, holding doxology and theodicy in tension. Now human sin has unleashed the chaos of sea level rise. End of century projections are for at least 60cm, and warming of 2° C above pre-industrial temperatures could result in a longer term rise of 6m.[23]

Cryosphere

Like the rain, snow is said to be under divine control, held in a storehouse above the firmament (Job 38:22) to water the Earth (Isa 55:10). Avalanches remind us that our recreational activities do not imply we have domesticated snow. Ice has been important in shaping the Earth as ice ages have

21. Robock, *20 Reasons Why Geoengineering is a Bad Idea*.

22. Mobley, *Return of the Chaos Monsters*, 21.

23. Dutton et al., "Sea-level Rise."

waxed and waned due to changes in the Earth's orbit, variations in the Gulf Stream and the configuration of the continents, covering large swathes or even most of the Earth.[24] Antarctica draws explorers, scientists and tourists alike, as the "enormity of its ice shelves and mountain ranges invariably heightens feelings of humanity's insignificance and nature's grandeur."[25]

Ice cover is a key climate feedback, reflecting sunlight back into space. This feedback is shifting into reverse with climate change, as glaciers and sea ice melt, uncovering less reflective land and ocean surfaces. Scientists are now suggesting that we will soon see Arctic sea ice free summers and the collapse of much of Antarctica's glaciers.[26]

Celestial Sphere

The ancients did not see the stars as other suns in the night sky, but as lights set in the celestial sphere or firmament.[27] The word meteorology retains this connection between space and the atmosphere. The night sky causes us to contemplate our significance in the universe (Ps 8).[28] Technology both aids and obstructs these existential considerations. While the science of astronomy means that we can see deeply into space, light pollution in our cities ensures that to experience this existential catharsis personally requires escaping to less populated areas.

Wilderness Management and the Myth of *Terra Nullius*

Given the context of the Anthropocene, a spirituality of creation demands we engage in restorative management. Creation as temple theology gives prominence to active dominion, where human beings are divine image bearers, representing God to creation (Gen 1).[29] Tilling and keeping of creation is an act of worship (Gen 2:15).[30] In the other tradition (e.g., Ps 104; Job 38–42), human agency takes second place to direct divine control.

---

24. Walker, *Snowball Earth*.

25. Lonely Planet, "Introducing Antarctica."

26. Maslowski et al., *The Future of Arctic Sea Ice*. Khazendar et al., "The Evolving Instability of the Remnant Larsen B Ice Shelf and Its Tributary Glaciers."

27. Walton, *The Lost World of Genesis One*, 16.

28. Leupold, *Exposition of the Psalms*, 103.

29. Walton, *The Lost World of Genesis One*, 68.

30. Walton, *The Lost World of Adam and Eve*, 104–15.

Human management in the Anthropocene is therefore a mixture of action and active letting be. Maintaining both the functional integrity and spiritual value of creation requires a number of management strategies, from fencing off to culling, reintroduction of lost flora and fauna, including rewilding by reintroducing predators.[31] More risky and speculative ideas include the introduction of analogues to extinct species, or even de-extinction via cloning. Forming sanctuaries where human activity is limited or forbidden can help increase species populations, although unless the larger issues of the Anthropocene are dealt with, such efforts will prove futile.

In the Australian context, the dichotomy of wilderness and civilization makes little sense to the First People's relationship to land. The Aboriginal Dreaming is an "all-encapsulating body of truths" which include the "past and ongoing activities of creative and life-giving forces."[32] Sites where such significant activities have occurred are "sacred sites," and care for these is a sacred duty to sustain people in the present to maintain religious, cultural, kinship and environmental balance. The Dreaming therefore represents a "beautifully worked out spirituality, complete with a full and coherent sacramental theology."[33] Western colonial powers and Western colonialism through the myth of *terra nullius* have failed to recognize this essential and spiritual connection to land, where "if the land is taken from you, or if you are taken from your land, your spirit will perish."[34] For Edwards, *terra nullius* represents a "lie, a horrendous distortion of truth, the claim that the land was unoccupied, that it was no-one's country," and suggests addressing this sin is our path to communal liberation through communal conversion.[35] This involves the recognition that through First People's spirituality and culture, God was already making himself known through the Holy Spirit before the arrival of Europeans.[36]

Such a path is laid out in *Rainbow Spirit Theology*.[37] Invoking Heb 1:1, the Elders claim that "God the Creator Spirit has been speaking through Aboriginal culture from the beginning," primarily through the land.[38] There are close parallels between First People creation stories and the ordering of creation in Gen 1 and 2; in particular, the understanding of responsibility

---

31. Monbiot, *Feral.*

32. Dodson, *The Land our Mother, the Church our Mother*, 83.

33. Ibid., 84.

34. Ibid., 85.

35. Edwards, *Sin and Salvation in the South Land of the Holy Spirit*, 91.

36. Ibid., 99.

37. Rainbow Spirit Elders, *Rainbow Spirit Theology.*

38. Ibid., 12.

towards the land comports well with Gen 2:15 in that "The Creator Spirit is the true landowner, and human beings are like trustees, responsible to the Creator Spirit for the care of this land."[39]

Conclusion

Jesus is the Creator Spirit who took human form and "built a humpy among us."[40] With echoes of Rom 8, Rainbow Spirit Theology understands the Gospel as "not a message limited to saving souls for heaven, but as a message of God in Christ freeing all creation."[41] We have much to learn from Aboriginal experience as we develop a contextualized spirituality of creation for the Anthropocene. Land is a place of mystery, silence and meeting, and the land can become a "revelatory symbol" if we allow Aboriginal peoples to be our mediators of this experience and see ourselves as their apprentices.[42]

Bibliography

Baly, Denis. *The Geography of the Bible*. New York: Harper, 1957.

Bar-Yosef, Ofer. "Climatic Fluctuations and Early Farming in West and East Asia." *Current Anthropology* 52.4 (2011) S175–S193.

Budden, Chris. *Following Jesus in Invaded Space: Doing Theology on Aboriginal Land*. Princeton Theological Monograph Series 116. Eugene, OR: Pickwick Publications, 2009.

Butler, Tom. *Plundering Appalachia: The Tragedy of Mountaintop Removal Coal Mining*. San Rafael: Earth Aware, 2009.

Colbert, Elizabeth. *The Sixth Extinction: An Unnatural History*. London: Bloomsbury, 2014.

Crutzen, Paul. "Geology of Mankind." *Nature* 415 (2002) 23.

deMenocal, Peter B. "Cultural Reponses to Climate Change during the Late Holocene." *Science* 292 (2001) 667–73.

Dodson, Pat. "The Land Our Mother, the Church Our Mother." In *Discovering an Australian Theology*, edited by Peter Malone, 83–88. Homebush, NSW: St. Paul, 1988.

Dutton, A. et al. "Sea-level Rise Due to Polar Ice-sheet Mass Loss during Past Warm Periods." *Science* 349 (2015). DOI: 10.1126/science.aaa4019.

Edwards, Denis. "Sin and Salvation in the South Land of the Holy Spirit." In *Discovering an Australian Theology*, edited by Peter Malone, 89–102. Homebush, NSW: St. Paul, 1988.

39. Ibid., 35.

40. Ibid., 59.

41. Ibid., 23.

42. Edwards, *Sin and Salvation in the South Land of the Holy Spirit*, 100.

Khazendar Ala et al. "The Evolving Instability of the Remnant Larsen B Ice Shelf and its Tributary Glaciers." *Earth and Planetary Science Letters* 419 (2015) 199–210.

Leupold, H. C. *Exposition of the Psalms.* London: Evangelical, 1972.

Lewis, Simon L., and Mark A. Maslin. "Defining the Anthropocene." *Nature* 519 (2015) 171–80.

Lonely Planet. "Introducing Antarctica." http://www.lonelyplanet.com/antarctica.

MacKinnon, J. B. "False Idyll." *Orion Magazine* 31.3 May/June 2012. http://www.orionmagazine.org/index.php/articles/article/6807/.

Maslowski, Wieslaw, et al. "The Future of Arctic Sea Ice." *Annual Reviews of Earth and Planetary Sciences* 40 (2012) 625–54.

Mobley, Gregory. *The Return of the Chaos Monsters—And Other Backstories of the Bible.* Grand Rapids: Eerdmans, 2010.

Monbiot, George. *Feral: Searching for Enchantment on the Frontiers of Nature.* London: Allen Lane 2013.

Pope, Mick. "The Earth is Full of Your Creatures: A Theology of Wilderness." *Anglican Ecocare Journal of Ecotheology* 1 (2014) 65–78.

Rainbow Spirit Elders. *Rainbow Spirit Theology: Towards an Australian Theology.* 2nd ed. Hindmarsh: ATF, 2007.

Robock, Alan. "20 Reasons Why Geoengineering Is a Bad Idea." *Bulletin of the Atomic Scientists* 64 (2008) 14–18.

Rolston, Holmes, III. "Disvalues in Nature." *The Monist* 75 (1992) 250–78.

Santmire, H. Paul. *Before Nature: A Christian Spirituality.* Minneapolis: Fortress, 2014.

Stanley, Bruce. *Forest Church: A Field Guide to a Spiritual Connection with Nature.* New York: Anamchara, 2014.

Steffen, Will, et al. "Planetary Boundaries: Guiding Human Development on a Changing Planet." *Science* 347 (2015) 1–17.

———. "The Trajectory of the Anthropocene: The Great Acceleration." *The Anthropocene Review* 2 (2015) 81–98.

Walker, Gabrielle. *Snowball Earth: The Story of the Great Global Catastrophe that Spawned Life as We Know It.* London: Bloomsbury, 2003.

Walton, John H. *Ancient Near Eastern Thought and the Old Testament: Introducing the Conceptual World of the Hebrew Bible.* Grand Rapids: Baker, 2006.

———. *The Lost World of Adam and Eve.* Downers Grove, IL: IVP Academic, 2015.

———. *The Lost World of Genesis One: Ancient Cosmology and the Origins Debate.* Leicester, UK: InterVarsity, 2009.

Wilderness Act. Public Law 88–577 (16 U.S. C. 1131–1136) 88th Congress, Second Session, September 3, 1964.

Part 3

Suffering in Creation

8

Disasters, Nature, and Acts of God

Robert S White

Sometimes it takes a natural disaster
to reveal a social disaster.[1]

Background

WE LIVE IN A world where the same natural processes that make it habitable can also be extremely dangerous. Disasters may kill thousands or even hundreds of thousands of people at a stroke. Natural disasters pull us up sharp and make us face head-on the hard questions of life and death. For atheists and agnostics they challenge humankind's hubris that we can control our environment—or that our cleverness can keep us from suffering. For Christians they raise the hard question of why an all-powerful, all-loving God allows such things to happen. Disasters bring into sharp focus the relationship between the creator God, his creation and humans made "in his image."

The Problem of Disasters

Despite the increase over the past century in our scientific understanding of the world in which we live, and our advancing technological abilities, the number of people affected by disasters is increasing with every decade that

---

1. Fletcher, "Katrina Pushes Issues of Race and Poverty at Bush."

goes by. In our increasingly interconnected world, a disaster in one country may not only cause large economic losses in that region, but may ripple out around the world. The long term trend of economic damage from natural disasters is now over US$100 billion per year. Today around 300 million people per year are affected by disasters. It is likely that in the not-too-distant future there will be an earthquake that kills over one million people.[2]

These increasing numbers of people affected by disasters is largely a result of the exponential increase in global population. The number of people on this planet has more than doubled in the last fifty years. Since 2010 the balance has tipped so that more than half the world's population lives in cities, where people are more vulnerable to disasters than they are in dispersed rural populations (see the chart below).

Global Population 1950 to 2050

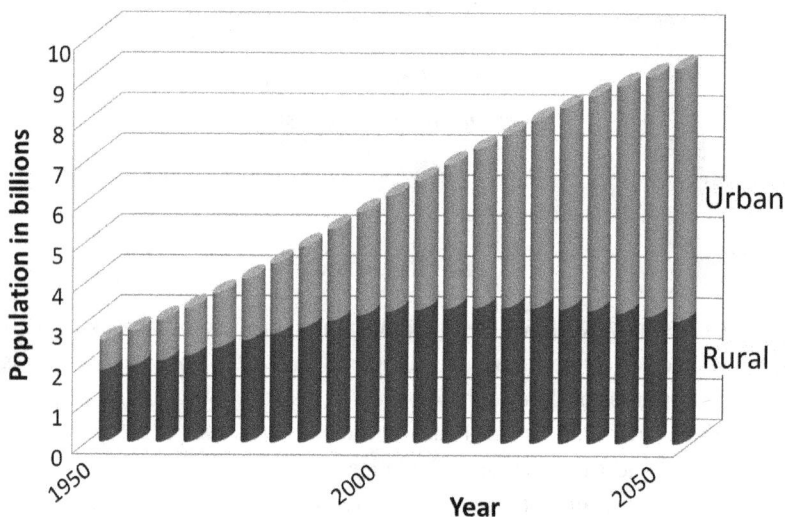

The percentage of city-dwellers is projected to increase still further over this century as people migrate to urban agglomerations from rural areas. Exposure to disasters is also increasing as population and economic pressures force more people to live in hazard-prone regions such as coastal and exposed areas.

We are accustomed to calling catastrophes arising from natural processes such as floods, earthquakes and volcanic eruptions "natural disasters," as if humans played no part in them. Yet once you scratch beneath the surface as we discuss later in this chapter, it becomes clear that almost always it

2. Musson, *The Million Death Quake.*

is the actions, or the inactions or neglect, of humans which turn otherwise beneficial natural processes into disasters. To this extent the term "natural disasters" is a misnomer and is actually highly misleading.

A Fruitful Earth

Far from being unwelcome intrusions, earthquakes, volcanoes, and floods are essential to the well-being of this planet and its inhabitants. They are what make the earth a fruitful, habitable place where humans and indeed the whole biosphere can live and thrive. Without them earth would be a barren planet without life as we know it. Planet Earth is astonishingly fruitful. Indeed, the term "anthropic principle" has been coined for the observation that the physical structure of the universe and the processes that control how it works are extremely finely tuned for the existence of life on Earth. This is a topic of serious academic research and debate by the secular world. For the theist it is a source of awe and wonder, but is entirely consistent with belief in the creator God, as for example Ps 104 proclaims.

Many of the processes that give rise to disasters are also what makes it possible for humans to live on Earth. For example, if there had never been any volcanoes on Earth then the main geological source of carbon dioxide in the atmosphere would be missing. The likely result is that the planet would have been frozen for most of its history.[3] Volcanic eruptions also continually cycle to the surface of the earth huge volumes of minerals essential for life. Volcanic islands such as Hawaii support lush growth of plants and animals, and are some of the most biodiverse areas on earth. Yet volcanic eruptions are often fatal to humans caught up in them. Another example of a normally beneficial natural process is floods. They are a means of distributing fertile soils. For millennia it was the annual flood of the Nile that enabled Egypt to prosper. When the Nile flood failed, as it did for example in 1784, one sixth of the population died.

Lastly, without plate tectonics and the accompanying earthquakes which are produced as the plates move, there would be no mountain ranges. The continual building and erosion of mountains provides a steady supply of nutrient-rich sediments which allows vegetation and crops to flourish and for life to thrive on this planet. Mountains also trigger rainfall which in turn makes the surrounding areas fertile and habitable. Without the Himalayan mountain range the annual monsoons which provide water for a billion people in India would not occur.

---

3. See Houghton, *Global Warming*.

Although natural processes are beneficial in generating a suitable home for humanity, it is when humans interact badly with them that an otherwise beneficial natural process can turn into a disaster. Unfortunately, it is often the actions of humans that hugely exacerbate the scale of disasters, as I discuss next.

Human Factors

Over the past century millions of people have died in disasters as a result of human failings. For example, an almost identical earthquake to the one that killed over 200,000 people in Haiti in January 2010 occurred over 20 years earlier in Loma Prieta, in the San Francisco Bay area of California. Yet the Californian earthquake killed only 57 people. The reason for such a low death toll? California enforced building codes that meant houses did not fall down in the quake. Indeed, most of the casualties in California were on a collapsed two-level freeway that was in the process of being prepared for earthquake strengthening at the time. In contrast, people died in Haiti when their poorly built concrete slab houses situated on landslide slopes collapsed on top of them. It is no coincidence that 70 percent of Haiti's population lives on less than $2 per day, making it the poorest nation in the western hemisphere.[4] By comparison of the two death tolls from identical earthquakes, you could say that 99.98 percent of the deaths in Haiti were due to human factors, largely derived from decades of endemic corruption, misrule and poverty.

A striking demonstration of the ability to build earthquake-proof buildings in the most seismically active place in the world is the massive magnitude 9.1 earthquake near Japan in March 2011. It released 1,500 times as much energy as the Haiti earthquake, yet only a handful of people died in the earthquake shaking. This was due almost entirely to the building codes in place in Japan. In addition, automated systems from over one thousand seismometers gave more than sixty seconds warning in Tokyo of the impending arrival of seismic waves. They also triggered automatic emergency braking on over thirty high-speed bullet trains travelling across the Sendai Plain at up to 300 kilometers per hour before the seismic waves arrived. This prevented derailing and almost certain large loss of life.

We could take an example of the human factors in causing a disaster from a volcanic eruption of the Mont Pelée volcano on Martinique in 1902. This, the worse known volcanic disaster in the world, killed the entire population of 26,000–36,000 people in Saint Pierre in the space of just

---

4. Farmer, *Haiti after the Earthquake*, 60.

a few minutes when a cloud of burning ash and gases from the volcano rolled across the town. Yet this disaster could, and should have easily been avoided. For two weeks prior to the eruption there had been earthquakes, ash falls, fires, sulphurous fumes and mud flows that had already killed over 600 people. Despite the self-evident danger from the ongoing eruption of Mont Pelée, barely six kilometers (3.7 miles) from St. Pierre there was no widespread evacuation. Indeed the mayor and the governor first discouraged and later prevented people leaving, using soldiers to block the trails.[5]

Why were the governor, the mayor, and the other authorities so keen to prevent people evacuating St. Pierre, against all common sense? It seems clear that the reason was that elections were due, and the governor wanted to keep St. Pierre's voters in town until the election was over because the demographics of those voters favored his party. It was an avoidable tragedy. The governor, his family, the rest of the inhabitants of St Pierre paid for it with their lives. We can hardly blame God for that.

Where floods are concerned, it is nowadays frequently possible to predict them well in advance. Yet still people die. A striking example is Hurricane Katrina which hit New Orleans in 2005. Despite it occurring in the most technologically advanced nation in the world, and having been tracked in its approach for several days prior to landfall, over 1800 people lost their lives. They were disproportionately the infirm, the elderly, and the poor who had no cars and could not evacuate the city as the storm approached. A report by the University of Louisiana into the causes of more than 50 breaches of the levees concluded that "failure of the NOFDS [New Orleans Flood Defense System] was a predictable, predicted, and preventable catastrophe." It went on to say that "this catastrophe did not result from an act of God. It resulted from acts of People."[6]

Famines caused an estimated 70 million deaths during the twentieth century alone. They are one of the disasters most readily averted by intervention from others who have food and resources available. Indeed famines, at least in the modern age, are often caused by the direct actions and decisions of autocratic rulers and by warfare. These famines are almost entirely attributable to human agency. It is sobering to realize that even today famine is a factor in over six million deaths annually of children under five years old. There were over 850 million people, or 16 per cent of the world's population, malnourished in 2001–03. Shockingly, there are also an estimated 1,000 million people in high-income countries who are damaging their health by being grossly overweight.

5. Thomas and Morgan-Witts, *The Day the World Ended.*
6. Team Louisiana, *Failure of the New Orleans Levee System.*

There are many examples of avoidable famines that caused enormous numbers of deaths. The Irish potato famine of 1846-51 is one such. About one million people died, one eighth of the population. Two million Irish were forced to emigrate to seek livelihoods elsewhere, many landlords using the famine as a pretext to evict tenants. Though initially in 1846 the potato crop failure caused shortage of food, after 1847 there was sufficient food available which would have prevented mass starvation if it had been properly distributed to reach the smallholders and laborers in the south and west of Ireland. The Irish famine occurred on the doorstep of Britain, then the richest nation in the world. But there wasn't the political incentive amongst the ruling Whig politicians and middle class of Britain to prevent mass starvation of the Irish poor.[7]

Another example comes from China, which has always been subject to famines, either as a consequence of frequent massive floods, which were common in the south of the country, or as a result of droughts, most often in the north. A particularly bad famine, following prolonged droughts, occurred in the north of China during 1876-79. An estimated 9–13 million people died, more than 10 percent of the population of that area. In the hardest hit province of Shanxi, one third of the people died in the famine. News of the Chinese famine led to one of the first major international aid appeals. Much of the relief effort in the field was administered by foreign Christians, including over seventy Protestant and Catholic missionaries.

One of those missionaries, Timothy Richard subsequently wrote that "at the close of the famine it occurred to me, that if I could show to the authorities the *causes* of their famines and the way to remove them, I would really be rendering them a far greater service than we did during the famine relief. The remedies I suggested were—the Christian religion, Education, Science and invention and investigation, new manufactures, new industries, engineering and better means of communication and distribution."[8] This, he suggested would lead to "the relief of the poor from starvation." Although Timothy Richards was perhaps a little too optimistic in his views, he was correct in pointing out that preparation for such events was better than waiting until they happened, and then sending relief. Famines were a frequent and recurrent occurrence in China prior to the particularly bad one in which he was caught up, yet the authorities did little to prepare for them or to put in place measures to mitigate their worst effects.

An example of a government causing the deaths of its own citizens occurred in China during 1958–62 as a result of Mao Zedong's policies of

7. See Donnelly, *The Great Irish Potato Famine.*

8. Bohr, *Famine in China*, 148.

the "Great Leap Forward."[9] At least 45 million unnecessary deaths resulted from his aggressive agricultural policies. They were often accompanied by coercion, terror and systematic violence largely against the poorest segments of the population. Even while his own people starved, Mao Zedong attempted to maintain his international reputation by putting exports above local needs. In 1959 China doubled its grain exports compared to the previous year. Culpability was compounded by continual failure to take remedial action even when the consequences of the "Great Leap Forward" were evident to all.

The famines caused by "natural" processes such as droughts or floods are relatively easy to deal with in our globalized world. Those due to warfare, and particularly civil wars or local insurrections are far harder for outside agencies to reach. Indeed, denial of food and starvation is often consciously used as a tactic in warfare. This has been the case for millennia, with for example the Bible reporting (in 2 Kgs 6:24-29) a famine resulting from a siege of Samaria which was so severe that some Israelites in the city resorted to cannibalism.

The common factor in all these disasters is that it is the poor and the voiceless who suffer most. That is also true for one of the most pervasive causes of disasters that humans are wreaking on the earth—that of global climate change. Many disasters are related directly or indirectly to climate change, including heat waves, floods, droughts, landslides and changes in weather patterns that impact agriculture and may lead to famines. Those of us in the high-income countries who have benefitted from burning cheap fossil fuels, thereby causing global climate change have a moral duty to help those in low-income countries, who largely are the people who suffer from climate change. At the very least, they deserve our assistance to help them adapt to the inevitable changes that result.[10]

A Christian Perspective

The problem of suffering is one which has exercised humanity from the earliest times. For example, the book of Job, possibly one of the oldest parts of the Bible, grapples with the question of why a righteous person should suffer. There are no easy or trite answers, and we should not expect to find them. But there are some things we can usefully say about disasters that may help us to respond to them. The first is that nature is not a force separate from God. As John Wesley wrote when he reflected on the 1755

9. Dikotter, *Mao's Great Famine*.

10. See Spencer et al., *Christianity, Climate Change and Sustainable Living*.

Lisbon earthquake: "What is nature itself, but the art of God, or God's method of acting in the material world?" A similar idea was expressed nearly two millennia ago by Augustine (AD 354–430) when he wrote that "nature is what God has made." Natural processes occur under the overarching sovereignty of God, and so too must natural disasters. This should underpin our thinking.

Some Christians have tried to get around the apparent problem of natural disasters by saying that processes such as earthquakes, volcanic eruptions and floods did not occur before the Fall, when humans chose to disobey their creator God. But this is simply not borne out by the evidence. There is no doubt from geological evidence that all those events were present on the earth long before humans first walked on it. Indeed, as we have already discussed, it is those very processes that have made the earth habitable and continue to do so.

What did happen at the Fall was that humans chose to put themselves first, rather than God. It is as if in a parody of the Lord's Prayer, they said to God "not your will, but mine be done on earth." The result was that humans put themselves out of relationship with God. They broke that intimacy that had prevailed before the Fall when God walked and talked with them "in the cool of the evening." And they spoilt the relationship not only between themselves and God, but also between themselves and the rest of creation. It now became toil to wrest food from the land, rather than a pleasure to work in the Garden, and there was an increase of pain in childbirth.

This was a failure to observe the very first commandment God gave humans in Gen 1:28, which was to have dominion over all the living things on earth. It is fashionable to think of this command in terms of stewardship, and indeed this was part of what God wanted humans to do: to be good stewards of his earth. But it was an even stronger command than that—humans were told to have dominion over the earth. That means taking positive steps to keep it in good order: for example to keep wild animals away from where they could do harm; actively to make use of the resources of the world for the good of both the human and the non-human inhabitants; and to actively manage and develop the world. To have dominion over the earth has overtones of ruling it. The sense is that God set humans to rule over the earth on his behalf. Our misrule is not hard to see in this age of environmental degradation, of species annihilation by humans, of widespread pollution of the sea, the land and the air, of all the changes wrought by unprecedented rapid global climate change. The result is that all creation is groaning, as the Apostle Paul put it in Rom 8:22.

God's creation is very good. That is made clear in Gen 1:31: "God saw all that he had made, and it was very good." That must include earthquakes, fires and floods. Although we are tempted to think that this world was made just for us, it is clear in the Bible that God's delight in his creation extends to everything. In Job 38:26-27 the writer portrays God as watering "a land where no one lives, an uninhabited desert, to satisfy a desolate wasteland and make it sprout with grass." As Ps 104:27 proclaims, all creatures, including both predator and prey "look to [God], to give them their food at the proper time." "The lions roar for their prey and seek their food from God" says the psalmist approvingly (Ps 104:21). God provides food "for the young ravens when they call" (Ps 147:9). God is sovereign over inanimate matter as well as living things. For example, he is portrayed in Ps 104:32 as someone "who looks at the earth, and it trembles, who touches the mountains, and they smoke." God desires all of his creation to flourish, both human and non-human, animate and inanimate alike.

As we contemplate disasters, it is helpful to see God's response to the trials suffered by Job. We know from the backstory that Job was a righteous man who never once lost that righteousness. Yet he suffered grievously at the hands of Satan, losing all that was most dear to him, including his possessions, flocks, family and even his own health. Some, at least, of the disasters were due to natural processes, such as the wind that blew down his eldest son's house and killed all his ten children (Job 1:18-19).

Job's so-called friends tried to rationalize the disasters that had befallen Job as being the result of some sin or failing on his part. Job rightly rejected those suggestions, but still he wanted an explanation from God. He wanted his day in court. When that day finally came, and God spoke to Job "out of the whirlwind," he didn't give any tidy explanations. Instead he spoke majestically of his power over all his creation, from the stars through the weather to all the animals, and in particular all the wild animals, which were far from the domesticated environment in which Job lived. Perhaps most tellingly, God showed himself to be sovereign over the most fearsome of animals, the Leviathan. It is terrifying beyond anything with which humans can deal: "When he rises up, the mighty are terrified." It is possible, indeed that the Leviathan represents Satan himself.[11] Yet God had complete control over him. God's power is unsurpassably greater than that of Leviathan. We can be reassured from the story of Job that God knows all there is to know about evil, that he constrains its reach and is ultimately sovereign over it.

Though God vindicates Job and indeed praises him, Job finally understands both that God's purposes cannot be thwarted and that God's knowledge and wisdom is far beyond anything to which Job could aspire. The lesson for us is that we should not and cannot expect to understand all

11. See Fryall, *Now My Eyes Have Seen You.*

of God's dealings this side of heaven. "Now I know in part; then I shall know fully" (1 Cor 13:12). But we can, and should, hold on to God's faithfulness and goodness as Job did, however dire our circumstances seem to be.

Another biblical story which hinges around a prolonged natural disaster is that of Joseph. Ultimately it was a seven-year famine which brought Joseph to the fore in Egypt. But Joseph was only on hand to oversee the storage of grain during the good years and its distribution during the bad, because of a series of evil actions by others. Initially his brothers had intended to kill him, but then sold him to some traders on their way to Egypt who providentially happened along. From the perspective of natural disasters, there is never the slightest hint that the famine is a punishment from God for particular wrongdoing or sin. The scriptural account just takes the famine as a given, as part of the fabric of life, although it does make God's sovereignty clear: "the matter has been firmly decided by God, and God will do it soon" (Gen 41:32). It is a warning to us not to rush to blame the latest natural disaster on punishment by God of some particular behavior that we choose to identify as especially sinful.

Even more strikingly, Joseph also makes a point of saying that the whole sorry episode of human sinfulness shown by his brothers' sale of himself into slavery was used in God's providence for God's purposes. Joseph tells his brothers after they had been forced by the famine to come begging for food and eventually to move to Egypt that "you meant evil against me, but God meant it for good, to bring it about that many people should be kept alive, as they are today" (Gen 50.20). The preservation of the Israelites became part of God's redemptive history of his people down through the ages.

Hope for the Future

Though we may not understand fully why disasters happen, or what God's plans in them might be, we can hold on to the certainty of God's sovereignty over this present world and that in the fullness of time this creation will be renewed. Nothing that happens is outside God's knowledge. So it is not meaningful to talk about natural disasters as things that happen outside his will. This sovereignty does not mean that the suffering a person experiences is necessarily God's direct punishment for their own sin. But we do need to recognize that even causes of suffering do not happen outside God's control. As the writer of Lamentations recognized "Although [the Lord] brings grief, he will show compassion, so great is his unfailing love" (Lam 3:32) and "Is it not from the mouth of the Most High that both calamities and good things come?" (Lam 3:38).

It is worth recalling that God's ways are not our ways, his thoughts are not our thoughts (see, for example Job 37:5 and Isa 55:9). Even when we can discern his purposes, we can do so only indistinctly, like seeing in a mirror dimly (1 Cor 13:12). Although scripture maintains that God has revealed to us everything necessary for our salvation, and all we need to know to live lives that please him, it also makes it clear that humans, being created beings, cannot second-guess the motives of the creator. For example, Isa 29:16 draws the analogy that it is ridiculous for a pot to claim that the potter who made it, didn't in fact do so, or didn't know what he was doing:

> You turn things upside down,
>   as if the potter were thought to be like the clay!
> Shall what is formed say to him who formed it,
>   "You did not make me"?
> Can the pot say to the potter,
>   "You know nothing"?

The apostle Paul makes the same point in the New Testament "Shall what is formed say to the one who formed it, 'Why did you make me like this?'" (Rom 9:20). Yet this is precisely what we are often tempted to do, saying things such as "If I were God, I wouldn't allow any suffering in this world." We often prefer to make God in our own image rather than the reality which is, of course, exactly the opposite.

We cannot make sense of the suffering and death in this world, and of the evil that is often its cause, without the perspective of the new creation to come, and of the kingdom of God that Christ proclaims has already been inaugurated in this world with his coming.[12] The certainty of the new creation is the cornerstone of Christian hope. The kingdom of God to which Christians look forward is not just a hypothetical construct, a psychological prop, a wishful "pie in the sky, by and by." It is a reality which ought to inform everything about the way we live in this world now. That includes our attitude to the natural environment and to the disasters which plague this world. We live in the in-between times, the "now but not yet" between the first coming of God to this world as the man Jesus, and his return to judge the world, when all things will be renewed in the new creation. That is when he will make this world the place he intended it to be, free from all death and mourning, free from all that has been made twisted and out of order by the rebellion of humans against their creator. The death and, crucially, the resurrection of Jesus are the seal and the proof of this reality. The kingdom

---

12. See Wright, *Evil and the Justice of God.*

of heaven is here now, albeit in a highly attenuated, veiled way, but will be fulfilled in all its glory when Jesus returns.[13]

The new creation will be the fulfillment of all that God intended for the Earth and for his people—where God will come down to live with his people, where all things will be renewed. This is the ultimate destiny God has promised. He promises to renew all of creation. We do not know whether or not there will be volcanic eruptions, earthquakes and the like in the new creation, and the Bible doesn't tell us, so we should not speculate. But if there are volcanic eruptions, then it is clear that they will not hurt anyone. Presumably they will be awe-inspiring spectator events, showing forth God's glory.

The new creation will be a place where God's people will feel perfectly at home. So our work in this creation should prefigure the new creation. It is part of our worship of God to use our various skills and understanding, our talents, our financial and natural resources to help reduce the effect of disasters in the future and to help those affected when they do strike. That is what will please God.

Hope for the Present

Of course we wish that disasters would not happen. The very fact that we now have the capability to construct buildings that do not collapse in earthquakes, that we can see storms, typhoons and hurricanes developing and can track them long before they hit land, that we can monitor and predict volcanic eruptions, mean that we should be able to prevent the great majority of casualties from these natural processes. I take it to be a sign of God's goodness to us that he has given us a stable, understandable world where we can use the fruits of science and technology for the good of others; that we have the capability to prevent disasters and to alleviate or mitigate the harmful effects on others of some of our actions, such as causing global climate change by burning large quantities of fossil fuels. The fact that we don't do so as much as we could or should is a sign of our selfishness—of what the Bible calls our sinfulness.

The story of Joseph gives a strong message that a right and proper way to honor God and to work within his purposes is for Christians to use their gifts and abilities to seek to ameliorate the harmful consequences of occurrences such as famines. Joseph clearly was insightful, resourceful, energetic, trustworthy and an extremely good administrator and organizer. But although at many times he wielded great power, he never failed to

13. Moo and White, *Let Creation Rejoice.*

acknowledge that God was sovereign over both him and his circumstances. He spent his life serving others, albeit often in high ranking positions, rather than being self-serving.

This is certainly an encouragement to believers in whatever sphere they work: to scientists or engineers who seek to understand the natural world and to use that knowledge for the good of humankind; to administrators, secretaries and government officials who enable society to function even when under stress; to aid workers and politicians who try to implement practical policies to ameliorate suffering; and indeed to everyone to be good stewards of resources. The story of Joseph tells us that there is nothing "unspiritual" about working hard at such mundane things, provided always that, like Joseph we remind ourselves that both we and our circumstances are firmly under God's providence if we are faithful to him.

The Christian perspective sees the reality of the brokenness of this world, but also the truth of God's sovereignty over it and of his ultimate plans for a new creation. Evil cannot derail those plans. That does not mean that we need not strive to improve things now. Rather it points in the opposite direction, that we should work for better scientific understanding of disasters, that we should enable communities to build resilience against them, that we should strive to remove the unjust disparities in wealth and resources that mean it is so often the poor who are most vulnerable and who suffer most. Even though we may not be able to prevent every last casualty of the next disaster, there is an enormous amount we can do even from our present understanding of natural processes to hugely reduce the impact of disasters. This is surely what Jesus would want us to do, using our understanding of his creation for the good of others, and working to enable his creation to reflect his glory as he intended it to do.

Meanwhile, as we struggle in this beautiful, yet suffering world, we have the assurance from Jesus himself that those blessings we shall experience permanently in the new creation can sustain us now: "Come to me, all you who are weary and burdened, and I will give you rest," says Jesus (Matt 11:28).

Bibliography

Bohr, Paul Richard. *Famine in China and the Missionary: Timothy Richard as Relief Administrator and Advocate of National Reform, 1876–1884.* Cambridge: Harvard University Press, 1972.

Dikotter, Frank. *Mao's Great Famine: The History of China's Most Devastating Catastrophe, 1958–62.* London: Bloomsbury, 2010.

Donnelly, James S. *The Great Irish Potato Famine.* Stroud, UK: Sutton, 2002.

Farmer, Paul. *Haiti after the Earthquake*. New York: Public Affairs, 2012.

Fletcher, M. A. "Katrina Pushes Issues of Race and Poverty at Bush." *Washington Post*, September 12, 2005, A02. http://www.washingtonpost.com/wp-dyn/content/article/2005/09/11/AR2005091101131.html.

Fyall, Robert S. *Now My Eyes Have Seen You: Images of Creation and Evil in the Book of Job*. Downers Grove, IL: IVP, 2002.

Houghton, John T. *Global Warming: The Complete Briefing*. 5th ed. Cambridge: Cambridge University Press, 2015.

Moo, Jonathan A., and Robert S. White. *Let Creation Rejoice: Biblical Hope and the Ecological Crisis*. Downers Grove, IL: InterVarsity, 2014.

Musson, Roger. *The Million Death Quake: The Science of Predicting Earth's Deadliest Natural Disaster*. New York: Palgrave Macmillan, 2012.

Spencer, Nick, et al. *Christianity, Climate Change and Sustainable Living*. Peabody, MA: Hendrickson, 2009.

Team Louisiana. *The Failure of the New Orleans Levee System during Hurricane Katrina*. Appendix VI. Baton Rouge: Louisiana Department of Transportation and Development, 2006.

Thomas, Gordon, and Max Morgan-Witts. *The Day the World Ended*. London: Scarborough House, 1991.

White, Robert S. *Who Is to Blame? Nature, Disasters and Acts of God*. Oxford: Lion Hudson, 2014.

Wright, N. T. *Evil and the Justice of God*. London: SPCK, 2006.

9

The Nexus between Divine, Human, and Creational Suffering

A Theological Reflection on Romans 8:15–25

Mark Worthing

IN THE CONTEXT OF Paul's discussion of sin and salvation in his letter to the Christian community at Rome we find what is at the same time one of the most unexpected, misunderstood and profound reflections on the relationship between God, humanity and the rest of creation. The apostle writes:

> For the creation waits with eager longing for the revealing of the children of God; for the creation was subjected to futility, not of its own will but by the will of the one who subjected it, in hope that the creation itself will be set free from its bondage to decay and will obtain the freedom of the glory of the children of God. We know that the whole creation has been groaning in labor pains until now; and not only the creation, but we ourselves, who have the first fruits of the Spirit, groan inwardly while we wait for adoption, the redemption of our bodies. (Rom 8:19–23)

While there is certainly a link between human sin and the suffering of creation, this text does not name human sinfulness as a cause of the suffering of creation. Instead, we are told creation suffers (or was subjected to futility) "not of its own will, but by the will of the one who subjected it." Likewise, this text does not diminish the centrality of Christ's suffering on the cross, yet it implies that divine suffering extends beyond the cross and is linked to the suffering of the whole of creation. Therefore we find that the hope of salvation and an end to suffering for God, humanity, and the whole of creation are inescapably bound together.

The Scope of Suffering

This is challenging perspective for a tradition that has tended to limit its thinking about the scope of the atonement to human beings, and then often to a very select portion of these. As a further challenge to our traditional thinking about the scope of atonement and reconciliation, the whole of creation in this text has broader reference than just to the animal kingdom. How, we might ask, do we conceptualize the suffering of plants, oceans, mountains, the atmosphere we breathe? Traditionally only sentient beings are seen as capable of suffering as only sentient beings can experience pain. Even then, there are questions about whether so-called lower forms of fauna experience as much pain as higher forms. Can a spider experience as much pain as a fish, a fish as much as a dog, a dog as much as chimpanzee, a chimpanzee as much as a human?[1]

Studies in comparative ethology suggest such presumed hierarchies of the capacity of various sentient life forms to experience suffering is problematic. Darwin himself, in *The Descent of Man,* concluded that "the difference in mind between . . . [humans] and the higher animals, great as it is, certainly is one of degree and not kind."[2] The implication is that pain and suffering are experienced far beyond the confines of the human. Simple observation suggests to us that animals indeed experience suffering in ways similar to humans. As Peter Singer observed: "Nearly all the external signs that lead us to infer pain in other humans can be seen in other species . . . The behavioral signs include writhing, facial contortions, moaning, yelping or other forms of calling, attempts to avoid the source of the pain, appearance of fear at the prospect of its repletion, and so on."[3]

Studies in ethology and comparative psychology have supported the view that however great the quantitative distinction between humans and other animals may be, it is just that—a quantitative and not a qualitative distinction. Studies such as those by Marc Hauser, *The Evolution of Communication*; Euan Macphail, *The Evolution of Consciousness*; and the several works by Donald Griffin, including *The Question of Animal Awareness,*

---

1. Cf. Stamp Dawkins, "Scientific Basis for Assessing Suffering in Animals." See also the discussion of this and the related question of intelligence in Worthing, "Human and Animal Intelligence."

2. Darwin, *Descent of Man*, 128.

3. Singer, *Animal Liberation*, 11.

Animal Thinking, and *Animal Minds*, suggest that the demarcation between animals and humans may be less clear cut than we are accustomed to assume. Theologically, only the attribute of the image of God in humans sets us apart—but this is not something we possess by virtue of some special innate human abilities, but is a gift of the creator. Therefore, also from the Christian point of view, there is great difficulty with insisting on a difference of kind in the areas of intelligence, consciousness, and ability to experience suffering.[4]

From a theological perspective, the biblical creation account, traditionally used to demonstrate the uniqueness of humans, must be considered from the perspective of the solidarity of humanity with other animals. Humans and animals are, after all, both made from the earth (Gen 2:7, 19), literally the dirt of the ground, the same ground out of which all plants grow (Gen 2:9). Both animals (Gen 2:7) and humans (Gen 1:30) are described as being "living souls." There is an inescapable boundness of human beings to the rest of God's creation. The discovery that all things living share the same building blocks of DNA served as a further reminder of this millennia-old theological truth.

This puts Paul's teaching that all of creation experiences suffering into a very concrete context. This suffering includes traditional ideas of pain, but also subjection to futility, which might be described as loss or distortion of purpose; and decay, which calls to mind the inescapable reality of the second law of thermodynamics. In the context of this passage, suffering must be understood as something broader and more intertwined than simply the experience of pain of individual sentient beings.

The Suffering of God

Similarly, we might ask whether Christ's suffering extends beyond his presence on the cross? Does the whole of God suffer? Does God take responsibility for all the suffering in creation? Does God intend to reconcile all of creation (and not only humans) through God's own suffering?[5] These are the kind of questions that arise through a close ecotheological reading of Rom 8. They are questions that go to the heart of key aspects of our faith.

---

4. This raises significant and unavoidable issues concerning the inherent value and rights of animals and their ethical treatment that we are not able to explore in the context of this discussion.

5. For a discussion of the suffering of God in relation to traditional understandings of the atonement see Worthing, "The Atonement in the Light of Human and Divine Suffering."

The suffering of God is not a new idea. God is not impassible, but feels pain at the broken relationship with humans. God's pain in the Old Testament is hard to overlook. It is a major theme in Isaiah, Jeremiah and Hosea, and occurs frequently in the Psalms and Ezekiel.[6] Japanese Lutheran theologian Kazoh Kitamori, strongly influenced by Luther's theology of the cross, wrote his ground-breaking *Theology of the Pain of God* after being deeply struck by two similar Old Testament passages: Isa 63:15 and Jer 31:20. Jeremiah 31:20, translated literally, reads: "Is Ephraim my beloved son? Is he a pleasing child? For since I spoke against him, I cannot forget him; I writhe in anguish for him." In the many complaints God raised against his people in the Old Testament, one detects more hurt than anger. Poignantly, we read in Jeremiah:

> My grief is beyond healing, my heart is sick within me. Hark, the cry of the daughter of my people from the length and breadth of the land: "Is the Lord not in Zion? Is her king not in her?" Why have they provoked me to anger with their graven images and with their foreign idols? For the wound of the daughter of my people is my heart wounded, I mourn, and dismay has taken hold of me . . . O that my head were a spring of water, and my eyes a fountain of tears, that I might weep day and night for the slain of my poor people! (Jer 8:18—9:1)

The picture gained from the Old Testament is of a God deeply pained by our rejection.[7] The radical thought that springs from this insight is that, on the cross, God is seeking neither a ransom nor someone to punish. God is seeking healing of a broken heart.

One of the most striking texts portraying the pain God experiences in his relationship with his people is found in the prophet Hosea. In Hos 9 the prophet announces that "the days of punishment have come" and that God "will remember their iniquity" (vv. 7, 9). At the end of chapter 10 God promises warfare and destruction, using some of the most angry and wrathful words of the Old Testament. Yet in chapter 11 we find a God who is angry because he is deeply hurt—a God portrayed as a rejected parent who does not at all want to punish his children, despite the rejection experienced at their hands.

---

6. Cf. Fretheim, *The Suffering of God*.

7. Cf. for instance, Fretheim, *The Suffering of God*; Heschel, *The Prophets*; Mauser, *Gottesbild und Menschwerdung*; Scharbert, *Der Schmerz im Alten Testament*; Robinson, *The Cross in the Old Testament*, and his earlier *Suffering, Human and Divine*; and Kitamori, *Theology of the Pain of God*.

> When Israel was a child, I loved him, and out of Egypt I called
> my son. The more I called them, the more they went from me;
> they kept sacrificing to the Ba'als, and burning incense to idols.
> Yet it was I who taught Ephraim to walk, I took them up in my
> arms; but they did not know that I healed them. I led them with
> cords of compassion, with the bands of love. I was to them like
> those who lift the infants to their cheeks. I bent down to them
> and fed them . . . My people are bent on turning away from me
> . . . [Yet] how can I give you up, O Ephraim! How can I hand you
> over, O Israel! . . . My heart recoils within me, my compassion
> grows warm and tender. I will not execute my fierce anger, I will
> not again destroy Ephraim; for I am God and no mortal, the
> Holy One in your midst, and I will not come in wrath to destroy.
> (Hos 11:1–4, 7–9)

The Scope of the Atonement

In light of the relatively recent re-discovery of the idea of divine suffering, and the rise in awareness of the inherent value of the non-human created order within theological discussions, the question of the connections between divine, human and whole creational suffering merits fresh consideration. The suffering of God, humans and fauna are all distinct, yet they are somehow bound together in both their causes and their resolution. The whole of creation exists in necessary relationship to its creator (Col 1:16ff). Christ holds all creation together. He is bound to it and we to him.

The fact that all of creation suffers along with us (and with God) is also a clear inference from the Old Testament eschatological visions of the lion and lamb lying down with one another (Isa 11:6–9). The fact that the benefits of the hoped for New Age extend to all creation also bears witness to the fact that the whole of creation presently suffers.

A restoration of the human-divine relationship brings with it a healing that extends to the non-human creation. As the Psalmist writes: "You save humans and animals alike, O Lord" (Ps 36:6). Paul's reflections in Romans, therefore, do not arise in isolation from the context of the Hebrew biblical tradition. We should not be surprised to hear the Apostle argue that just as the whole of creation suffers, so also it shares in the benefits of the atoning work of Christ. As biblical scholar James Dunn had pointed out in relation to this text: "Paul's vision of God's saving purpose drives him beyond any idea of a merely personal or human redemption. What is at stake . . . is creation as a whole."[8]

This brings the question of the scope of the atonement firmly into the discussion. Elizabeth Johnson, in her recent book *Ask the Beasts*, suggests something of the extent of the rethink needed in our thinking about the atonement with the concept of "deep incarnation." Johnson writes: "God's own self-expressive Word personally joins the biological world as a member of the human race, and via this perch on the tree of life enters into solidarity with the whole biophysical cosmos." It is this perspective that allows her to conclude that the "logic of deep incarnation gives a strong warrant for extending divine solidarity from the cross into the groan of suffering and the silence of death of all creation."[9]

The concept of "deep incarnation," originally put forward by Danish theologian Niels Gregersen,[10] has been taken up by many as a means of expressing theologically the magnitude of God's involvement with the creation. Gregersen, in light of biological evolution, described the incarnation as an "incarnation into the very tissue of biological existence, and system of nature." Significantly, for consideration of the Rom 8 text, he claimed that when seen in this way "the death of Christ becomes an icon of God's redemptive co-suffering with all sentient life . . ."[11] Australian theologian Denis Edwards takes the implications of deep incarnation even further when he argues that the flesh embraced by God is not limited to humanity but "includes the whole interconnected world of fleshy life and, in some way, includes the whole universe to which flesh is related and on which it depends."[12]

This leads us to consider the related concept of the cosmic Christ. This has been most notably developed by Matthew Fox, particularly in his *The Coming of the Cosmic Christ* (1988). Fox makes the point that the idea that salvation as an individual or private matter is actually nothing more than a popular heresy. He argues that "those who indulge exclusively in their personal salvation and their personal Savior do so in direct contradiction to the entire teaching of the Cosmic Christ crucified for all. Salvation must be universal in the sense of a comprehensive healing of all the cosmos' pain, or it is not salvation at all."[13] Again, Fox points out, that "since the pain, suffer-

---

8. Dunn, *Romans 1–8*, 487.

9. Johnson, *Ask the Beasts*, 198.

10. Gregersen, "The Cross of Christ in an Evolutionary World."

11. Ibid., 205.

12. Edwards, *Ecology at the Heart of Faith*, 58.

13. Fox, *The Coming of the Cosmic Christ*, 151.

ing and sin are cosmic—bigger than we can control and far more complex in space and time than we can imagine—the redemption must be cosmic as well."[14]

The insights of evolutionary biology and cosmology indicate an interconnectedness of all creation which helps contemporary Christians make sense of Paul's words in Rom 8. We are able to see that the radical implications of the theology of this text have a clear foundation in the interconnectedness of the evolving cosmos. The rich potential for dialogue between science and faith is seldom so profound as at this point. The evolutionary themes of new life out of suffering and death are paralleled in the theological insights of the suffering of humans and of all creation finding common healing and new life through the suffering of God in Christ.

The point is significant. A God who creates all things suffers with all things, and finally redeems all things. God's act of becoming human flesh as well as God's act of vicarious death on the cross, have universal implications. Although humans are seen to occupy a special place in this nexus of creation, suffering and reconciliation, no part of creation can be excluded. As Sallie McFague put it: "Creation is not one thing and salvation something else . . . Salvation is for all of creation. The liberating, healing, inclusive ministry of Christ takes place *in* and *for* creation."[15]

God's suffering on the cross is universal in the sense that it is unrestricted. Nothing is withheld, nothing excluded. So, too, the significance of this divine suffering is universal. Paul goes so far as to declare that through Christ and his suffering "God was pleased to reconcile himself to all things, whether on earth or heaven, by making peace through the blood of the cross" (Col 1:20). An anthropocentric understanding of the atonement has long caused us to begin and conclude our reflections on what God accomplished on the cross with human beings. The biblical texts make it clear that we are not the exclusive focus of Christ's atoning work. Paul's radical insights on the co-suffering of divine, human, and all of creation in Rom 8 are foundational for a full understanding of the richness of the reconciling work of Christ on the cross. The cross brings healing to all of creation in ways we cannot yet fully comprehend.

14. Ibid., 152.
15. McFague, *The Body of God*, 182.

Bibliography

Darwin, Charles. *The Descent of Man, and Selection in Relation to Sex.* London: Murray, 1871.

Dunn, James D. G. *Romans 1–8.* Word Biblical Commentary 38A. Dallas: Word, 1988.

Edwards, Denis. *Ecology at the Heart of Faith.* Maryknoll, NY: Orbis, 2006.

Gregersen, Niels. "The Cross of Christ in an Evolutionary World." *Dialog: A Journal of Theology* 40 (2001) 192–207.

Fox, Matthew. *The Coming of the Cosmic Christ: The Healing of Mother Earth and the Birth of Global Resistance.* San Franciso: Harper & Row, 1988.

Fretheim, Terence E. *The Suffering of God: An Old Testament Perspective.* Overtures to Biblical Theology. Minneapolis: Fortress, 1984.

Griffin, Donald. *Animal Minds.* Chicago: University of Chicago Press, 1992.

———. *Animal Thinking.* Cambridge: Harvard University Press, 1984.

———. *The Question of Animal Awareness.* New York: Rockefeller University Press, 1976.

Hauser, Marc D. *The Evolution of Communication.* Cambridge, MA: MIT Press, 1996.

Heschel, Abraham. *The Prophets.* New York: Harper & Row, 1962.

Johnson, Elizabeth. *Ask the Beasts: Darwin and the God of Love.* London: Bloomsbury, 2014.

Kitamori, Kazoh. *Theology of the Pain of God.* 1965. Reprinted, Eugene, OR: Wipf & Stock, 2005.

Macphail, Euan. *The Evolution of Consciousness.* Oxford: Oxford University Press, 1998.

Mauser, Ulrich. *Gottesbild und Menschwerdung: Eine Untersuchung zur Einheit des Alten und Neuen Testaments.* Beiträge zur historischen Theologie 43. Tübingen: Mohr/Siebeck, 1971.

McFague, Sallie. *The Body of God: An Ecological Theology.* Minneapolis: Fortress, 1993.

Robinson, H. Wheeler. *The Cross in the Old Testament,* London: SCM, 1955.

———. *Suffering, Human and Divine.* New York: Macmillan, 1939.

Scharbert, Josef. *Der Schmerz im Alten Testament.* Bonner biblische Beiträge 8. Bonn: Hanstein, 1955.

Singer, Peter. *Animal Liberation.* 2nd ed. New York: Avon, 1990.

Stamp Dawkins, Marian. "Scientific Basis for Assessing Suffering in Animals." In *In Defense of Animals: The Second Wave,* edited by Peter Singer, 26–39. Malden, MA: Blackwell, 2006.

Worthing, Mark. "The Atonement in the Light of Human and Divine Suffering." *Lutheran Theological Journal* 48 (2014) 132–44.

———. "Human and Animal Intelligence: A Difference of Degree or Kind?" In *God, Life, Intelligence and the Universe,* edited by Hilary D. Regan and Terence J. Kelly, 85–110. Adelaide, SA: ATF, 2002.

10

Lord of the (Warming) World

Bonhoeffer's Ecotheological Ethic and the Gandhi Factor

Dianne Rayson and Terence Lovat[1]

Introduction

BONHOEFFER'S ECOETHIC, EMANATING LARGELY from his understanding of God who would be "Lord of the World"[2] in Christ, provides a framework for approaching the challenge of climate change. This chapter explores the relationship between Gandhi's—and, hence, Indian—natural theologies, on the one hand, and, on the other, Bonhoeffer's own evolving natural theology concerning humanity's relationship with the rest of creation. The case rests partly on clear coincident thinking between the two, but also sufficient evidence in Bonhoeffer's writings to raise the question of this coincident thinking being possibly more a case of Gandhi's direct influence on him. Common to both Bonhoeffer's and Gandhi's thinking are notions of interrelatedness, nonviolence and suffering. It is argued that Bonhoeffer's ecotheology, to be seen principally within the framework of his overarching Christology but with unusually plain influence from Indian natural theologies, can provide a suitable foundation for a contemporary ecotheology and

1. Originally published in longer form as "'Lord of the (Warming) World.'" Reprinted with alterations and with permission.

2. "Lord of the World" is an enduring motif throughout Bonhoeffer's work with special importance in the prison writings: see Bonhoeffer, *Letters and Papers*, 365.

allied ecoethic that can assist the global community's search for solutions around the issues associated with climate destabilization.

The Ethical Issue

Climate change has been repeatedly described as the great moral challenge of our generation. Because the climate catastrophe is driven by human constructs and behaviors, we need to address the issue theologically and develop a response which addresses both the causal factors and the consequences, including the theological dimensions in both cases. In Christian, indeed Abrahamic, theological terms, the effects of anthropogenic climate change on the earth's flora and fauna, and on the entire inanimate portions of creation,[3] require a re-examination of such concepts as stewardship and dominion, the relationship between human and other-than-human creation, and our very conception of who God is in relation to Earth. In this context, it is contended that Bonhoeffer's notion of God, in Christ, as "Lord of the World" offers a valuable point of reflection, as does the possible influence of Gandhi on Bonhoeffer, what we refer to as "the Gandhi factor," and, in turn, those Indian natural theologies that comprise Gandhi's own influences. In developing the case for a stream of influence that reached from these Indian theologies to Bonhoeffer's tentatively emerging natural theology, and specifically ecotheology, we turn first to the Gandhi factor.

Gandhi's Ecotheological Ethic

Human ecology considers the relationships between people and their environments, especially the impact of humans and social systems on and within ecosystems. Gandhi has been described as a human ecologist insofar as his examination of human society was not separated from where and how humans live; social organization was seen as taking place within the context of the natural and constructed environment and, in turn, influenced by it.[4] The model Gandhi proposed for sustainable living opposed the trajectory of modern civilization toward materiality and consumption and instead sought limitation of wants and "harmony among different elements of the social and natural order."[5] In what follows, one can see the connection between interrelatedness and nonviolence as markers of Gandhi's ecotheology.

3. Stocker et al., *Climate Change 2013*.

4. Moolakkattu, "Gandhi as a Human Ecologist," 152.

5. Ibid.

Gandhi's evolving worldview and personal lifestyle reveal an eco-theological ethic best ascribed to Jainism, a religious influence that Gandhi openly acknowledged.[6] In Jainism, release from the cycle of rebirth is eventually attained through developing understanding of the true nature of reality, ethical practice, and commensurate purification. These are represented by "right faith, right conduct, and right knowledge"—the three "jewels" of Jainism.[7] The Jain relationship to the environment at one level is one of deep connectivity, and this relationship is enhanced through the practices of nonviolence, truthfulness, not stealing, sexual restraint, and nonpossession.[8]

Ahimsa, or nonviolence, became a key tenet of Gandhi's teaching regarding human interactions, dealings with the environment and training the inner self. The Jain discipline of *ahimsa* requires that one not only remove violent behavior from one's life, but remove also the ability to commit violence and, furthermore, the ability to conceive of it.[9] Gandhi's personal commitment to these disciplines and his ethical practice were both attractive to Bonhoeffer and, it would appear, influential, even from afar.[10]

In Jain natural theology, life and soul are present throughout all things, moving and inanimate:[11] *jiva* (life force) is defined according to the sense-organs possessed. Whereas animals have five senses, Earth, air, water, and vegetation have but one, that of touch.[12] Humans alone have the sixth sense of thought, and thus have additional responsibility to care for and protect *jiva*,[13] on behalf of all "life." "Treading lightly" on the earth, therefore, recognizes and respects the sense of touch that Earth possesses.

All behavioral restraints demonstrate the Jain paradox: namely, both the distancing of oneself from the material and, at the same time, the deep care for and connection to its *jiva*. *Ahimsa*, then, has implications for humanity's relationship not only with itself, both internally and behaviorally, but in its essential relationship with the entire biosphere. Bonhoeffer himself describes this in the 1932 lecture, "The Right to Self-Assertion," by referring to the Upanishad phrase "*tat tvam asi*"—deriving from the refrain "That which is the subtle essence, this whole world has for its self. That is

---

6. Nojeim, *Gandhi and King*. Rajachandrea Mehta, a Jain layman, was Gandhi's guru; see Long, "Jainism," 505.

7. Dundas et al,, "Jainism."

8. Pániker, *Jainism*.

9. Nojeim, *Gandhi and King*.

10. See Bethge, *Dietrich Bonhoeffer*, 105.

11. Chapple, "Jainism, Ethics and Ecology," 3–4.

12. Sinha, "Religion and Creation," 9.

13. Dundas et al., "Jainism."

the true. That is the self. You are that."[14] It is a phrase denoting the oneness with the rest of existence and to which Bonhoeffer credits the Indian immersion in the natural: the "distant, fertile, sunny form- and idea-rich world of India,"[15] where:

> the soul breathes the life that surrounds it in its abundance, penetrating the experience of life in the midst of this great abundance, uniting itself with it, probing and pondering its rhythm and its depths, which are basically the depths of the soul itself, and the expanses of the Indian soul are the expanses of all living things. In this way the submerging soul recognizes itself again in all that lives, as if in thousands of mirrors; out of every form of nature it hears the quiet answer: *tat tvam asi*, this is you, you yourself.[16]

According to Bonhoeffer, the Indian approach, immersed in nature, allows freedom of the soul "for surrender and self-deepening."[17] Surrender inherently involves suffering and responsibility.

Further to the case being put, in Buddhist literature, *ahimsa* is referred to as *pranatipapt-virmana*, conveying the same meaning. Whilst Buddhism recognizes the universality of suffering within a transitory frame—hence, the life and death cycle of both flora and fauna—the Eightfold Path still demands discipline which serves to protect both the human and other-than-human elements of the Cosmos from harm.[18] Buddhism and Jainism, both broadly Eastern and specifically Indian traditions emerging from a similar period, require overt behaviors commensurate with the nonviolence of a disciplined mind and spirit. Gandhi, schooled in both these traditions,[19] recognized the affinity with the life and teachings of Jesus, perhaps insofar as beliefs and ethics are expressions of authentic faith, and in Jesus' commitment to nonviolence. Again, in that same lecture, Bonhoeffer recognizes the fundamental thread between eco-relationality and nonviolence:

> And the eternal awe of the sanctity of all life comes over the soul.
> It aches if nature suffers violence; it is torn apart when living

---

14. See footnote 15 in Bonhoeffer, *Ecumenical, Academic, and Pastoral*, 251.

15. Ibid., 250.

16. Ibid.

17. Ibid.

18. Morgan, "Buddhism."

19. It is likely that Bonhoeffer also had some understanding of the Jain, Buddhist and Hindu influences on Gandhi's worldview given his deep interest in the Mahatma and his interactions with Gandhi's associates such as C. F. Andrews at the World Alliance. See Bethge, *Dietrich Bonhoeffer*, 194, 249–52.

things are injured. You should not kill, for life is the soul, and life is you yourself; you should not do violence to any living thing; you should resist and reject anything in you that stimulates you to get your way with violence; you should tame the thirst of your passions, your hatred and your love, if they drag you to assert yourself and hurt another life. Learn to suffer, learn to go by, learn to die, all this is better than to assert oneself and to violate and live. Only in this way will your soul, which indeed is the soul of the Universe [das All] be uninjured and holy. Through love and suffering, we enter the Universe and overcome it.[20]

Tolstoy's analysis of Christianity in relation to violence also had an important resonance with Gandhi. Gandhi was deeply drawn to Jesus' teachings and in particular the Sermon on the Mount. Tolstoy examines the Sermon and finds Christianity wanting in relation to the commands against violence, both in behavior and attitude. To the extent that Gandhi and Tolstoy corresponded over general and specific issues around nonviolence and justice, Gandhi considered himself a "humble follower" of Tolstoy, indicating an enduring influence on the Mahatma's developing position.[21] Gandhi's social experiment in South Africa from 1910, Tolstoy Farm, was an early attempt to demonstrate *satyagraha* (his own version of nonviolence) as a lifestyle.[22] Whilst it is unknown when, or to what extent, Bonhoeffer was aware of the Tolstoy Farm experiment, he was certainly interested in Gandhi's ashram and in the other Christian communities in India. In any case, the subsequent resonance with Bonhoeffer's own experience in communal living is noteworthy.

Bonhoeffer and Gandhi

Bonhoeffer intended to visit Gandhi in India, making three attempts from 1929 to 1936[23] with letters of introduction and an invitation from the Mahatma.[24] It seems that Bonhoeffer saw in Gandhi, and the Indian natural theologies that underpinned his own eco-ethic, the authenticity for which he strove, particularly within the Confessing Church of Germany as well as in the ecumenical context.[25] Bonhoeffer's attraction to Gandhi's "exempli-

20. Bonhoeffer, *Ecumenical, Academic, and Pastoral*, 250–51.

21. Murthy, *Gandhi and Tolstoy Letters*.

22. Ibid., 62–78.

23. Bethge, *Dietrich Bonhoeffer*, 105, 148, 407.

24. Ibid., 407.

25. Ibid.

fication of the Sermon on the Mount" was in the duality of inner spiritual discipline coupled with social action.[26] Bonhoeffer was seeking a "prototype for passive resistance that could induce changes without violence."[27] As events transpired, he chose to remain in Germany to open his alternative seminary and, as Bethge describes it, "he would have to form his own ashram—the seminary—without prior experience in the Far East."[28]

We see parallels between Bonhoeffer's authentic spirituality and Gandhi's consistency concerning the inward and outward *ahimsa*. Jainism's three jewels, where none is complete without the others, finds resonance in Bonhoeffer's theology (even in his first work)[29] and he later explores this desire for authenticity as part of the construct of "religionless Christianity," whilst still situated within the limits and constraints of life: for him, this denotes the tension between the ultimate and the penultimate.[30] When he asks from his prison cell "Who is Christ for us today?" Bonhoeffer is, in part, exploring an authentic spirituality which pervades all aspects of life and which, it seems, he found apparent in Gandhi. Similarly, when Bonhoeffer considers a God who would be, in Christ, "Lord of the World," he is seeking out the authentic expression of faith which infiltrates all relationships. It is to this concept that this chapter is now directed.

Bonhoeffer's Ecotheology

The persistence and continuity of the key Christological emphasis throughout the Bonhoeffer corpus has been well documented.[31] Bonhoeffer's ontological understanding of humanity and creation can be seen as one of sociality rather than domination, reflecting the nature of the relationship between humanity and God, first glimpsed in the creation narrative (and considered by Bonhoeffer in the idea of participating in the "one reality").[32] This relationship is mediated, made possible, through the work and nature of the Suffering Christ. Bonhoeffer appreciates in the Indian experience that suffering for and through nature demonstrates an intrinsic understanding

---

26. Lovat, "Dietrich Bonhoeffer."

27. Bethge, *Dietrich Bonhoeffer*, 409.

28. Ibid.

29. Bonhoeffer, *Sanctorum Communio*.

30. Bonhoeffer, *Ethics*, 137. Note that another key element of these questions is the historical context in which they are asked and which is beyond the scope of this chapter.

31. For a review, see Lenehan, "Reading Bonhoeffer."

32. Bonhoeffer, *Ethics*, 33.

of our oneness with it.[33] Further, reaching a position of willingness to suffer is the ultimate freedom, and this becomes possible as a manifestation
of apprehending the Suffering God.[34] As Lenehan summarizes it: "We can
clearly see Bonhoeffer's conviction that in Christ the interrelationality of
all reality has been reconciled and restored, and that Christ is the *Mittler*
[Mediator] of reality who continually makes that re-created relationality
possible within reality."[35]

As the Suffering Christ is present throughout all of creation, relationships throughout the biosphere are therefore both made possible and mediated by Christ. Humanity's position in relation to other-than-human nature
reflects the sociality possible from human to human: we acknowledge and
respond to the Suffering Christ in the face of the other—whomever or whatever that "other" is.[36] The God who suffers is both paradoxical and essential:
"In a world where success is the measure and justification of all things, the
figure of him who was sentenced and crucified remains a stranger and is at
best an object of pity . . . the figure of the Crucified invalidates all thought
which takes success for its standard."[37] With Bonhoeffer, the logical extension of the above is that we recognize the Suffering Christ in creation
around us. He explored this theme in *Creation and Fall* wherein creation is
described as being "subject to God in devout worship;" even the formless,
mute world was already worshipping God before creatures were made.[38]
Humanity's behavior toward creation has reflected the desire for domination borne of selfishness, rather than dominion of care and servanthood
which would better reflect and represent Christ. In Bonhoeffer's words,
"originally man was made in the image of God, but now his likeness to God
is a stolen one."[39] Old theologies which do not move humanity toward the
ultimate reconciliation and restoration[40] are artifacts and, in the context of
climate crisis, a barrier to people of faith participating in the reality of the
world[41] that Bonhoeffer describes.

---

33. Bonhoeffer, *Ecumenical, Academic, and Pastoral Work*, 246–57; Moses, *Reluctant Revolutionary*, 92. See Moses' full critique of "The Right to Self-Assertion," 90–97.

34. Bonhoeffer, *Ethics*, 197.

35. Lenehan, *Standing Responsibly*, 522.

36. Bonhoeffer, *Letters and Papers*, 35, 543.

37. Bonhoeffer, *Ethics*, 77.

38. Bonhoeffer, *Creation and Fall*, 36.

39. Bonhoeffer, *Ethics*, 22.

40. Williams, "Renewing the Face of the Earth," 3.

41. Bonhoeffer, *Ethics*, 195.

"Stewardship," then, assumes a preferential place for humanity, an ontological difference between human and other-than-human nature. What is evident in Bonhoeffer's theology, and where there is more than a measure of perceived similarity with the Eastern theologies he was investigating, is the sense of the interrelatedness of all creation, living and nonliving, rather than hierarchy, and where suffering is inherent. James Lovelock would later describe the whole of Earth as a self-regulating super-organism, *Gaia*,[42] but Bonhoeffer emphasized how a deep Christology must be reflected in the human relationship to the rest of creation: "The ground and animals over which I am lord constitute the world in which I live, without which I cease to be . . . I am not free from it in any sense of my essential being, my spirit, having no need of nature, as though nature were something alien to the spirit. On the contrary, in my whole being, in my creatureliness, I belong wholly to this world; it bears me, nurtures me, holds me."[43]

The continuity of the above with Jainism's paradigm of interconnectedness, neatly characterized in the classic motif *Parasparopagraho Jivanam* (living souls render services to one another),[44] is evident. Jainism recognizes the paradox which exists. One can, indeed must, engage in careful nurturing of the world whilst concurrently shunning all things material. Bonhoeffer's theology allows also for this tension: the world requires care (dominion and suffering) whilst contemporaneously we recognize our oneness with it, our essential relationship to it. So, in humanity's relationship with God, we recognize a role in bringing about restoration and reconciliation with the world. Our relationship with other-than-human nature should be one of servanthood: "We do not abandon it; we do not repudiate, despise or condemn it. Instead we call it back to God, we give it hope, we lay our hand on it and say: God's blessing come upon you, may God renew you; be blessed, world created by God, you who belong to your Creator and Redeemer."[45]

Indian natural theologies have engendered a relationship with Earth that is respectful and useful to the development of a contemporary ecotheological ethic. We suggest that the discipline of nonviolence which Gandhi articulated is appealing to Bonhoeffer precisely because of its consistency with the latter's inherent Christology. For him, a relationship of nonviolence with other-than-human nature better reflects the meaning of "dominion" in

---

42. Lovelock, *Gaia*.

43. Bonhoeffer, *Creation and Fall*, 66.

44. Dundas et al., "Jainism."

45. Bonhoeffer, *Conspiracy and Imprisonment*, 632.

the creation narratives of Genesis.[46] In an allied sense, Bonhoeffer is moved to ask if our actions toward Earth conform to the image of Christ precisely because his theology is grounded in the centrality of Christ: "In Jesus Christ we believe in the God who became human, was crucified, and is risen. In the becoming human we recognize God's love toward God's creation, in the crucifixion God's judgment on all flesh, and in the resurrection God's purpose for a new world . . . In Christ the reality of God encounters the reality of the world . . . Christian life is participation in Christ's encounter with the world."[47]

Bonhoeffer would argue that the relationship enabled through the mediation of Christ requires an attitude, and commensurate behavior, of servanthood. How can Christ be Lord of the World if the community of believers rejects its essential task of servanthood? How can the task of reconciliation, commenced in Christ, be fulfilled in the world unless humanity participates in that very work? Christ's life and teaching demonstrate that servanthood is not dependent on being ontologically identical. Christ demonstrated both service toward, and dominion over, creation.

Behavior toward the other via a relationship of sociality thus becomes an ecotheological ethic, driven by the interrelatedness described equivalently across faiths. Gandhi's attraction to the Jain ethic of treading lightly, and Bonhoeffer's relationship to the Christ in the other, recognize a truly ecological view of creation, that is, one of interrelated networks and systems of which humanity is but one part. One senses that this is moving closer to what Bonhoeffer affirms when declaring Christ to be Lord of the World, where "Christ would then no longer be the object of religion, but something else entirely," and where "religionless-worldly Christians" understand themselves not "as privileged, but instead . . . as belonging wholly to the world." In the next breath, Bonhoeffer asks "is this where the 'arcane discipline' . . . [has] new significance?" in a similar way to that of Gandhi—where the outward behavior characterized by nonviolence becomes merely a manifestation of the shared, secret discipline.[48]

Conclusion

In searching out a Bonhoefferian ecotheological ethic that we believe can be found implicit in Bonhoeffer's Christology, we have made reference to

46. Gen 1:26–28. Concepts of "dominion" and "subduing the Earth" have frequently been isolated from this passage.

47. Bonhoeffer, *Ethics*, 157–58.

48. Bonhoeffer, *Letters and Papers*, 362–65.

a coincidence of thought between him and Gandhi that, evidence suggests, may amount to a veritable influence by Gandhi and his own underpinning Indian natural and eco-theologies, as well as by Western influences. In essence, this chapter poses its own version of the great Bonhoefferian Christological question: "Is this who Christ is for us today?" Is Christ throughout the Cosmos, in the form of the other, demanding a sociality which requires humanity to respond to the rest of the ecology in a relationship of mutual service and edification rather than domination? Is dominion, in the form of responsible service to the ecology, arguably Christianity's most urgent and potentially powerful expression of faith midst the current challenges of climate change? Herein, it is proposed, Bonhoeffer's inherent Christology provides in part for an ecotheology with potential to inform, enliven, and embolden that expression.

Bibliography

Bethge, Eberhard. *Dietrich Bonhoeffer: A Biography*. Rev. illus. ed. Translated by Eric Mosbacher. Edited by Victoria Barnett. Minneapolis: Fortress, 2000.

Bonhoeffer, Dietrich. *Conspiracy and Imprisonment 1940–1945*. Translated by Lisa E. Dahill. Edited by Mark S. Brocker. DBWE 16. Minneapolis: Fortress, 2006.

———. *Creation and Fall: A Theological Exposition of Genesis 1–3*. Translated by Douglas Stephen Bax. Edited by John W. de Gruchy. DBWE 3. Minneapolis: Fortress, 2004.

———. *Ecumenical, Academic, and Pastoral Work: 1931–1932*. Translated by Anne Schmidt-Lange. Edited by Victoria J. Barnett et al. DBWE 11. Minneapolis: Fortress, 2012.

———. *Ethics*. Translated by Reinhard Krauss et al. Edited by Clifford J. Green. DBWE 6. Minneapolis: Fortress, 2005.

———. *Letters and Papers from Prison*. Translated by Isabel Best et al. Edited by John W. de Gruchy. DBWE 8. Minneapolis: Fortress, 2010.

———. *Sanctorum Communio: A Theological Study of the Sociology of the Church*. DBWE Vol. 1. Translated by Reinhard Krauss and Nancy Lukens. Minneapolis: Fortress, 1998.

Chapple, Christopher Key. "Jainism, Ethics and Ecology." *Bulletin for the Study of Religion* 39.2 (2010) 3–7.

Dundas, Paul et al. "Jainism." http://www.britannica.com/EBchecked/topic/299478/Jainism/59016/Jiva-and-ajiva.

Lenehan, Kevin. "Reading Bonhoeffer." In *Standing Responsibly between Silence and Speech: Religion and Revelation in the Thought of Dietrich Bonhoeffer and René Girard*, 5–33. Leuven: Peeters, 2012.

———. *Standing Responsibly between Silence and Speech: Religion and Revelation in the Thought of Dietrich Bonhoeffer and René Girard*. Louvain Theological & Pastoral Monographs. Leuvan: Peeters, 2012.

Long, Jeffrey. "Jainism: Key Themes." *Religion Compass* 5 (2011) 501–10.

Lovat, Terence. "Dietrich Bonhoeffer: Interfaith Theologian and Practical Mystic." *Pacifica: Australasian Theological Studies* 25.2 (2012) 176–88.

———. "'Lord of the (Warming) World': Bonhoeffer's Eco-theological Ethic and the Gandhi Factor." *The Bonhoeffer Legacy: Australasian Journal of Bonhoeffer Studies* 2 (2014) 57–74.

Lovelock, James. *Gaia: A New Look at Life on Earth.* Oxford: Oxford University Press, 2000.

Moolakkattu, John S. "Gandhi as a Human Ecologist." *Journal of Human Ecology* 29.3 (2010) 151–58.

Morgan, Peggy. "Buddhism." In *Ethical Issues in Six Religious Traditions*, edited by Peggy Morgan and Clive A. Lawton, 61–117. 2nd ed. Edinburgh: Edinburgh University Press, 2007.

Moses, John A. *The Reluctant Revolutionary: Dietrich Bonhoeffer's Collision with Prusso-German History.* New York: Berghahn, 2009.

Nojeim, Michael J. *Gandhi and King: The Power of Nonviolent Resistance.* Westport, CT: Praeger, 2004.

Pániker, Agustín. *Jainism: History, Society, Philosophy and Practice.* New Delhi: Motilal Banarsidass, 2010.

Sinha, Atul N. "Religion and Creation: Ecological Concerns in Jainism and Buddhism." *Bulletin of the Christian Institute of Religious Studies* 27.1 (1998) 3–13.

Srinivasa Murthy, B., ed. *Mahatma Gandhi and Leo Tolstoy Letters.* Long Beach, CA: Long Beach Publications, 1987.

Stocker, Thomas F. et al. *Climate Change 2013: The Physical Science Basis. Working Group I Contribution to the Fifth Assessment Report of the Intergovernmental Panel on Climate Change.* Edited by IPCC. Cambridge: Cambridge University Press, 2013.

Tödt, Heinz Eduard. *Authentic Faith: Bonhoeffer's Theological Ethics in Context.* Translated by David Stassen and Ilse Tödt. Edited by Glen Harold Stassen. Grand Rapids: Eerdmans, 2007.

Williams, Rowan. "Renewing the Face of the Earth: Human Responsibility and the Environment." In *Christianity and the Renewal of Nature: Creation, Climate Change and Human Responsibility*, edited by Sebastian C. H. Kim and Jonathan Draper, 1–13. London: SPCK, 2011.

Part 4

Wisdom in Creation

11

Where Can Wisdom be Found?

Re-discovering Wisdom in God's Creation

Norman Habel

Invitation

WISDOM IS NOT SIMPLY an ancient concept that informed the cosmology of the wise in the ancient Near East. Wisdom was discerned as a dynamic reality in the universe by the "scientists" of that world, a force of nature to be explored and investigated. Wisdom was more than an intellectual mystery; it was recognized as a natural dimension of the cosmos and a governing factor in God's creation, to be observed, studied and interpreted as a pivotal force throughout creation.[1] You are invited to join these ancient scientists in their investigation of Wisdom. We will not, at this point, seek to correlate or harmonize the approach of these ancient scientists with the various contemporary scientific methods. Rather, we will seek to explore core dimensions of the world of the Wisdom School on their terms.

The Wisdom School

The Wisdom School is a world of ancient science that deserves to be heard on its own terms rather than on the terms of those with a contemporary

---

1. A more detailed analysis of this subject can be found in Habel, *Discerning Wisdom in God's Creation*, written for, and distributed at the 2015 conference "Rediscovering the Spiritual in God's Creation."

theological or scientific mindset. This process is not to be viewed as a leap of faith but a rational investigation. The fact that our investigation focuses initially on a tradition in the Hebrew Scriptures is no reason to treat its orientation as in conflict with the principles of scientific research or radical religious thought. As we explore the approach and findings of the wise— the scientists of the ancient world—we are challenged to discern Wisdom for ourselves, and to discover those dimensions of Wisdom integral to the design, domains and deeps of creation in our own world. We are also challenged to identify specific experiences in our own lives where we have discerned Wisdom in God's creation. The question that naturally arises, given our contemporary perspective on the sciences and the context of the "Rediscovering the Spiritual in God's Creation" conference, is whether the understanding and observation of nature by the wise also incorporated what we would today call a "spiritual dimension."

Modus operandi

To appreciate the *modus operandi* of the wise in ancient Israel, especially their way of interpreting nature, we will begin with key technical terms used to describe the process of analysis in the Wisdom School.

"Observe"—rāʾā

Like good scientists, the wise are expected to discern through "observation" and rational analysis. This practice is abundantly clear in the following passage:

> Go to the ant, *observe* its ways and be wise (Prov 6:6).

In this example the wise person "observes" or "watches critically" a specific phenomenon of nature: the ant. As the wider use of this verb indicates, the process is more than a chance "seeing." The task is to "observe" closely and discern the "way:" a determining characteristic of that phenomenon.

"Discern"—bîn

While the noun "discernment" is found in parallel with "Wisdom" in some passages, such as Prov 4:7, the verb *bîn* refers to a process of empirically distinguishing one factor from another. The aim of discernment is, more specifically, to determine the "way" (*derek*) and/or the "place" (*māqôm*) of a particular phenomenon of nature.

"Acquire"—qānâ

To "acquire" Wisdom is the mission and task of every student of Wisdom (Prov 4:7). The wise over the centuries observed the behavior of humans and society, observations that led to an accumulation of acquired Wisdom known as proverbs. Acquiring Wisdom could also be achieved by observing and analyzing nature where Wisdom may be discerned as an innate force.

"Place"—māqôm

In the ordering of things on Earth, in the thinking of the Wisdom School, everything has its "place." In Job 28 the "place" of things is made explicit. The rocks of Earth, for example, are the "place" of sapphires. Precious gems have a "place" in stones (Job 28:6); gold has its "place" in the Earth (Job 28:1); Earth has its "place" in the cosmos (Job 14:18; 18:4) and the East wind has its "place" in the heavens (Job 27:23). It is central to the role of a student of the Wisdom School to determine the locus or "place" of a given phenomenon in the world of nature. The ultimate question to be explored later is the "place" of Wisdom in the cosmos.

"Way"—derek

Just as the term *māqôm* has Wisdom significance, so too does the key term *derek*, which is usually translated "way." In Wisdom contexts we hear about the "way" of the eagle in the sky and the "way" of a snake on a rock (Prov 30:18).

Every phenomenon of nature has its own inner formative force, its driving characteristic.[2] This concept of *derek* (way) is crucial for an understanding of the basic Wisdom interpretation of nature in the ancient world. The *derek* of something is the Wisdom programmed into its nature as part of the ecosystem. In the analysis that follows, I will seek to retrieve dimensions of Wisdom from three major domains of creation where Wisdom is innate, namely (a) living creatures of the natural world, (b) inanimate forces and realms of nature and (c) the cosmos as a whole.

---

2. Habel, "The Implications of God Discovering Wisdom in Earth," 286.

Wisdom—An Innate Life-Force

Wisdom is a life-force innate in all living creatures of the natural world, a force that determines their driving characteristics and the distinctive roles of their existence. The first dimension of Wisdom that we will explore—and hopefully experience—is Wisdom as a life-force within all life-forms, whether they be amoebae or ants, eggplants or elephants. I used to call this life-force "instinct," the capacity of animals to know what to do in the routines of their lives. The Wisdom School has taught me that this innate life-force programmed into all living creatures, is called Wisdom by ancient scientists, an innate capacity that enables living beings to be true to their nature.

In the Wisdom School, a person interested in becoming wise was expected to observe nature and understand its "ways" closely. Following this practice, the individual may not only learn lessons about life, but also about the phenomenon itself, its way" or inner wisdom. The *derek* or "way" of a phenomenon, as we outlined above, is the Wisdom programmed into its very being so that it remains true to its essential nature.

The "Way" of the Ant

The novice is encouraged by wise mentors to watch the ant, for example, and observe its distinctive code of behavior—the innate Wisdom found in ants—and so gain some personal Wisdom:

> Go to the ant, you lazybones!
>
> 'Observe' its 'way' and be wise!
>
> Without having any chief
>
> or officer or ruler,
>
> it prepares its food in summer,
>
> and gathers its sustenance in harvest (Prov 6:6–8).

The Wisdom in an ant colony is, according to these ancient scientists, an inner capacity to function as a corporate body without any hierarchy—without any bosses or leaders—a mystery that modern scientists still find fascinating.

Another dimension of ant Wisdom, according to this ancient scientist, is its instinctual/intellectual capacity to gather food in summer and store it for the winter when conditions for finding food are difficult. The Wisdom embedded in the ant enables it to anticipate the future and plan ahead.[3] It

3. Habel, "The Way of Things!" 3.

may seem surprising that ants were chosen by the wise as an exemplar of Wisdom in living creatures on our planet. I was delighted to discover recently that Tim Flannery, in his chapter on "super-organisms," also explores the amazing capacity of ants, especially attine ants, to construct complex ecosystems we might well call societies, even agricultural societies.[4] The wise in ancient times called this interconnected and programmed intelligence of ants the "way" or Wisdom dimension of the ant. And as Flannery outlines, this inner capacity is apparent in all areas of the ant ecosystem—from the ingenious techniques used to locate and prepare a new habitat to the sophisticated practices developed for the agriculture of fungus. These inner capacities may have developed over millions of years, but they testify to a deep dimension of such creatures in nature that may be designated their innate Wisdom.[5]

The "Way" of Living Creatures

The author of Prov 30 explores a range of mysteries both in society and in nature. He claims that he lacks the capacity to understand the mysteries that surround him (Prov 30:1–3). There are four things in nature, he declares, that are too wonderful to comprehend:

> The way of an eagle in the sky,
>
> the way of a snake on a rock,
>
> the way of a ship on the high seas,
>
> the way of a man with a girl. (Prov 30:18–19)

When Job is led by God into the kingdom of the wild, he is confronted by the "ways" of creatures in the wild. The assumption in this context is that all such creatures have an innate Wisdom that enables them to survive in the wild.

One creature, however, seems to demonstrate the opposite—the ostrich. She is a creature with grand plumage and high spirits but she, according to popular tradition, leaves her eggs on the ground, lets them get hot in the dust and be crushed by wild beasts. She also treats her young harshly, as if they were not hers (Job 38:13–16). The reason given is that Eloah deprived her of Wisdom and withheld her portion of discernment (Job 39:17). The ostrich is here presented as the exception to the rule. The implication is quite clearly that all living creatures are imbued with innate

---

4. Flannery, *Here on Earth*, 15.

5. Habel, "The Way of Things!" 3–4.

wisdom or discernment. In the preceding verses the ibex is portrayed as a nurturing mother, quite the opposite of the ostrich. The ibex has the innate Wisdom needed to determine the time of birth and how to watch over her young so that they grow into healthy animals who can leave home and be self-sufficient (Job 39:1–4).

The wild ass has the Wisdom needed to survive in the salt flats of the wilderness, find sustenance without a taskmaster and the capacity to laugh at the furor of the city (Job 39:5–8). The wild ox (Job 39:9–11) stands as a testimony to the Wisdom of creatures who know they are not subject to the mandate to dominate found in Gen 1:26–28.[6] Even the horse, who may appear to have been domesticated and dominated by humans, exhibits the fierce spirit of the wild (Job 39:19–25). Hawks are explicitly said to soar through the sky and spread their wings on high because of their inner "discernment" or Wisdom. Similarly the eagle has the innate knowledge required to dwell on rocky crags and build a nest safely in the heights (Job 39:26–30). Birds like the eagle, and animals like the ibex, are testimony to Wisdom innate in living creatures.

Celia Deane-Drummond, in her discussion of natural wisdom in evolutionary biology, returns to the example of the ant and asks whether we are now better informed than the "way" of the ant. She distinguishes between natural Wisdom and cosmic design, which implies a deliberate designer. She concludes: "Natural wisdom by contrast puts more emphasis on the process of the evolutionary searchlight scanning forms of biological diversity. Convergence across all traits simultaneously has not yet been found, for the way/wisdom of each species is unique."[7] The Wisdom School would also argue that each species has its own unique "way," its innate Wisdom. From each species we can learn new dimensions of the Wisdom embedded in all life forms.

A Wisdom Experience: Gazing at Godwits

Some years ago
I was seated on a grassy area by a shoreline
on a bay in Auckland, New Zealand.
As I waited and watched I observed
hundreds of bar-tailed godwits gather
from all around the island.

6. Habel, "Is the Wild Ox Willing to Serve You?"
7. Deane-Drummond, *Wisdom and Wonder*, 70.

All day they raced around in a feeding frenzy
communicating with extreme agitation.
Suddenly,
they heeded a signal deep within each of them,
began to circle round
and form a spiral of spinning life.

Slowly the spiral swirled out to sea
and the godwits set out across the ocean.
They fly across vast waters,
through storms over the equator,
on their way to a chosen location in Siberia
where they feed, breed and nurture their young
before they return.

At that moment I could sense their Wisdom—
the Wisdom of flight and the Wisdom of memory—
encoded in their spirit.
I discerned an amazing intelligence
of fellow Earth beings,
guiding themselves non-stop
to a place across the ocean
more than ten thousand kilometres away!
As they vanished into the distance
I had sense of sheer wonder.

I had discerned Wisdom in nature,
the innate force driving their evolution
over millions of year.

Wisdom as System of Codes in Nature

Wisdom is a "system of codes" programmed into the cosmos, a system that governs the domains of creation and controls the laws of nature.

We now move our focus from the world of living creatures to the discernment of laws and forces at work in the so-called inanimate domains of creation. The Wisdom dimension for this tradition is preserved in Job 28 where the ultimate question is posed: Where can Wisdom be found? Or in other words, what is the "place" of Wisdom in the operation of the cosmos? The significance of this chapter was demonstrated in the Netherlands when an entire conference was dedicated to the topic of *Job 28: Cognition in Context.*[8]

"Place" in Nature

Crucial for an understanding of this chapter is the Wisdom School concept of "place" *(māqôm),* the locus or habitat of a phenomenon/factor in the ecosystem network of the universe. As outlined above, there is an appointed place for each domain, creature or component of nature (cf. Ps 104:8). In Job 28, the poet takes the question of the essential *māqôm* of everything in the universe and even asks the question: Where is the *māqôm* of Wisdom itself? The answer to that question might seem to be obvious: the source or the original *māqôm* of Wisdom is within God. In the course of this poem, however, the Wisdom poet leads us on a search that ends in another location—the world of nature!

The opening verse of the poem immediately focuses on the question of the *māqôm* of various phenomena in creation, entities such as silver and gold: "Truly, there is a source for silver and a place *(māqôm)* for the gold they refine" (Job 28:1). As indicated above, everything has its appointed "place" in the order of creation, and more specifically on Earth. By establishing that precious commodities have a specific "place" in the design of the universe, the poet prepares the way for posing the ultimate question about the "place" of Wisdom, the most precious find of all (Job 28:12).

The crucial question about the location of Wisdom in Job 28:12–14 is made explicit in Job 28.20:

> But Wisdom, where does she originate?
> Where is the "place" of Discernment?

---

8. See Habel, "The Implications of God Discovering Wisdom in Earth." For a more detailed analysis of Job 28, see Habel, *Finding Wisdom in Nature,* chapter 3.

In this version of the refrain, the "place" of Wisdom in the cosmos is linked to the mystery of its origin. The "place" of Wisdom is a wonder that harks back to its very origins at the time of creation. In the final verses of Job 28 we learn that God is the one who first undertook a successful search for Wisdom. As the divine Sage-cum-Scientist, God searched far and wide across Earth to find Wisdom. Unlike like other deities of the ancient world who claimed to possess great Wisdom, the God of the Wisdom School undertakes the ultimate search for Wisdom. In the ancient Near East, the God Ea was known as "the wisest of the gods who knew every sort of thing." The wisdom of Marduk was considered a mystery never understood by humans. And the sun god Shamash was not only wise and mighty, "he was his own counselor."[9]

God the Scientist

The "place" where the God of the Wisdom School begins to search for Wisdom is not a distant realm among the gods or the council of heaven. The "way" of Wisdom that God the observing "scientist" discerns is not the "mind" of God or a personal capacity. Rather,

> God discerned (*bîn*) her way (*derek*),
>   and came to know her place (*māqôm*),
> for God looked to the ends of Earth
>   and observed [*rā'â*] everything under heaven. (Job 28:23–24)

God searches the ends of Earth including every domain "under heaven." God reads the entire landscape of the planet. The "place" of Wisdom is on/in Earth! As we begin this search with God, we become acutely aware that God is searching for the *māqôm* and the *derek* of Wisdom: the appointed locus of Wisdom in the cosmos and the driving characteristic of Wisdom in the domains of creation.

We finally reach the climax of the poem: God discovers Wisdom in nature. God's discovery of Wisdom, however, is not a recent event. God found Wisdom at the very beginning, during the process of creation. It is specifically when God is creating meteorological domains that God the scientist discerns Wisdom. These specific domains, it would seem, are representative of all the domains of nature.

> When God fixed the *weight* of the wind
>   and meted out the waters by *measure*,

9. Kalugila, *The Wise King*, 30–45.

> when God made a *rule* (*chôq*) for the rain
>   and a *way (derek)* for the thunderstorm,
> then God observed (*rā'ā*) her and appraised her,
>   established her and probed her. (Job 28:25–27)

The "Laws" of Nature

A significant dimension of God's search for Wisdom lies, not in the specific domains themselves, but in that feature of these domains where Wisdom is to be found. The use of the technical terms *derek* and *chôq* indicates that God is discerning the inner character of these phenomena—whether they be the wind, the waters, the storms or the rain. God does not merely observe a given phenomenon. God "discerns" its "way" (*derek*), its inner code, its innate character. By discerning the "ways" of these phenomena of nature, God discovers innate Wisdom. Wisdom, then, is not separate from these phenomena of nature, but an innate dimension of nature. God discovers Wisdom as a "network of forces" or "laws" in nature!

It is striking that this understanding of these "laws" of nature was anticipated by the scientists of ancient times. Significantly a "law" of nature was viewed as "intelligent," as the innate Wisdom or knowledge of a given phenomenon that guided its behavior. Wisdom, then, is a powerful code innate in all the domains of nature, a code that today is understood as integral to the laws of nature. The search for Wisdom in the laws of nature, the network of codes that govern and balance the forces of nature—from gravity and anti-gravity to summer and winter—persists as a challenge for the scientists and thinkers of today, whether they are geologists or astrophysicists. Given the specific "place" of Wisdom in Job 28, we may well consult meteorologists and climate scientists about the innate laws of nature in our atmosphere and ask whether the excessive use of greenhouse gases by humans has upset the network of forces innate in the ecosystems of the weather.[10]

---

10. Cf. Habel, "The Way of Things!"

A Wisdom Experience: Lightning Flashes

On Reformation Day (26 October) 2014,
black clouds filled the sky to the West
as if announcing a momentous hour.
In that hour
80 thousand lightning strikes penetrated the darkness
and landed on South Australia
as the sun set behind the thunder clouds.
The sight was stunning.
Even more stunning
was the mystery in full view,
clouds and lightning guided by innate Wisdom
filling the sky with wonder.

God asked Job:
Who put wisdom in the clouds?
Yes, and who put wisdom in the lightning?
It's innate, Job,
a mystery on display for all to see
on such a day.

A Primal Blueprint

Wisdom is the "primal blueprint" that preceded creation—a dynamic impulse for the evolution and design of the cosmos.

The third dimension of Wisdom in nature takes us back to the primordial: the time before time, to the infinite beginning of the beginnings of the cosmos. The Wisdom School tradition has an understanding of the primordial that is radically different from that found in Genesis or other creation traditions of the Hebrew Scriptures. In my opinion, Wisdom as a natural force in the primordial, as represented in the Wisdom Literature, has no parallel in the other traditions in the Hebrew Scriptures about the creation of the cosmos or the beginning of space, time and matter.

In the Wisdom School, Wisdom exists as a primordial factor that precedes creation, a primal capacity whose nature and function will be explored as we analyze this dimension of innate Wisdom. It is interesting to note that many astral scientists, who have explored the primordial through their observation of the components of space, believe that prior to the "Big Bang" there was a tiny ball of energy as big as the head of a pin. They believe that inside that ball was a cosmic impulse that caused the ball to explode and send blazing bits of energy in all directions.

God "Acquires" Wisdom

In the primordial we discover that, according to the Wisdom School, God "acquires" Wisdom prior to the processes of creation. This is explicit in the speech of Prov 8 where Wisdom explains her nature and role in the primordial and thereafter. The following translation of Wisdom's opening words is a literal—and I believe accurate—rendering, unlike the interpretive versions found in many translations. Wisdom declares:

> YAHWEH acquired (*qānā*) me first,
>   his way (*derek*) before his works.
> From of old, from antiquity I was established,
>   from the first, from the beginnings of Earth. (Prov 8:22–23)

Wisdom introduces herself as the "way" that God "acquires" before any of the works of creation. Wisdom is the primal "way," the primal dimension or impulse in the pre-creation universe. The verb translated "acquired" (*qānā*) is the standard term employed in Proverbs for acquiring Wisdom (see Prov 4:3, 7). The repeated injunction of the Wisdom teacher is to "acquire Wisdom"! The aim of the wise is to "acquire" Wisdom as an essential skill for a positive life.

Given this context, it seems logical to understand this term in the standard way.[11] God "acquires" Wisdom and in so doing is portrayed as a primordial sage, the ideal "scientist," the one who introduces the *modus operandi* of the wise as primal and powerful. God is introduced as the first student in the Wisdom School.

The Primordial "Way"

Crucial for an appreciation of the nature and role of Wisdom in this text and elsewhere is the designation of Wisdom as the "way" that precedes the "works" of creation. As we indicated above, the "way" (*derek*) of something

---

11. Cf. Lenzi, "Proverbs 8:22–31," 692.

refers to its inner formative force or, as I suggest, its driving characteristic.[12] The *derek* of something is its essential nature as part of the cosmos. In Prov 8, *derek* is identified as the primordial formative force or factor that precedes the works of creation. Scholars have long sought to discern precisely what this primal dimension might be. McKane declares: "I would hold with von Rad that the intention here is to emphasize the vast intelligence of Wisdom by assigning to her an architectonic function in the ordering of the world."[13] McKane's recognition of wisdom's "architectonic function" is consistent with the approach of von Rad and others who speak of Wisdom as "primeval order," "world reason" or "cosmic design."[14] I believe that "cosmic blueprint" is an appropriate description of the essential nature of wisdom as a primordial factor "acquired" by God for the design and creation of the cosmos.

In Prov 8 Wisdom is not a deity: Wisdom is a force that precedes all creation. Wisdom as a primordial blueprint reflects a dynamic understanding of the physical universe that extends, as we shall see, beyond the primordial into the present. This dimension of innate Wisdom is not a memory of ancient mythology, but a dynamic natural force discerned by the scientists of old. The architectonic or design dimension of Wisdom is also evident from the description of the various stages of creation depicted in Prov 8. After emphasizing her primordial nature, Wisdom declares she is present as the design agent or factor during a range of "works" of creation.

Wisdom is not only present before the existence of mountains: Wisdom is prior to the "shaping" of mountains (Prov 8:25). The implication is that Wisdom was involved in the designing of mountains. Wisdom is not only present before the creation of Earth, but is also aware that the "world" is composed of land, fields and bits of dust/soil from which vegetation may emerge (Prov 8:26). Wisdom is not only present when the skies are established, but also conscious of a "circle" or "vault" stretching over the "deep" both to contain it and a way to maintain the clouds above (Prov 8:27–29).

Elsewhere in biblical texts, the focus is on the word of God rather than Wisdom as the agency of creation:

> By the word of the Lord the heavens were made
>   and all their host by the breath of his mouth. (Ps 33:6)

It is important to recognize, I believe, that creation by the word of God and creation with Wisdom as the primal impulse represent two radically different perspectives. Creation by the word implies an all-powerful deity who brings

12. Habel, "The Implications of God Discovering Wisdom in Earth," 286.

13. McKane, *Proverbs*, 351.

14. von Rad, *Wisdom in Israel*, 156–57.

things into existence by divine command, as in Gen 1. In the Wisdom School, by contrast, Wisdom pre-exists as a cosmic blueprint or intelligence that God appropriates for the work of creation. A dimension of nature called Wisdom is acquired by God to design the domains of the cosmos.

A Wisdom Experience: Discerning the Primordial

The date is 8 March 1986.

I am on a mountain in Tamil Nadu in South India

on the day that Halley's Comet

appeared for all to see.

The comet will return in 2061.

With me are scientists, scribes, and students

who have come to observe the comet,

completing its long but spectacular circuit

around planet Earth.

As we watch the comet move across the sky,

leaving its long trail of icy gases,

we see a genuine piece of stardust before our very eyes.

The comet appears before us as a classroom model,

a microcosm of the universe,

an image of the cosmos in miniature;

matter and energy and mystery in endless motion

from the beginning of time

to the moment the comet appears before us.

When we see the comet appear,

we may also see a microcosm of the design of the universe

reflected in the image of the comet spinning across the sky,

and discern an image of Wisdom,

as the blueprint of the cosmos—

a blueprint that is dazzling and dynamic,

a blueprint shimmering with primal intelligence,

a blueprint wired for motion and mystery,

a blueprint that evokes sheer wonder,

and a vivid cosmic consciousness.

Wisdom: A Profound Mystery

Wisdom is "a profound mystery" that manifests itself in the many natural phenomena of the universe, phenomena that may also arouse, in the wise, a sense of sheer wonder, a Wisdom consciousness and a spiritual awareness.

The more that scientists—whether they be the wise of old or the astrophysicists of today—explore the intricacies of the universe, the more they are faced with a vast world of mysteries. Whether they are investigating the option of alternative universes or the origins of genetic codes, the influence of gravity on dark matter or the evolution of an ant's nests, they are faced with a panorama of mysteries.

The many dimensions of Wisdom suggest comparable worlds of mystery that challenge the wise of all generations. The dimension of Wisdom as a primal blueprint ordering the seemingly endless parameters of space evokes a sense of sheer amazement. No wonder God is portrayed as filled with delight when God acquires this blueprint to create the cosmos.

Wisdom Consciousness

One way of responding to an experience of innate Wisdom as mystery is a sense of awe—whether as quiet amazement or sheer wonder. To be in the presence of such a pervading mystery may cause us to be mesmerized in amazement. Or the challenge of such a mystery may move us to delve even deeper into a phenomenon filled with mystery and seek for meaning or ultimate causes. A typical Wisdom-related experience of wonder is found in Prov 30:18–19.

Scientists may be struck with wonder as they contemplate the origins of the universe. The very design of the cosmos evokes sheer amazement amongst nuclear physicists. They are likewise astounded by the very existence of atoms when it might be expected that all matter and corresponding antimatter would cancel each other out and leave but a glow of cosmic radiation.[15] In the light of our preceding insights into Wisdom, I believe it is appropriate to speak of "Wisdom" consciousness as: an acute sense of the presence, power and significance of Wisdom in all domains of our environment; a mindset that recognizes Wisdom as an innate force driving nature and, ultimately, the cosmos. For some, Wisdom consciousness may be comparable to cosmic consciousness or ecological intelligence.

---

15. Deane-Drummond, *Wisdom and Wonder*, 22.

Spiritual Awareness

As profound as these experiences may be, we may ask whether they could lead to a spiritual awareness or a spiritual experience. *A priori*, we need to recognize that "spiritual awareness" or "spiritual experience" in the Wisdom tradition may differ from that in the prophetic world or in the priestly tradition. The experience of sheer wonder or Wisdom consciousness may be tantamount to spiritual awareness for some of the would-be-wise observing nature or exploring the cosmos.

I suggest, however, that the response of Job to his Wisdom consciousness experience may offer another appreciation of spiritual awareness. Job's ultimate challenge was to comprehend how all these domains where Wisdom was a driving force contributed to the "design" of the cosmos. The Wisdom consciousness that Job acquires is indeed a form of "cosmic consciousness." But is his new awareness also a "God consciousness," or a "spiritual experience"?

Job's response to his tour of the cosmos is perhaps surprising (Job 42:1–6). He recognizes that God was challenging him to understand the *'ētsā*: the primordial design, the blueprint for the cosmos. Job admits that he had not been true to his Wisdom tradition, that he had not used his "discernment" to interpret the cosmos or what is happening in his physical world. Previously, he had focused on the question: Where can justice be found? Now he is faced with the question: Where can Wisdom be found? He declares:

> I heard of you with my ears,
> but now my eyes "see/observe" you. (Job 42:5)

What does Job mean when he claims to have "seen" God? Surely such a cry is an admission that he has now had a spiritual experience of some kind. What kind of experience? The context is the Wisdom School; the meaning of this pivotal cry is relevant to our understanding of his response.

The first significant feature is the use of the term *rāā* (see/observe). As we noted above, this verb is a technical term in the Wisdom School. A key step of the wise scientist of old was to "see" or "observe" a particular phenomenon closely to "discern" its nature. Now Job, the newly initiated wise scientist, claims to have "seen/observed God." How? Where? Or, in the language of the Wisdom School: "Where can God be found/seen?" How can Job claim to have seen God as an "observable phenomenon" of the universe?

Job has been challenged to discern all the dimensions of cosmic design, including: the foundations of Earth; the "place" of the dawn; the "way" of lightning and thunderstorms; the "laws" of the skies; the "wisdom" in the clouds; the "discernment" of the hawk (Job 38–39). Job's education in the world of innate Wisdom is comprehensive. Job has clearly "seen" and "discerned" Wisdom as a force in all realms of nature. Job has acquired Wisdom consciousness. How then has Job "seen" God?

Cosmic Wisdom, as we have come to recognize, is a force of nature with many dimensions. In line with Wisdom School thinking, it would seem that by "seeing" or "experiencing" Wisdom as *a cosmic force in nature,* Job has also experienced God as *present in that force of nature* in its many manifestations. We may discover another dimension of this experience if we return to Job 28 and ask the question: "Where can God be found?"

As we discussed earlier, God is portrayed as the primal scientist exploring creation to discover where Wisdom can be found. Significantly, however, God the Sage discerns the presence of Wisdom in the laws and domains of nature when God is creating them. Clearly, Wisdom as a force of nature and the Creator as the source of nature are closely interrelated. A similar interrelationship is evident in the primordial account in Prov 8.

In sum, innate Wisdom may not only be discerned as the *primal force of nature* but also *the medium through which the spiritual presence of the Creator may be discerned in nature.* Job, it seems, is claiming a dynamic spiritual experience. Discerning Wisdom as a multi-dimensional force of nature encoded throughout creation also involves "seeing" the Creator Spirit throughout the forces in the design of creation. The Wisdom factor and the creation process are integrated dimensions of cosmic ecology; Job's experience of this mystery is identified as "seeing" God.

After seeing the cosmos in all its diversity, wonder and mystery, God is, for Job, no longer located in a celestial court dispensing blessings and curses. Job recognizes that God is present in all the complex worlds of the cosmos, worlds governed by Wisdom. God, in ecological terms, is the spiritual dimension that is interrelated with, and inter-relates, all dimensions of the cosmos and, according to Job, is discernible through the many.

Bibliography

Deane-Drummond, Celia. *Wonder and Wisdom: Conversations in Science, Spirituality and Theology.* Philadelphia: Templeton Foundation Press, 2006.

Flannery, Tim. *Here on Earth: An Argument for Hope.* Melbourne: Text Publishing, 2010.

Habel, Norman. *Discerning Wisdom in God's Creation: Following the Way of Ancient Scientists.* Northcote: Morning Star, 2015.

———. *Finding Wisdom in Nature. An Eco-Wisdom Reading of the Book of Job.* Earth Bible Commentary Series 4. Sheffield: Sheffield Phoenix, 2014.

————. "The Implications of God Discovering Wisdom in Earth." In *Job 28: Cognition in Context,* edited by Ellen van Wolde, 281–98. Biblical Interpretation Series 64. Leiden: Brill, 2003.

————. "Is the Wild Ox Willing to Serve You? Challenging the Mandate to Dominate." In *The Earth Story in Wisdom Traditions,* edited by Norman Habel and Shirley Wurst, 179–189. Earth Bible 3. Sheffield: Sheffield Academic, 2001.

————. "The 'Way' of Things! Earth-Wisdom and Climate Change." In *Climate Change Cultural Change: Religious Responses and Responsibilities,* edited by Anne Elvey and David Gormley-O'Brien, 1–9. Eugene, OR: Wipf & Stock, 2013.

Kalugila, Leonidas. *The Wise King: Studies in Royal Wisdom as Divine Revelation in the Old Testament and Its Environment.* Lund: Gleerup, 1980.

Lenzi, Alan. "Proverbs 8:22–31: Three Perspectives on Its Composition." *JBL* 125 (2006) 687–714.

McKane, William. *Proverbs: A New Approach.* Old Testament Library. Philadelphia: Westminster, 1970.

Rad, Gerhard von. *Wisdom in Israel.* Translated by James Martin. Nashville: Abingdon, 1972.

12

Windows to the Divine Spirit in Creation

Between Species Encounters, Wild Justice and Image Bearing in an Ecological Perspective

Celia Deane-Drummond

H OW IS CREATION REFLECTIVE of God's presence in the world? And more specifically: How do human beings deeply experience that presence? I hope to show in this chapter that such questions are puzzles best understood through the language of wisdom. I am not going to rehearse the fascinating approach to Hebrew wisdom that Norman Habel suggests—in the previous chapter and elsewhere[1]—makes the Hebrews the very first scientists. Rather, this chapter deals with the implications of close observation of the natural world through a wisdom lens arising out of some of the insights of contemporary scientific knowledge. Scientists, of course, as natural scientists today, would resist any sense that the Spirit works as a "life force" in the natural order, a position that, according to Habel, seemed to be presupposed by the Hebrew scientists and their wisdom tradition.

But belief in an active force pushing change in the natural world was a respectable position to hold even during the heated debates in the nineteenth century that followed in the wake of Charles Darwin's publication of the *Origin of Species*. Further, while the fear of "vitalism" is strong among contemporary biologists, long put to bed by a strong theory of natural selection, the possibility of a spiritual dimension as operative in the living world that is not detectable by contemporary science cannot be ruled out of court. And it is significant, also, that many scientists and philosophers are

---

1. See Habel, *Discerning Wisdom*, and previous chapter.

starting to find purely reductionist accounts of the dynamism of the living world rather less than satisfactory, opening up once more the possibility of discourse about the sacred or the transcendent. Finding a way to express what that is and how a sense of transcendence works is a challenge for contemporary theologians, who believe in faith that the Spirit is operative in creation, but still search for a language that still makes sense today.

The specific focus for this chapter is *between species* encounters, especially those between humans and other creatures. Ecotheologians have focused for years on how to think about the interrelation between different creatures and their natural habitat, but getting to the particular implications for how humanity and other creatures might be changed through that encounter is left in the background. And I push this further, too, in arguing that such encounters bring us something of a felt and transformative sense of the divine, the Spirit of God as present to each and every creature and made especially conscious in human minds and hearts. That enlargement of knowing is a form of wisdom, and in so far as it includes a sense of God, it is divine wisdom made manifest.

Perhaps, as a Christian community, we should not forget that Job's insights about God as both natural scientist and sage came in the wake of acute trauma and suffering. Once we tune into what is happening in the world through climate change, that suffering and trauma becomes only too obvious to behold, reverberating in the whole of the created order and especially in the lives of the most vulnerable members of society. What I hope to express here is to show more clearly where God's presence in a community can be witnessed through encounters with other creatures, and how that experience opens up the presence of wisdom. The Spirit of wisdom, then, it seems to me, is a *communal term* that sits at the boundary between creation and new creation, showing forth not just the goodness of creation, but also, in the cases where it is suffering, the possibilities for its redemption.

Encountering Creaturely Others

Vicky Balabanski portrays wonderfully the symbiotic presence of living creatures in each and every living human body with reference to the hymn to wisdom in Col 1.[2] Such intimate relations in us are a hidden presence now made visible by biological science. There is intricate wisdom here, certainly, in the mutual dependence within each complex form of life, for such associations reverberate throughout the creaturely world as we know

2. See next chapter in this volume, Balabanski, "Do not handle, do not taste, do not touch."

it. There are also likely to be many thousands of relations that have not yet been found, given that our own knowledge of different creaturely kinds is still limited. Scientists estimate that only a small fraction of the different creatures in the world come under close scrutiny and study; many are going extinct without even being named or identified. The task that God gave Adam to name the creatures in the Garden of Eden is still unfinished. But what I would like to open up in this chapter is the presence of others on the journey of human becoming: others that exist in communion with human beings in surprising ways. I am going to do that by three case studies on human interspecies relations with hyenas, elephants, and macaque monkeys.

Case Study 1: Hyena Human Relations

Human beings have been associated with hyenas for as long as their history permits. This might seem surprising, since we are used to thinking of hyenas as disgusting animals, associated with carrion and death, animals with whom our only response is likely to be one of fear rather than delight. But I am beginning by naming hyenas deliberately in the context of this chapter, for it is all too easy to romanticize the natural world, especially once we bring in religious and even more constructive theological considerations of the work of the Spirit in creation. The work of the Spirit that surfaces in human encounters, I suggest, is not simply about warm fuzzy relationships with those domesticated animals who have become part of our social world. Rather, it is also those encounters with predators that have shaped who we have become. It is for this reason that deep evolutionary history is highly relevant to a discussion of ecological relations. For if we have little sense of where we have come from, we will not know where we are going.

It is only recently that hyena distribution has become constricted to those areas of the world where we know them today, predominately in the African subcontinent. Even as far back as *4.4 million years* ago there was an association between hyenas and one of the earliest of subspecies or hominins in the *Homo* genus lineage, namely, the *Ardipithecines*. If hyenas had not been present many, many more hominin remains would have turned up; the hyenas crunched up the bone remains as part of their feeding habits. But half a million years later, we find hominin *Australopithecus anamensis* still associated with hyena remains. 3.6 million years ago further evidence for such association continues. Such facts are not contested; there is no doubt that these remains show evidence of mutual interaction in the course of a complex social history that evolutionary biologists term co-evolution. The damaged bones of our earliest ancestors had previously been interpreted as evidence for a violent hominin, a "killer ape," persisting in the literature for three decades. Instead, close examination of the bones revealed they were not killer apes at all, but falling prey to carnivores, and the most likely culprits were leopards and hyenas.

Homo ergaster, *Megantereon whitei* and *Pachycrocuta brevirostris* (giant hyenas almost as tall as the hominins themselves) all co-evolved. Half a million years ago the giant hyenas became extinct and were replaced by spotted hyenas, *Crocuta cocuta*. It is remarkable that the only African species persisting in Europe after the various glacial cycles were hyenas and humans, with hyenas finally disappearing from Europe and Asia a little before ten thousand years ago.[3] Why is this so crucial? I suggest it is crucial because our deep human history has not happened in isolation from other species, but in co-evolutionary contexts, and with, to our present context at least, some surprising others. So while we can use a microscope to look at the way symbiotic species have helped shape why we are alive and make life possible, the lens of deep history brings in another perspective on the dynamics of creation that we can all too easily miss.

Like the symbionts in our bodies, such a view challenges narrowly conceived perceptions of the human as being *most human* in isolation from and in sharp separation from other species. Rather, these companions on our way have helped to shape and re-shape human communities, alongside a mutual human influence on those communities of other animals.

Australian anthropologist Marcus Baynes-Rock has done some fascinating work on human hyena relations in the Muslim town of Harar. He develops an argument for what he terms the "interspecies commons" between humans and hyenas by very close and detailed observations. He describes in great detail a dramatic chain of events after a specific hyena in that town became poisoned. At first the dying hyena attracted the attention not just of the local people, who tried matches, smoke from burning rags, lime, milk, and other attempts to revive the hyena. He noticed that eventually "the large female picked up the hyena in her mouth and marched off into the darkness with him. She was followed by thirty-one other hyenas, growling and whooping, their manes and tails bristling."[4] The story continues. "On the second night after the above incident, there was some unusual activity at the place outside Yusuf's house. One hyena was uttering a series low

3. Baynes-Rock, "Hyenas Like Us," also published as *Among the Bone Eaters*. For discussion of this and other aspects of theological anthropology see Deane-Drummond, *The Wisdom of the Liminal*.

4. Baynes-Rock, "Life and Death in the Multispecies Commons," 210–27. I have discussed this article in more detail in Deane-Drummond, "Deep History, Amnesia and Animal Ethics."

groans while the other hyenas present were agitated. They were scratching at the ground and gathering around at various places, sniffing together."[5] A few minutes later about six hyenas arrived at the normal gathering space of hyenas at the Argobberi gate and appeared in an aggressive relationship with a group of other hyenas.

Baynes-Rock unravels the puzzles of the behavior he observes by considering the social and biological significance of the entangled human-hyena relations. It is important to note that hyenas in Harar are entirely dependent on human food sources. The disappearance of hyenas in other regions of Africa seems to be related to the threat to pastoralists, while in Ethiopia "unlike colonization in other parts of Africa, the Abyssinians did not bring radically new ways of managing the landscape, nor did they bring ideologies of extermination."[6] Lions, which used to prey on hyenas have largely disappeared in this region. Hyenas scavenge on left over carcasses, as well as occasionally breaking into unguarded livestock pens. But hyenas are also fed directly, and the locals exploit this practice as a tourist attraction. The place—Yasuf's house, where the rest of the pack found the poisoned hyena—was one such feeding place. Baynes-Rock suggests that this practice makes the hyenas bolder in the company of people, even though the kind of food they are given is much the same as they would find in garbage dumps by their own scavenging.

The Argobberi gate where the hyenas clashed has a human history, but also a hyena history, as it is the site of exchange between three hyena clans. The different hyena clans occupy different territories in different parts of the town, and enter it through different gates. Human feeding is confined to the Sofi clan, and, on encountering the dying hyena Yusuf assumed the hyenas were Sofi; but Baynes-Rock's observations on the angry reactions of the hyenas made this much less likely. The Aboker hyenas were angry as one of their clan was taken off and presumably killed by the Sofi clan.

Did the Aboker clan know that one of their members was missing? Baynes-Rock refuses to be drawn on this except to say that they would have been aware of the commotion a few nights before which had involved one of their clan, since the feeding place is so close to the Aboker territory. And it is at the Argoberri gate that is the place where disputes between hyena clans are resolved. Baynes-Rock suggests that the Argoberri gate "is a mutually constructed, historicised, politicised, meaningful place in the minds of both hyenas and humans who participate in the dramas which are enacted there."[7]

5. Baynes-Rock, "Life and Death," 213.

6. Ibid., 215.

7. Ibid.," 221.

And in the minds of the local people these spotted hyenas are *agents* just like humans, for, according to them, "hyenas hold meetings, make supplications for food, and communicate detailed messages to conspecifics and to humans who can understand hyena language."[8] They also believe that hyenas will punish other hyenas who attack livestock, and humans who poison or kill hyenas will, in turn, receive retribution. So when the hyena got poisoned the local people treated it like a person in the same situation, since waving a match under the nose is standard treatment in this region for those with an epileptic seizure. Lime-juice is also standard treatment in those cases where a girl has swallowed bleach, which occasionally happens where a girl is forced to marry against her will. The milk was Baynes-Rock's own idea, and Yusuf followed his advice after his own attempts failed.

Hyenas are also thought to be spiritually powerful animals that are able to mediate messages from the local town saints and pass these messages onto people that can understand hyena language. The messages are thought to be quite specific, including information about the number of "*jinn*" in the town, jinn being unseen spirits that can possess their owners or cause mischief. Hyenas are thought to be able to catch and eat jinn. So this also explains the behavior of reciting the Qu'uran after the hyena was taken away by the hyena pack. And it also explains the long-term persistence of hyenas: far from being a threat, they are thought to be able to protect people from negative spiritual forces.

The connection between religious practices and the hyenas understood as agents in a theological drama is fascinating, for it implies that other animals in some sense are viewed as mediating agents with the divine. And it is this mediating influence that also colors Christian religious history as well, for lurking in the story of Adam and Eve we find the ubiquitous appearance of the snake.[9]

Case Study 2: Ethnoelephantology

Elephants also have a long history of association with humans, representing weapons of war, prestige, even symbols of divinity, entertainment, icons of conservation, vehicles for labor, as well as companion animals. As Piers Locke suggests in a review of the current anthropological literature, elephants are "caught up in human enterprises of power, wealth, worship,

8. Ibid.

9. I have commented on the particular significance of this as it relates to Christian teaching about the fall of humanity in Deane-Drummond, "The Birth of Morality and the Fall of Adam."

pleasure, and preservation. Feared or worshipped, killed or conserved, captured or maimed, appropriated for stories and symbols, they are animals with whom humanity is profoundly entangled."[10]

Elephants are capable of considerable learning, retaining and transmitting practical skills and social information. Perhaps most poignant of all, it is the individual personalities of elephants that are capable of influencing patterns of interaction according to particular social conventions in the elephant community. So they can recognize each other as individuals as well as: "appreciate the thoughts and feelings of other sentient beings and engage in strategic behavior. Like humans elephants have a high encephalization quotient (brain/body weight ratio), a highly developed neocortex and a high neuron density, all of which are associated with complex learning skills and behaviors."[11]

Locke makes no hesitation, then, based on his own experience with observing elephants in Chitwan National Park in Nepali, in challenging a common presupposition in much of the scientific and popular literature that animals cannot make judgments based on knowledge of the thoughts or feelings of others, sometimes termed "theory of mind." He adds, "Finally, like humans, elephants grieve for lost friends and relatives."

Locke proposes a research program called *ethnoelephantology* characterized by three principles:[12] (1) subjective agency of both humans and elephants, i.e. both have sentient and affective lifeworlds; (2) coevolution of humans and elephants in their mutually entangled social, historical and ecological relationships; (3) bio-cultural methodology that draws on both the natural and social sciences.

The last remaining wild elephants in China also play a significant, albeit unequal role in the network of interrelationships that link up scientists, government officials, farmers, conservationists and tourists, especially those that deal with elephant-human conflict, species survival and animal welfare. Human decision making about how to act wisely in this particular context is significantly *also* dependent on how elephants themselves act, including more destructive habits such as colliding with cars or destroying houses. Locals claim that elephants' protected status has led to them changing their habits and exploiting their even greater freedom. So in this context human indigenous rights start to be asserted afresh as a further *counter reaction* to elephant destructive behavior.

10. Locke, "Explorations in Ethnoelephantology," 80.

11. Ibid., 79–80.

12. Ibid., 80. Similar arguments have been made for developing ethnoprimatology as developed by Agustin Fuentes in Fuentes, "Naturalcultural Encounters in Bali."

Case Study 3: Macaques & Ethnoprimatology

Agustin Fuentes has conducted a fascinating study of the long-tailed macaques living in the temple forest complex at Padangtegal, Bali. Here the boundary between nature and culture is blurred, so that in "naturalcultural contact zones" we find "subtle behavioral and ecological interactions against the backdrop of the longue durée of human histories and paleohistories."[13] So this is not as simple as either strict competition or purely reciprocal association between humans and other primates. In the temple complexes resident monkey groups are participants in ritual practice.[14] For the Balinese "all actors in this scenario are part of a natural ecology."[15] It is important to stress that as in hyena and elephant cases the macaques are thought of as actors as well. On a biological scale, human alteration of the landscape has shaped the population genetics of the macaques in particular ways, where gene flow is channeled down specific riverine corridors created by the Balinese agricultural system.[16] The main point here is that there is an *interlacing* of human and macaque histories so that their environments are constructed on particular lines, shaped by particular decisions made in human societies.

Theo-drama and the Spirit

I would like to weave in a theological interpretation at this juncture. How might we envisage the particular role of humanity in such exchanges? Where does, in other words, our *particular* responsibility as human beings lie? What does it mean to bear the divine image?[17] My own preference, given the cases I have discussed, is that this makes most sense through the category of *performance*, or *drama*, for the dynamic movement through that drama also speaks of the presence of God in creation. Encounters, be they of joy or suffering, are woven into a theo-drama that reminds us that God is not absent from God's creation, but present with and through

13 Fuentes, "Naturalcultural Encounters in Bali," 606.

14. They are viewed in diverse ways by the Balinese, either as just part of the environment, as a nuisance, or as emissaries of spiritual-natural forces: ibid., 608. Macaques seem largely to be able to anticipate when they are permitted to feast on the food offerings from their experience of human contact.

15. Balinese do not generally distinguish between material or non-material agents, so the natural and supernatural worlds and niches coexist, simultaneously and equally: ibid.

16. Ibid., 609.

17. For full discussion in a more accessible format, see, Deane-Drummond, *Re-Imaging the Divine Image*.

it in the rich entanglements of human and creaturely history. In theological terms this movement reflects an eschatological orientation towards redemption, for theo-drama takes its bearings from the life, passion, death and resurrection of Christ.

But what more specifically do I mean by theo-drama? I take this term from the work of the Swiss Catholic theologian Hans Urs von Balthasar, whose monumental five-volume work on *Theo-Dramatic Theory* was published after his ten-volume work on theological aesthetics, called the *Glory of the Lord*. His own theology, however, said virtually nothing about relationships with other creatures, and concentrated on human history in a much more limited sense, rather than opening this up to wider evolutionary and ecological history.

I take theo-drama as an orientating one for theology, and make it more inclusive. Such a constructive approach is connected with the ecological idea of ecological niche, *oikos* or home, but stresses its forward dynamism. A *niche* in ecology is the living environment in which a particular species is found. Human niche construction that charts the changing ecological relations of the whole system through deep history is not detached from other animal kinds, but as anthropologist Tim Ingold has suggested, in some sense *entangled with* them.

This renders the theo-dramatic task as *inclusive* rather than *exclusive*, a way of seeing the active presence of God in relation to humans and other creaturely kind in terms of *dynamic performance*, incorporating insights from evolutionary science, while still being self aware of different methodological and metaphysical presuppositions. Yet, the relationship between theological and particular biological modes of expression is, I suggest, still importantly an *analogous* one. Talk about God is in a limited sense always *analogous* to what might be found and discovered in the human sphere, as we are using culturally bound *human* language even when speaking of humans as made in the image of God. I am not suggesting here some kind of reduction to a naturalistic view, where the only compass for knowing comes from the scientific world. Rather, the kind of knowledge that theology brings is not just discovered in the created world, but is also *revelatory* knowledge, one that takes religious experience seriously, so orientated on faith in a loving Creator and Redeemer of the world.

In this way, understanding creation through theological reflection can never be reduced to or even contained within evolutionary or anthropological insights. So there are certainly family resemblances in anthropology and the kind of theology I am inviting here, but metaphysical differences as well. Such intersection articulates I believe, in a richer sense what it means to say God is present in creation.

Wild Justice

In the final section of this chapter I am going to build on additional insights on fairness in social communities that come from close observations of the behavior of social animals. Ethologist Marc Bekoff and philosopher Jessica Pierce have discussed social rules of animal societies in their book *Wild Justice*.[18] Bekoff and Pierce define fairness in other social animals as "a desire for equity and a desire for and capacity to share reciprocally;" so reactions to equity in expressions of "pleasure, gratitude and trust" and reactions to inequity, including "retribution, indignation and forgiveness."[19] Some biologists prefer the term *inequity aversion,* rather than the more anthropomorphic language "wild justice."[20] Biologists are hesitant to use the term "freedom" for other animals, preferring the more generic term "agency." Until comparatively recently, most biologists studying social animals hesitated to use the term "justice" when referring to the cluster of behaviors that seem to be connected with a sense of fairness.

Bekoff and Pierce use the following evidence:

a. a keen sense of justice as fairness is universal in humans;

b. even very young babies have a strong sense of fairness even without language; and

c. indicators from direct observation of animal behavior.

Bekoff's close study of play behavior provides an important bridge between a sense of fairness expressed by individual animals in reaction to rewards given to them and others, and particular social rules. The rules of social play depend on fairness, cooperation, and trust; accordingly: "During social play individuals can learn a sense of what's right and wrong—what's acceptable to others—the results of which is the development and maintenance of a social group (a game) that operates efficiently."[21] Animals also learn to take turns and set up "handicaps" in order to make play fair between different ages or sizes. The rules of engagement include: ways of agreeing to play, how

18. Bekoff and Peirce, *Wild Justice*. For further discussion of wild justice, see Deane-Drummond, "Natural Law Revisited."

19. Bekoff and Pierce, *Wild Justice*, 113.

20. Bekoff has defended such use of language in a number of articles, including, for example, Horowitz and Bekoff, "Naturalizing Anthropomorphism." In as much as this language enables a richer understanding of other animal societies, I believe it is justified. The layperson must take care not to assume that what fairness or justice or indignation or even forgiveness means in animal societies is necessarily in direct continuity with that in human societies.

21. Bekoff and Pierce, *Wild Justice*, 116.

hard to bite, avoiding mating attempts, assertion of dominance minimized, and what to do in the event of a mistake.

Play teaches its participants social skills and cements social bonds. By definition, play cannot be unfair—if it were it would become something else and cease to be play. There is even some evidence that play stimulates brain development in young animals and the growth of larger brains.[22] Psychologist Gordon Burghardt finds evidence of play behavior one million years ago, among placental mammals, birds, and even crustaceans.[23]

If, by definition, play cannot be unfair, then it is different from other collective social activities such as caregiving or hunting. Bekoff believes that this makes play a form of wild justice in that it is "a set of social rules and expectations that neutralize differences among individuals in an effort to maintain group harmony."[24] Are these hints in the animal world "justice" or not? I believe the answer is *yes*, as long as it is clear what is meant by the term, and it is clear that justice making in animal societies is not intended to be either identical to *or* necessarily precede that in humans.

Wild justice seems to lack a reflective and deliberative concern for the other that is integral to human justice. Perhaps the best evidence for second order fairness, which is designed to test for sensitivity to inequity observed *in others*, is in Sarah Brosnan and Frans de Waal's work on chimpanzees, where chimpanzees are sensitive not only to inequity in distribution, but inequity in *another's* reward following a task.[25] So those that received grapes (the preferred food) also reacted when their partners received a lower reward for doing the same task. This implies, at least, sensitivity to what the other is receiving—that is, a second order sense of fairness.

Can we go on to say that wild justice reflects the presence of God in creation? My own perception is this. If we are prepared to say that, for example, there is a *quality* to creaturely life and encounters between creatures that speaks of ecological wisdom, then we can pair that with wild justice. How far and to what extent are such forms of wisdom and justice *also* signs of either the presence of God in creation or perhaps the Spirit in a new creation?

I suggest that there are analogous relations between them. So wild justice speaks of God's presence in creation that bears *some relation to* human justice that again bears *some relation to* the eschatological goal of perfect

22. Ibid., 11 8–9.

23. Burghardt, *The Genesis of Animal Play*.

24. Bekoff and Pierce, *Wild Justice*, 121.

25. Brosnan et al., "Mechanisms Underlying Responses to Inequitable Outcomes in Chimpanzees," 1229–37.

Divine Justice. Similarly, ecological wisdom bears *some relation to* human wisdom, which in turn looks to Divine, transcendent Wisdom. Human wisdom therefore occupies a middle space between ecological wisdom and divine Wisdom, and, to some extent, is dependent on both simultaneously. This is true even for those who deny the possibility of transcendent wisdom, since the wisdom arising out of openness to encounters with other creatures is itself a window onto the divine. It may be a clouded window, marred by human sin and the violence that already is present in the natural world, but it still has the capacity to say something about God's presence in the world.

A Christian believer, or perhaps those from other religious traditions, will perceive more in such encounters, but this imaginative religious capacity is itself a corrective to those dogmas that arise when science is falsely assumed to be value free. Science, including ecological science and evolutionary anthropology, no less than philosophy, are therefore like handmaids in the theological birthing of insights arising from paying attention to the created world. A Christian will encounter the natural world with the background belief that God as Trinity is both creator and redeemer, and therefore will already be open to some extent to the possibility of a form of nature mysticism. That divine presence is received by those who are, through a kind of poetic sensitivity, attuned to the pathos of both beauty and horror in the natural world, so, like Gerard Manley Hopkins, ready to consider Christ in all things. The new creation that is dependent on the active presence of the Spirit is not, therefore, presupposing a destruction of the existing order but its renewal. This also fits with the intent of the book of Revelation, where the new heaven and the new earth is not so much a replacement as a *renewed* heaven and earth.

Human beings in the image of God, by mediating between creaturely and divine, occupy a middle ground. Image bearing is about human performance in relation to others, but, as divine image, humans bear a special responsibility to act for the common good as perceived according to divine Wisdom. The common good is not narrowly prescribed in the human community, but opens up in dynamic relation with other creatures. Humans are richly embedded in a life with others. Ethics, in other words, needs to take account of the deep creaturely reality from which we have come, only fragments of which arise through *paying attention* to that world by close and detailed observations and experiential encounters.

If the Christian calling is to see Christ in the suffering face of the downtrodden and the oppressed, then Christ too is the mask through which we can encounter creaturely others. This is, I suggest further, the outcome of a Christology of deep incarnation in practice and not just in theory, for God's agents are multifarious, including those we are least likely to suspect:

the hyenas. And that ability to pay attention to the created order is rooted in that ancient Hebrew tradition of discerning wisdom in God's creation.

Bibliography

Baynes Rock, Marcus. *Among The Bone Eaters: Encounters with Hyenas in Harar.* Pennsylvania: Pennsylvania State University Press, 2015.

———. "Hyenas Like Us: Social Relations with an Urban Carnivore in Harar, Ethiopia." PhD diss., Macquarie University, 2012.

———. "Life and Death in the Multispecies Commons." *Social Science Information* 52.2 (2013) 210–27.

Bekoff, Marc, and Jessica Peirce. *Wild Justice: The Moral Lives of Animals.* Chicago: University of Chicago Press, 2009.

Brosnan Sarah et al. "Mechanisms Underlying Responses to Inequitable Outcomes in Chimpanzees." *Animal Behavior* 79 (2010) 1229–37.

Burghardt, Gordan M. *The Genesis of Animal Play: Testing the Limits.* Cambridge, MA: MIT Press, 2005.

Deane-Drummond, Celia. "The Birth of Morality and the Fall of Adam through an Evolutionary Inter-species Lens." *Theology Today* 72 (2015) 182–93.

———. "Deep History, Amnesia and Animal Ethics: A Case for Inter-Morality." *Perspectives on Science and Christian Faith* 67.4 (2015) 1–9.

———. "Natural Law Revisited: Wild Justice and Human Obligations for Other Animals." *Journal for the Society for Christian Ethics* 35.2 (2015) 159–73.

———. *Re-Imaging the Divine Image: Humans and Other Animals.* Kitchener, ON: Pandora, 2014.

———. *The Wisdom of the Liminal: Evolution and Other Animals in Human Becoming.* Grand Rapids: Eerdmans, 2014.

Fuentes, Agustin. "Naturalcultural Encounters in Bali: Monkeys, Temples, Tourists and Ethnoprimatology." *Cultural Anthropology* 25 (2010) 600–24.

Habel, Norman, *Discerning Wisdom in God's Creation: Following the Way of Ancient Scientists.* Northcote: Morning Star, 2015.

Horowitz Alexandra and Marc Bekoff. "Naturalizing Anthropomorphism: Behavioral Prompts to Our Humanizing of Animals." *Anthrozoos* 20 (2007) 23–35.

Locke, Piers. "Explorations in Ethnoelephantology: Social, Historical, and Ecological Intersections Between Asian Elephants and Humans." *Environment and Society: Advances in Research* Vol. 4 (2013) 79–97.

Part 5

Eco-Readings In Creation

13

"Do not handle, do not taste, do not touch" (Col 2:21)

Rediscovering our *Selves* as Community, in Order to Re-imagine our Interconnectedness with Creation

Vicky Balabanski

Introduction

IN 1962 ON AUSTRALIAN television, an advertisement for *Mortein* insecticide went to air. The jingle was an early contribution of Bryce Courtenay[1]:

I'm Louie the Fly, Louie the Fly,

Straight from rubbish tip to you.

Spreading disease with the greatest of ease,

Straight from rubbish tip to you.

I'm bad and mean and mighty unclean,

Afraid of no-one, except the man with the can of *Mortein*.

Hate that word *Mortein*.

One spray and Louie the Fly

1. Bryce Courtenay emigrated from South Africa via the U.K. to Australia in 1958. The first Louie the Fly advertisement was launched in 1957; Courtenay's advertising brilliance took the concept and transformed it to great effect.

173

(Apple of his old mother's eye was Louie).

Poor dead Louie, Louie the Fly, a victim of *Mortein. Mortein!*[2]

The advertisement shows a sleeping baby under siege from Louie's trail of dirt. It has become something of a cultural icon in Australia, and has given rise to further iterations of Louie the Fly advertisements right up to the present, not only in Australia, but also in India, Pakistan, Bangladesh, many Middle Eastern countries and more recently in South East Asia.

For those of us who grew up with Louie the Fly advertisements, it evokes feelings of pleasure, amusement and nostalgia. There is something delightful in Louie's death throes. But notice those words with which Louie describes himself: "Bad and mean and mighty unclean." Those words evoke concepts of danger, pollution and contagion. The words appear to be about hygiene, but their potency draws on cultural and spiritual roots that shape our perception of the world around us.[3] What is "bad and mean and mighty unclean" is learned in early childhood, before there is a neat division between scientific and spiritual concepts. Even for the adult viewers of that 1962 advertisement who were of course aware of the bacterial transmission of disease, there was no neat distinction between issues of hygiene and the sacred trust that is invested in parents to protect a helpless infant from danger. It was in the very blurring of those categories that the power of the imagery lay—the message appears to be about rescuing an infant from the dangers of the world. The 1962 advertisement also had an element of humorous compassion—the death throes of Louie are charmingly memorable, and the mock dirge or lament for Louie as the "apple of his old mother's eye" is a powerful element that is lacking in the subsequent iterations of Louie. The more recent scripts clearly do not want to mitigate our disgust at Louie's filth with this element of compassion.[4]

---

2. The advertisement can be viewed on You Tube, https://www.youtube.com/watch?v=UupBBVDXol4, starting at 1.09 minutes. This and all websites cited in this paper were accessed 24 April 2016 to reconfirm their accuracy and currency.

3. This is recognized by Mary Douglas as she sets out ideas of secular defilement: "There are two notable differences between our contemporary European ideas of defilement and those, say, of primitive cultures. One is that dirt avoidance for us is a matter of hygiene or aesthetics and is not related to our religion . . . The second difference is that our idea of dirt is dominated by the knowledge of pathogenic organisms. The bacterial transmission of disease was a great nineteenth-century discovery. It produced the most radical revolution in the history of medicine. So much has it transformed our lives that it is difficult to think of dirt except in the context of pathogenicity. Yet obviously our ideas of dirt are not so recent. We must be able to make the effort to think back beyond the last 100 years and to analyze the bases of dirt-avoidance, before it was transformed by bacteriology . . ." Douglas, *Purity*, 36.

4. Intriguingly, I think that excising the (mock) compassion has reduced the power

The reason that I begin here is that our attitude to Louie the Fly is comparable to our attitude to other "bugs"—the bacteria that surround and inhabit us. With the exception of those specific bacteria in certain foods like yoghurt and cheese, bacteria are widely perceived as "bad and mean and mighty unclean." Never before in the history of the world has the human population been so focused on sanitizing our surroundings with anti-bacterial and anti-microbial products. There are anti-bacterial soaps and body-washes, antibacterial creams and paints and household cleaners, and anti-bacterial plastics. There are some contexts like hospitals where such products are vital, but the fact that we are tackling general hygiene this way suggests that we perceive the microbial world as a threat.

This is particularly striking given that each of us is home to some hundred trillion microbes—vastly more than the human population of the earth. Those hundred trillion microbes are our constant companions and collectively constitute our life support system.[5]

This chapter develops the premise that we humans have lost touch with our interconnectedness with creation, the creation that we can see, hear, touch, smell, and taste. In fact we are yet to grasp our interconnectedness with the vast creation that is not accessible to our senses—the nano-cosmos which lives in and on us. We are intimately connected with and dependent on our internal and external microbial community for our health and well-being, yet we conceptualize our relationship with microbes as a constant defensive war against invasion. With a few notable exceptions, our culture currently calls on us to view bacteria as "bad and mean and mighty unclean." While science is progressing in leaps and bounds to show us that in fact bacteria are crucial for health and well-being, there is a cultural disconnect with nano-creation that inhibits us from seeing the world as an interconnected whole. Or to put it theologically, we find it very difficult to grasp that "all things, in heaven and on earth—things visible *and invisible*—all things have been created through Christ and for Christ" (Col 1:16).[6]

The first section of this chapter examines biblical concepts of purity, pollution and contagion, looking first at the Levitical purity code, and then at Jesus' attitude to these issues. On this basis I then turn to the letter to the Colossians, where we find the new community of Christ's followers grappling with what they may handle, taste and touch (Col 2:21). We meet them as a community of people who are re-configuring themselves in relation to

---

of the advertisement.

5. See a summary of the findings of the Human Microbiome Project in Kolata, "In Good Health?"

6. This and all quotations from the Bible are drawn from the NRSV unless otherwise indicated.

the cosmos and learning to perceive themselves as safely connected with all things, the whole cosmos, in Christ. After this, I gather the strands covered thus far. Then in the final part of this chapter I draw out some practical implications of the theological insights for how we live. While I draw on scientific research, this chapter is essentially a contribution to biblical eco-theology/eco-hermeneutics.

Purity, Pollution and Contagion

Levitical Purity

Concepts of purity and pollution are deeply embedded in the biblical tradition. In Leviticus, an ancient priests' manual, the priests are charged not only with ritual actions in relation to the sanctuary, but also to teach the people of Israel to "distinguish between the holy and the common, and between the clean and the unclean" according to the statutes they have received through Moses (Lev 10:10–11). The two pairs of antonyms—holy and common, clean and unclean—are not simply two ways of describing the same set, as though holy means clean and common means unclean.[7] There are things that are clean and common—in fact we might say that this was most of daily life for the people of Israel. And then there are holy things which, in the wrong place, at the wrong time or with the wrong people, "defile the hands" and render the person unclean. The two axes which define the world prove more complex than meets the eye.

The clean and the unclean encompass bodily states that involve death, blood, semen, and scale-disease. This affects human beings, but it also encompasses the paraphernalia of life—houses, water cisterns, clothes, crockery and other articles. The clean/unclean distinction relates to all living creatures—animals, birds, and insects; it is an ancient form of classification or taxonomy, which does not allow easy explanation.[8]

The holy pertains to God, to the place where God's presence is perceived and sought, particularly the sanctuary in earlier times and later the Jerusalem Temple. The holy or sacred also pertains to the people and things that are set apart for God's purposes. Holiness is both a ritual and an ethical reality; to transgress it can mean death.[9] Holiness can be thought of as a

7. Milgrom, "Rationale," 108.

8. See for example Kugler, "Holiness." Kugler distinguishes the purity system of Lev 1–16 from Lev 17–26, arguing that the latter represents a democratization and laicization of holiness.

9. Aaron's two oldest sons, Nadab and Abihu, next in importance after Moses and Aaron, took a censer/pan and offered incense on *unauthorized coals*; "fire came

series of concentric circles with the sanctuary at the center, the land of Israel as a wider circle and the earth and its inhabitants as an outer circle. Concentric circles also help us conceptualize the ancient biblical view of humanity, with priests at the center, people of Israel further out and all humanity further out still. The animal world can be thought of in this way as well, with the sacrificial animals (which are edible, domesticated and unblemished) at the center, clean animals further out, and unclean and wild animals on the periphery.[10]

I want to set out a particular aspect of biblical holiness, via the issue of contagion.[11] If something is contagious, it passes on an aspect of itself, for good or for ill. We can think of a contagious laugh that sets people smiling; and of course we readily think of a contagious disease that infects those who come in contact with it. The biblical purity and pollution statutes are premised on a contagious world—a world in which impurity is contagious between people, clothing, objects and houses, and people's impure ethical behavior can infect the land and the sanctuary.

It is also a world in which holiness is contagious. God is holy, so the people of God are to be holy (Lev 11:43–45; 19:2). This is not just an exhortation, but articulates that what the people do directly affects God's holiness:

> You shall not make yourselves detestable with any creature that swarms; you shall not defile yourselves with them, and so become unclean. For I am the Lord your God; sanctify yourselves therefore, and be holy, for I am holy. You shall not defile yourselves with any swarming creature that moves on the earth. For I am the Lord who brought you up from the land of Egypt, to be your God; you shall be holy, for I am holy. (Lev 11:43–45)

This is a contagious world. Touching sacred ash from the burnt offering transferred holiness, but not in a risk free way; this holiness transfer had to be managed with great care (Lev 6:8–11). The holiness of the land sets apart not only its citizens, but aliens as well (Lev 18:25–29), and the contagion can go both ways.

This is a worldview in which both the contagion of impurity and the contagion of holiness affects all people, all creatures and all objects, including the land itself; and people were schooled to see—for better or worse—everything as interconnected. There were no isolated actions; every ritual

---

out from the presence of the Lord and consumed them, and they died before the Lord" (Lev 10:1–2).

10. Milgrom, *Leviticus*, 722–25.

11. See the discussion by Majer, "Contagions."

and moral action could either maintain the holiness of the community, or could endanger the community though contagion.[12]

Jesus' Approach

When we turn to Jesus' relationship to the system of holiness, purity, impurity and contagion, it would be wrong to think that Jesus critiqued it as an outsider. Jesus was concerned for the holiness of God's name; he taught his disciples to pray as their very first petition that God's name be hallowed (Mt 6:9).[13] However we can say with certainty that Jesus spent a great deal of time with the very people that the system declared unclean. Jesus touched them, ate in their houses (Mk 14:3), and he did not spend time constantly ritually cleansing himself. Jesus shifted the focus of purity from outward to inward; we might say that Jesus radicalized[14] (or perhaps spiritualized[15]) the purity statutes. While his actions were offensive to the religious elite, the fact that he didn't live within the purity code probably wasn't very surprising or shocking to the peasants who gathered around him, and who were constantly in contact with bodily secretions and other things that rendered them unclean.[16]

There were various views among Jesus' educated contemporaries about the flow of contagion.[17] Jesus' actions show that he did not see the contagion of the unclean flowing back toward the holiness of God and sullying it. Jesus modeled a different perception (Mk 7:17–23): "whatever goes into a person

12. Much important research has been done on purity as the core value structuring the social world of Israel and as an ideology of the ruling elites. See for example Borg, *Contemporary Scholarship*, 107–12.

13. There is good reason to affirm that Jesus sent the lepers he healed to undergo the ritual process of being declared clean by the priests (Mark 1:40–44; Matt 8:2–4), and if that process was by-passed by the healed person (as it was in Mark's account), this does not prove that Jesus was intent on dismantling the purity system.

14. Borg, *New Vision*, 110.

15. Ibid., 140.

16. So Rohrbaugh, "Social Location," 158.

17. That the statues concerning purity were contested among the first century sages is indicated by the disputes recorded in *m. Yadayim* 4:6–7: "The Sadducees say, We cry out against you, O ye Pharisees, for ye say, 'The Holy Scriptures render the hands unclean', [and] 'the writings of Hamiram do not render the hands unclean.'" See http://www.sefaria.org/Mishnah_Yadayim.4.6?lang=en&layout=lines&sidebarLang=all. According to the Pharisees, sacred Scriptures' holiness is contagious (and therefore has to be handled with great care and respect), whereas secular writings are common but not unclean. See the discussion in Cohen, *Three Crowns*, 131–33.

from outside cannot defile . . . It is what comes out of a person that defiles." By that he doesn't mean bodily secretions, but evil intentions and actions.

Jesus modeled the conviction that God's holiness has the power to infect the unholy and impure, re-sanctifying them to receive God's grace. The fear of contagion, which had kept the boundaries secure between Jew and Gentile, pure and impure, men and women, clean and unclean animals, began to be dismantled. Jesus' ministry re-defined the understanding of contagion, with the power of God's gracious holiness primarily a movement from the divine to the unclean, not from the unclean to the divine.

Jesus did not live as though the unclean were contagious. Instead he modeled a world in which sacred contagion only moved toward the needy and the marginalized, not from them to God. For Jesus, God's holiness was not vulnerable to human sin and distortion; it was powerful to reach out and embrace the unlovely, the blemished and unclean.

No wonder he was accused of being a friend of tax collectors and sinners. The ritually pure, those with full health and right standing did not welcome Jesus' type of good news. They saw it as transgressing their connection with the Holy God, the Holy Sanctuary and the Holy Land. They saw it as inciting people to break the covenant which lay at the heart of the community's identity as God's people. This called into question the sort of interconnected world that they had been taught according to the Levitical commandments (Lev 10:10–11)—a world in which ritual and ethical transgressions against the laws endangered not only the individuals who committed them, but the community as a whole. What they perceived in Jesus was a man inciting people to transgression, and the crowds—who didn't know any better—being misled.

In fact, what proved to be contagious was Jesus' teaching and example. It was a contagion that even his humiliating and unclean death did not put a stop to—the contagion of a Gospel which redefined the nexus between God's holiness and human holiness. We (Gentiles) are beneficiaries of that change—we venture across boundaries into the sacred with the assurance that the Holy God has torn open that veil and welcomed us in.

But alongside the liberation, healing and hope that this Gospel brought to the unclean and the marginalized, there was also an unexpected shadow. Just how the world was interconnected was no longer clear. Jesus broke the holiness connection—sacred people, sacred land, sacred God—in favor of a sanctifying God reaching out to unclean people and places. But was there now any sense of interconnection between people and place? I put that question on hold for a moment.

Colossians

I want to fast forward now some twenty years to a small city in the broad Lycus River valley in Asia Minor, modern Turkey. It is a city of diverse shrines, surrounded by thriving agriculture and a center of a distinctive black wool industry. The city's name is Colossae. Alongside the river god of the Lycus, the regional goddess of fertility "Great Mother" Cybele and the Phrygian god Mên,[18] there is also a Jewish synagogue at Colossae, as there is in most urban centers in the region. For the synagogue members in Colossae, statues about holiness could no longer simply be about the interconnection between God's holiness, the people's holiness and the land of Israel, as set out in Leviticus. Issues of purity, pollution and contagion had to do with identity in a context far removed from the Holy Land; for them, these issues were about marking the boundary between the worship of the God of Israel and worship of the many gods of their neighbors.

Into this mix of cultures and layers of identity, someone by the name of Epaphras arrived in Colossae[19] proclaiming the good news of Jesus Christ, and gathered some Gentiles who received his message gladly. Epaphras proclaimed this good news in keeping with the message of Paul and his associates (Col 1:7–8). Those Gentiles who were willing to receive the grace of God through the death and resurrection of Jesus were not required to practice the purity regulations of the Jewish statutes. Through their baptism they had been buried with Christ and had died to those statutes and their requirements: "So if you have been raised with Christ, seek the things that are above, where Christ is, seated at the right hand of God. Set your minds on things that are above, not on things that are on earth, for you have died, and your life is hidden with Christ in God" (Col 3:1–3).

Because they had died through baptism, the Levitical statutes were no longer boundary markers for them. Theirs is now a spiritual circumcision: "In him also you were circumcised with a spiritual circumcision, by putting off the body of the flesh in the circumcision of Christ; when you were buried with him in baptism, you were also raised with him through faith in the power of God, who raised him from the dead" (Col 2:11–12).

But at the time when the letter to the Colossians was written, Epaphras was no longer in Colossae to offer guidance, and the letter reflects the fact that this fledgling Christian community was turning for guidance to the synagogue and its boundary-marking practices. This must have seemed to those early Gentile believers to be a logical step—after all, they had been

18. Cadwallader, *Fragments*, 49–52.

19. Epaphras had also worked in the other cities in the region—Laodicea and Hierapolis, according to Col 4:12–13.

grafted into the worship of the God of Israel, and their closest allies were their neighbors at the Jewish synagogue.

In Colossians chapter 2 we see that the Colossian Christians were adopting particular practices in relation to food and drink, and in observing festivals, new moons and Sabbaths. Col 2:16–17 states: "Therefore do not let anyone condemn you in matters of food and drink or of observing festivals, new moons, or Sabbaths. These are only a shadow of what is to come, but the substance belongs to Christ."

It seems that they have already adopted practices around what may be handled, tasted and touched: "Why do you submit to regulations, 'Do not handle, Do not taste, Do not touch'? All these regulations refer to things that perish with use; they are simply human commands and teachings" (Col 2:20–22).

Circumcision is also an issue; Col 2:11 affirms that they have already been "circumcised with a spiritual circumcision, by putting off the body of the flesh in the circumcision of Christ." If they have spiritual circumcision, why should they be considering undergoing physical circumcision? Colossians experts may object at this point that I am oversimplifying the problems at Colossae, which appear to have both a Jewish and a pagan set of issues, evident in the mention of philosophy (Col 2:8), the elements of the cosmos (Col 2:8 and 2:20a),[20] ascetic practices, angelic worship (Col 2:18)[21] and visions (Col 2:18). I take these to be practices by which the Colossian believers were seeking to sanctify themselves, fearing that they may in the end be disqualified from the sacred presence of God. They were "allowing themselves to be disqualified" (Col 2:18).

---

20. Col 2:8 and 2:20a refer to the *stoicheia* of the cosmos, which is translated in the NRSV as "elemental spirits." The meaning of this term is much disputed, and the interpretation of it in this context is closely related to the wider question of what the "Colossian problem" actually was more generally. Were these new Gentile believers succumbing to certain pagan deities or practices? A fuller discussion of this issue lies beyond the scope of this chapter. However, I consider this term is better translated as "elementary principles" or the "rudiments." These same words—the "basic elements of the world"—were used by Paul in Gal 4:3, where they described the sorts of practices that were our task masters while we were minors, namely the Jewish purity laws and customs. In Colossians as in Galatians, the phrase "elementary principles of the cosmos" therefore can best be understood as describing the views and practices that no longer govern those who have died with Christ in baptism.

21. "Worship of angels" or "angelic worship" (*thrēskeia tōn angelōn*) can be understood as a subjective or objective genitive. If the issue were one of idolatry or participation in pagan (or heterodox Jewish) practices of worshipping angels, one would expect a greater level of attention given to it. It is mentioned in passing, and I take it as a subjective genitive—striving to participate in a level of worship of God truly associated with angels.

The clustering of issues about food and drink, Sabbath observance, the concern with handling and bodily contact and the reference to circumcision all suggest strongly that the new Christ followers at Colossae were developing their practices according to what their Jewish neighbors condemned or recommended. That would mean seeking to live inside the boundaries of the purity code and rejecting a world full of unclean people, animals, objects and food.

The letter to the Colossians urges them not to see either their bodies or the cosmos that way. Instead, it calls on them to see that "all things in heaven and on earth were created [through Christ], things visible and invisible, whether thrones or dominions or rulers or powers—all things have been created through him and for him" (Col 1:16). They can be confident that because all things have been created through Christ and for Christ, nothing need be feared as unclean or impure. They share their origin with all things in heaven and on earth in Christ. This is part of the mystery of God that they share: the world is interconnected—not through purity, pollution and contagion, but through Christ. This interconnection is described quite literally in bodily terms. Colossians 2:9 states that "in Christ, the whole fullness of deity dwells *bodily*." The word "bodily" (*sōmatikōs*) is in an emphatic position in the Greek. Notice the present tense of the verb: dwells, not dwelt. This is not an affirmation just of Christ's incarnation,[22] but of the ongoing embodied presence of Christ here, now and everywhere. This is a remarkably biological way of talking about the presence of Christ, and it's a phrase worth meditating on: in Christ, the whole fullness of deity dwells bodily! The whole creation is in view! Col 2:9 challenges us to perceive Christ's presence in all things, not just in other human beings, and not just in a disembodied way. Christ is the one through whom all things in heaven and on earth were created, and in Christ the whole fullness of deity continues to live (*katoikei*) bodily.

The passage goes on to address our bodiliness: just as the whole *fullness* of deity dwells bodily in Christ, we too are described as having come to *fullness* in him (Col 2:10). Instead of the Levitical connection between a holy God and a holy people, this letter connects the whole fullness of God with fullness of God's people. There is an echo of Ps 24:1 (LXX Ps 23:1): the Earth is the Lord's and its *fullness*. This is a different type of interconnected world, not connected through holiness, purity and contagion, but through the fullness of Christ.

The passage goes on to urge the believers to see that they have fulfilled the holiness code by being buried with Christ in baptism. This is described

---

22. Cf. Col 1:22

as a spiritual circumcision, the circumcision of Christ. Baptism is a symbolic and spiritual dying, a symbolic and spiritual putting off the body of flesh. Through this act of identification with Christ's death, God raises us beyond the demands of the Levitical statutes (Col 2:13–14).

The passage has spoken of the bodily presence of God in Christ and our own bodies as mirroring that presence. It also talks of the community of God's people as a body, which holds fast to the head, "from whom the whole body, nourished and held together by its ligaments and sinews, grows with a growth that is from God" (Col 2:19).

This is a wonderfully interconnected vision of reality. I think it is a vision that has not yet shaped Christians' view of ourselves in relation to the cosmos deeply enough. We have tended to compartmentalize biological and spiritual aspects of reality, as though they exist on different planes. But the genuine bodiliness of Christ in the incarnation is connected with the ongoing *bodily* presence of Christ in all things, which were created through him and for him.

Gathering the Strands

To draw some threads together, I have set out biblical models of how God, humanity, and the rest of creation are connected. The first is what I have called contagion: God's holiness sets apart places, people, animals and objects to participate in God's sacredness. In both continuity and discontinuity with that, the second model is how Jesus lived out God's holiness, demonstrating that it embraced the blemished and the unclean, and showing that it was not limited to the sacred sphere or land, but reached out in grace and mercy to invite all people, all places and all creatures to participate. The third model is the one articulated in Colossians, which affirms that in Christ Jesus, we see the invisible God revealed—made visible—the God who creates, sustains and reconciles all things. Here Christ is seen as the mystery of God's presence and saving power throughout the world. We can call this a model of interconnection, with Christ now understood cosmically, and the church as those who are sanctified into the mystery of Christ (Col 1:26–27). I posed the question earlier as to how God, people and place can be seen as interconnected once the purity code is dismantled. I think this vision of the Cosmic Christ offers an answer.

In each of the biblical models we glimpse a God who is holy, transcendent, and beyond our capacity to comprehend. Each model affirms God's immanence as well, though in different ways—the first with great fear and awe in the face of the sacred, the second with great compassion and love, and the third by explicitly affirming God's immanence in all things (Col 1: 15–20).[23] I think that the third model remains very difficult for us to grasp.[24]

It may be that science can help us grasp this interconnected vision in a new and deeper way, through seeing ourselves each as an eco-system. Claire Ainsworth describes the work of the International Human Microbiome Consortium, which aims to identify and study all the microbes living in and on our bodies:

> It is transforming our understanding of the organisms that colonize our gut. It turns out that the "germs" we do our best to exterminate with antibacterial sprays are not our enemies after all. In fact, we are locked in an intimate and vital relationship with them, and it shapes our physical development, helps train our immune systems and equips us with a set of metabolic abilities we would otherwise lack. Each of us is part of a vast and complex microbe-human ecosystem—less an individual than a "superorganism." This realization is forcing researchers to develop a more holistic approach to studying human biology . . .[25]

Each of us—each individual—is a nano-cosmos, an inter-connected reality. The word individual—which literally means *inseparable*—reminds us that we aren't separate from the wider Earth community. The boundaries of the self are equally inseparable from the miniature cosmos of living creatures for which we provide a home. If we can imagine our bodies as an interconnected reality in themselves, which rely upon our interconnection with the Earth community, we may be able to conceptualize something more of the way the transcendent God is present to and in all things; the bodily presence of the Cosmic Christ to which Col 2:9 refers: "in Him the whole fullness of deity—the divine presence—dwells bodily."

Conclusion

In the final part of this chapter, I am going to explore what it means to live as community—not just with other humans or other creatures we encounter—but with our *selves,* including our constituent members. First I want to invite you to imagine this with me.

23. Col 1:23 even states that this good news has been proclaimed to "every creature under heaven."

24. Rohr states that "It seems that either we acknowledge that God is in all things or we have lost the basis for seeing God in anything, including ourselves." *Hope*, 136.

25. Ainsworth, "Gut Reactions." She goes on to say, "We may soon be worrying as much about the biodiversity inside our bodies as we do about our external environment."

Let's stop for a moment and think about ourselves as a community of 100,000,000,000,000 microbes living and working together. Can we think of them with acceptance? Thankfulness? Can we view them with compassion? Can we acknowledge that we are community?

What if we acknowledge that our microbial citizens play a part in who we are? What we avoid? What we enjoy?

What if God is not only the God of humanity, but of the microbial world as well? Can we imagine ourselves as a cosmos, and as part of an interconnected world, connected by God's impulse to life and energy to love?

And finally, if we can find compassion for our own microbial cosmos—can we find it also for microbes beyond ourselves?

I want to return to talking about dirt. There is a bacterium found in soil, which, when it comes into contact with us, has a positive, even vital effect on us. *Mycobacterium vaccae,* this friendly bacterium, was shown in 2007 to have an anti-depressant effect, activating brain cells to produce the brain chemical serotonin.[26] Lead author of this study, Dr Chris Lowry from Bristol University said, "These studies help us understand how the body communicates with the brain and why a healthy immune system is important for maintaining mental health. They also leave us wondering if we shouldn't all be spending more time playing in the dirt."[27]

What does the biblical witness say? "you are dust, and to dust you shall return" (Gen 3:19).

Instead of spending time playing in the dirt, we are much more inclined to reject our connection with the dust and ask for a nice clean tablet. Scientist Charles Akle, who is the chair of Immodulon Therapeutics, a biopharmaceutical company in London,[28] is on record as suggesting that "if the precise mechanism [by which *Mycobacterium vaccae* affects mood] can be uncovered, it might be possible to develop drugs that mimic the bacterium's effect."[29]

While I am absolutely in favor of scientific research into such mechanisms and in favor of developing new medicines, I want to suggest that in an interconnected world, a drug developed to mimic the effect of a soil bacterium will never have the same life-giving effect as cultivating an interconnected lifestyle. The good which follows when we allow our own microbial community to spend time with old microbial friends in the soil is not just a

26. Lowry, "Identification."

27. Paddock, "Soil Bacteria."

28. Immodulon Therapeutics is a private biopharmaceutical company developing novel immunotherapeutic products for cancer.

29. Geddes, "Infectious moods."

simple chemical mechanism. It's an interconnected biological exchange. We need to return to the garden. We need to learn and relearn our friendship with the whole earth community, the very soil itself, if we are to teach our children the kinship of all creation.

I want to conclude with one practical suggestion. One act of befriending the microbial world that is in keeping with the Christian tradition is to choose to be buried. Instead of expending the huge load of energy required to cremate our body, imagining that we are not part of the microbiome, we can choose to allow our bodies to decompose. I have booked a site on the Yorke Peninsula, South Australia, a place on and in the earth that has special significance to me. After all, "I am dust, and to dust I shall return."

I hope that as part of rediscovering the spiritual in God's Creation, we can live as creatures who have a deep and abiding connection with the soil. Maybe one day we may even discover that Louie the Fly and his trail of soil has a place in God's interconnected world.[30]

Bibliography

Ainsworth, Claire. "Gut Reactions: The Microbes that Make You." *New Scientist* 2812, 11 May 2011. www.newscientist.com/article/mg2102812 2–6 00-gut-reactions-the-microbes-that-make-you.

Borg, Marcus J. *Jesus: A New Vision.* San Francisco: Harper & Row, 1987.

———. *Jesus in Contemporary Scholarship.* Valley Forge, PA: Trinity, 1994.

Cadwallader, Alan H. *Fragments of Colossae: Sifting through the Traces.* Hindmarsh: ATF, 2015.

Cohen, Stuart A. *The Three Crowns: Structures of Communal Politics in Early Rabbinic Jewry.* Cambridge: Cambridge University Press, 1990.

Douglas, Mary. *Purity and Danger: An Analysis of Concepts of Pollution and Taboo.* London: Routledge, 2001.

Geddes, Linda, "Infectious Moods: The Happiness Injection." *New Scientist* 2795, 19 January 2011. www.newscientist.com/article/dn19951-infectious-moods-the-happiness-injection/.

Kolata, Gina. "In Good Health? Thank Your 100 Trillion Bacteria." *The New York Times*, 13 June, 2012. www.nytimes.com/2012/06/14/health/human-microbiome-project-decodes-our-100-trillion-good-bacteria.html?_r=4&ref=science.

Kugler, Robert A. "Holiness, Purity, the Body, and Society: The Evidence for Theological Conflict in Leviticus." *JSOT* 76 (1997) 3–27.

Landau, Elizabeth. "I Won the Nobel by Experimenting on Myself." In *New Scientist*, 2981, 9 August 2014. www.newscientist.com/article/mg22329814–900-i-won-the-nobel-by-experimenting-on-myself.

---

30. The intention of this essay is not to downplay the importance of hygiene, nor to argue that all bacteria are "friendly." However, even "unfriendly" bacteria such as the *Helicobacter pylori* which causes peptic ulcers is being investigated as potentially having immune benefits by Nobel Prize winner Barry Marshall. See Landau, "Nobel," 25.

Lowry, Christopher A., et al., "Identification of an Immune-Responsive Mesolimbo-cortical Serotonergic System: Potential Role in Regulation of Emotional Behavior." *Neuroscience* 146 (2007) 756–72. www.sciencedirect.com/science/article/pii/S0306452207001510.

Majer, Gerald "On Contagions: Leviticus and the Fascination of the Abomination." *Journal for Cultural and Religious Theory* 2.2 (2001) www.jcrt.org/archives/02.2/index.shtml.

Milgrom, Jacob. *Leviticus 1–16*. Anchor Bible 3. New York: Doubleday, 1991.

———. "The Rationale for Biblical Impurity." *JANESCU* 22 (1993) 107–11

Paddock, Catharine. "Soil Bacteria Work in Similar Way to Antidepressants." *Medical News Today*. 2 April 2007. www.medicalnewstoday.com/articles/66840.php.

Rohr, Richard, and John B. Feister. *Hope against Darkness: The Transforming Vision of Saint Francis in an Age of Anxiety*. Cincinnati: St Anthony Messenger, 2003.

Rohrbaugh, Richard L. "Social Location: Jesus' World." In *The Social World of the New Testament: Insights and Models*, edited by Jerome H. Neyrey and Eric C. Stewart, 141–62. Peabody, MA: Hendricksen, 2008.

14

Who Stirs Up the Sea so that its Waves Roar?

The Interconnectedness of All Reality in Jeremiah 31:35–37

Emily Colgan

FOR MORE THAN TWO decades now, scientific leaders have warned that climate change is real and it is already causing irrevocable damage to the planet. Where questions of human complicity once dominated the climate change discourse, scientific consensus now holds humanity responsible. Debate no longer centers primarily around whether or not climate change exists, or even whether humanity can avert it; rather, the dialogue has become one of mitigating the potentially catastrophic consequences of this global shift. Yet despite climate change being acknowledged as among the most critical issues faced by the Earth community, this unprecedented threat to the planet has failed to galvanize humanity, and the global environmental situation does not seem to be improving. Scientific fact alone, it seems, is not enough to counter what Thomas Berry calls the "deep cultural pathology" that enables humanity to cause such damage without thought of long-term consequence.[1]

For these warnings to challenge the well-established patterns of human ecology, it seems they must also find a degree of coherence with the religious and philosophical foundations that underlie the way in which human communities perceive themselves and their relationship to the surrounding environment. In this article I suggest that such coherence can be

1. Berry, "Into the Future," 410.

found in the depiction of an interconnected reality in Jer 31:35–37. It is my contention that an ecological reading of these verses reveals a rhetorical vision of relationality which has the capacity to contribute positively to the formation and sustenance of an alternative ecological sensibility for Christian communities.

Invitation and Response:
Non-hierarchical Relationality in Jer 31:35

My reading is located within the Book of Restoration, a collection of texts located at the periphery of the Jeremianic imagination in their emphasis on re-assurance and hope. The interaction between God and Cosmos in 31:35 is initially evident at a structural level, as verbs of action and encounter characterize the parallelism which constitutes the core of the verse:

YHWH

gives (lit. "gives," *nātan*)	the Sun	to light	by day
(and)	the Moon and Stars	to light	the night
stirs up (*rāga'*)	the Sea	to roar	its waves

YHWH

Although the verbs "to give" and "to stir" have been translated variously to support the anthropocentric agenda, a close examination of these terms from an ecological perspective yields new insights which confound conventional interpretations of a one-way relationship between God (as Maker/Designer/Agent) and the material realm (that which has been made/designed). Translations of the verb *nātan*, for example, range from "fixed" (NET) and "established," (JSB) to "appoints" (NIV) and "command[s]," (CEV), renderings which imply the authoritative action of a deity who is extrinsic to the creative process being described. In this interpretation, however, I have chosen to nuance the literal translation of *nātan* (to give),[2] using instead the verb "to enable." This translation picks up on and makes explicit the suggestion—implied in the verb "to give"—of performative force that is non-hierarchical, and yet still facilitates action. Something of this nuanced meaning is also discernible in the Hebrew, where the participial form of this verb indicates that the divine activity here is both interactive and on-going. Rather than being reduced to a set of events in the distant past promulgated by an all-controlling deity, God's creative activity—God's enabling—is construed as continuous engagement with the cosmic order.

---

2. ASV, ESV, KJV, and NRSV.

Existence is made possible through the dynamic interrelationship between deity and materiality.

This creative agency is not restricted to the divine figure alone, however. God's enabling results in the action of the celestial beings themselves, as the Sun, Moon, and Stars respond to the divine encounter by providing light (*leʾōr*) for the day and night respectively. Contrary to predominant interpretations of God's creative activity as asserting authority over the material world, the divine enabling here appears to be a continuous call into newness of being, to which the cosmic elements are invited to respond. This understanding marks a shift away from traditional portrayals of power, which contrast the passive and dependent Cosmos with a creative and independent deity. Instead, this reading implies an interdependent relationship between characters whose interactive agency makes them co-equal subjects in their own right. Just as the cosmic beings depend upon divine empowerment, so too does this deity depend upon the response of the Cosmos, for such empowerment is futile without corresponding action. In other words, just as the Sun is dependent upon God's enabling activity, so too is God dependent upon the Sun's response in providing light. Relationality, as it is understood from this ecological perspective, is thus an on-going and dynamic encounter between God and Cosmos.

From the celestial realm, the reader is drawn to the more immediate sublunary realm or, more specifically, to the surging oceanic domain of Jer 31:35b. The evocative imagery of this line depicts God "stirring up" the Sea, so that its waves "roar." Once again, the participial form of the verb "to stir up" (*rāgaʿ*) suggests that the divine interaction with the Ocean is an on-going or sustained encounter. Again also, the material subject (the Sea) actively answers God's stirring, in this case, through the roaring (*hāmā*) of its waves. In his reading of these verses, Bob Becking suggests that the interaction between deity and Ocean here should be read through the warrior traditions of neighboring Ancient Near Eastern cultures, and thus understood as an allusion to the divine battle with the Sea.[3] Against this backdrop, the Ocean is seen as a pelagic wilderness; an hostile power that threatens the cosmic order. Standing in combative opposition to this unruly force, God is presented as the heroic conqueror of chaos, whose engagement with the Ocean demonstrates the divine control over the powers present in the realm of this vast unknown. In seeking an alternative ecological interpretation of this text, I endeavor to re-read this so-called antagonistic relationship between God and the Ocean, and attempt to challenge the rhetoric

---

3. Becking, *Between Fear and Freedom*, 266.

of mastery and subjugation which inevitably emanates from the prevailing interpretations.

Read against the background posited by Becking, God's stirring in Jer 31:35b appears menacing and provocative, while the "roaring" of the Sea is seen as the hostile response to such goading. The intent behind these verbs changes dramatically, however, when they are read through the Bible's positive oceanic traditions,[4] in which the Sea's thunderous roar bespeaks pleasure and celebration. If, in line with these traditions, the Sea's utterance here is understood as an answering roar of spontaneous delight, then God's instigative stirring—which elicits such a response—can be interpreted as a playful gesture of joy-filled fun. Far from being an angry altercation, this interaction is conceived as light-hearted and amiable. In playing with the Sea, God demonstrates delight in the Ocean, taking pleasure in its wild and tempestuous character. Through such enjoyment, God implicitly acknowledges and respects the Sea's inherent subjectivity, for, as Joseph Sittler argues, "To enjoy means to let a thing be itself and rejoice in it."[5] God's stirring touch and the Ocean's pleasured response also affirms the sensual delights of the material realm, creating a kind of ecological *jouissance*. Such interaction destabilizes the dichotomized thinking that underlines traditional interpretations of the God-Sea relationship in that it depicts relationality beyond hierarchy. The playful reciprocity of this relationship seems to resist domination, circumscription and violent manipulation. Mutual enjoyment and its associated phenomena (pleasure, celebration, and delight), thus contribute to an alternative vision of relationality in their affirmation of non-hierarchical interconnectivity. In Jer 31:35, then, God's relationship to the Cosmos is not one that orders, controls, or directs, but is rather a continuous, moment-by-moment connection which (playfully) enlivens and empowers all matter. Ruth Page's expression "pan-syntheism" (God-with-all) seems an appropriate description of this presence in that it uses the preposition "with" to denote God's relationship to the material realm.[6] It is a term that encapsulates the subjectivity and unencumbered agency of both God and Cosmos outlined above, while at the same time conveying the impossibility of existence without the Other. God's being *with* the Cosmos here, allows for individuality without relinquishing interconnectivity.

God's presence with all that is inherently challenges the rigid hierarchical binaries of traditional Cartesian dualisms, questioning their relevance and rhetorical force. The well-established designation of the material

---

4. 1Chr 16:32; Pss 96:11; 98:7; Isa 42:10.

5. Sittler, "The Sittler Speeches," 134.

6. Page, *God and the Web of Creation*, 40–42.

realm as passive, static or mechanistic, for example, is replaced here by the assertion that the Cosmos is active, dynamic and inherently relational. Contested here also is the strict dichotomy between order and chaos, where order (embodied by the Sun, Moon, and Stars) is perceived as a positive that stands in direct opposition to the negative of chaos (embodied by the Sea). The presence of God (who epitomizes the positive—ordered—side of the conceptual hierarchy) amid the turbulent forces of the Ocean contradicts the absolute separation between these two realms, and casts doubt over the negative assessment of the pelagic domain. In blurring these binaries, Jer 31:35 refutes the conventional distinction between spiritual and material, affirming instead an on-going and intimate relationality between these orders. Far from having a disjointed relationship of dominance and subjugation, God and matter are inextricably interconnected here; bound together as a meaningful whole.

Reality, as it is presented in this verse, is fundamentally, joyfully and non-hierarchically relational. And such relationality seems to be characterized by interdependence, mutual empowerment, and the sincere enjoyment of an/Other. It is an image of interaction that both respects and allows space for the creative agency of life in all its forms—alien and threatening as they may seem—without totalizing or profiting from them. This imagery asserts that relationality is not fixed or static, but rather is a dynamic process that is continually constructed through negotiation in the form of on-going invitation and response. Up to this point, I've focused exclusively upon the relationship between God and (other-than-human) matter. Bearing in mind the image of relationality that has emerged from v. 35, I turn now to consider the interaction between humanity and that which is Other(-than-human) in v. 37.

Immeasurably Vast and Inconceivably Complex: Earth in Jeremiah 31:37

The final verse of this passage deals with the Heavens above and the Earth below. Rhetorically speaking, v. 37 employs a protasis-apodosis sequence, in which an impossible or unthinkable scenario negatively expresses an assurance. Here, it is the impossibility of the Heavens and the Earth being measured or explored that underlines the equally inconceivable rejection of Israel's descendants. Interpretive investigations into this verse tend to focus upon Israel's permanence as the people of God. In this alternative analysis, however, I focus my investigation on the (divine) assertion that the Earth

('erets) cannot be explored (chāqar, lit. "to search"), and consider the ecological implications that might emerge from such a claim.

To the contemporary reader, the text's insistence in v. 37 that the Earth
is unexplorable seems somewhat antiquated, reflective of an ancient worldview that is now obsolete.[7] Beneath the literal inaccuracy of the divine claim,
however, lies an awareness of Earth as immeasurably vast and fundamentally unknowable. In its extraordinary complexity, the Earth is ultimately
beyond human comprehension. God's assertion in this verse thus identifies
Earth as mystery. Here, the elusive character of Earth is not limited to that
which is not yet known; rather, unknowability is constitutive of the Earth itself.[8] Mystery, it seems, does not exclusively belong to God, but to the Earth
also. Such identification is insufficient in isolation, however, and it is in this
vein that I seek to examine the Earth's mysterious/unknowable character in
the broader context of relationality.

The image of Earth as unknowable to humanity counters anthropocentric modes of interaction with the environment, which have traditionally
been based upon conquest, domestication, and exploitation. God declares
that for humanity to perceive the Earth is both to know it and not to know it;
comprehension, writes Mark Manolopoulos, cannot be comprehensive.[9]
To encounter Earth is thus to encounter mystery, and to be faced with the
limits of human knowledge before such mystery. In the same way that the
unknowability of God shapes the human/divine relationship, so the Earth's
unknowability will have implications for the ways in which humanity relates
to their surroundings.

Contemplating the vast and unknowable character of Earth as it is
imaged here quells the reductionist compulsions of the mastering subject,
engendering instead an overwhelming sense of wonder and awe. Like Job
who is rendered speechless when confronted by the divine mystery,[10] so
humanity responds with silence in Jer 31:37 when presented with the unfathomable mystery of Earth. Such silence, however, is neither fearful nor
disinterested; rather, nuanced by the context of awe and wonder, it reflects
an attitude of reverence and gentle receptivity towards Earth. It is in this
silence that humanity is able to assimilate its own insignificance in the face
of this immeasurable and inconceivably complex Other. Acknowledgement
of this dynamic results in an attitude of humility and self-restraint that rec-

7. Brueggemann, *Commentary on Jeremiah*, 298, for example, notes that in our modernity "the heavens *can* be measured and the earth *can* be explored . . ." (my emphasis).

8. I have drawn on the work of Manolopoulos, *Creation*, 113, to explore the notion of "mystery" as it appears in relation to the Land in Jer 31:37.

9. Ibid., 115.

10. Job 40:3–5.

ognizes and respects the Earth in itself, for itself. At the heart of the mode of relationality imagined in v. 37, then, lies the interrelated categories of mystery, awe, silence, and humility.

Interconnected and Interdependent: The Cosmic Community in Jeremiah 31:36

And so we move now to the only remaining verse left in this passage. Like its succeeding verse, Jer 31:36 employs a protasis-apodosis motif, and is also commonly interpreted as a divine guarantee of Israel's permanence. The rhetorical assurance contained here relies primarily upon the absolute dependability of the "fixed order," an allusion to the Sun, Moon, and Stars of v. 35. Such dependability, argues Brueggemann, shifts the protasis from being a statement of conditionality to one of confident negation: as the cosmic order will never cease, so also shall Israel never cease to be a nation before God.[11] Bearing in mind the ecological emphasis of my analysis, however, I have chosen to nuance this dependability by taking the protasis-apodosis sequence at face value, as a statement of cause and effect: if the Cosmos were to cease from existing, then so too would (the "seed" of) Israel come to an end. In this reading I follow Lundbom, who suggests that the reference to "seed" (*zera'*) in this verse be understood in the broader sense as pertaining to the seed of every living entity on Earth.[12] From an ecological perspective, then, God's claim here is nothing short of an unqualified affirmation of the interconnected and interdependent relationality that exists between God, Cosmos, and life on Earth. The divinely enabled Cosmos (identified in v. 35) makes possible the existence of Earth and *all* its inhabitants.

In its cosmic perspective, Jer 31:36 images reality as a unified, integrated and meaningful whole which is characterized by the diversity of its member parts. The image assumes an infinite multiplicity of relationships, which form a complex web of dynamic and continuous connection-events. Everything that exists is interrelated. Relationality here is thus not incidental or additional to any given entity, but rather constitutes the very essence of all that is. With the recognition of this capacity for relationship—for action and connection—comes the acknowledgement that all modes of being are subjects, and agents of influence in their own right, who are themselves vulnerable to the influence of Others. In the image of reality depicted in this verse, human beings are not distinguished or separated from this cosmic

---

11. Brueggemann, *Exile and Homecoming*, 297.

12. Lundbom, *Jeremiah 21–36*, 486. See also Jer 31:27 where the "seed of humans" appears in conjunction with the "seed of animals."

ecosystem, but exist instead on the same ontological level as individuals who are related intrinsically and inescapably to all Others in this interconnected community. Within this text, humanity finds a place, not as a spirit among bodies but, as Sallie McFague suggests, as a spirited body among the innumerable spirited bodies of the Cosmos.[13]

The interconnectedness observed in Jer 31:36 builds upon the image of interdependence seen in v. 35, but here, *all* individual entities rely upon each Other for their existence. As the Sun, Moon, and Stars depend upon the divine lure calling them into being,[14] so the "seed"—that is, every living entity—is seen here as dependent upon the presence of this fixed order for its existence. Such dependence is not exclusive, however, for reliance upon this fixed order is, by extension, reliance upon the divine lure. Like the multiple nature of relationality, interdependence also is multi-layered and infinitely diverse. Directly or indirectly, all entities depend simultaneously upon both the divine empowerment and the myriad of other entities that have responded to that empowerment in the past. To exist within this cosmic reality is thus to be utterly dependent upon Others, although this dependence is not unilateral. In the same way that the interdependent relationship between God and the cosmic elements took the form of an invitation and reply (v. 35), so the dependence depicted in v. 36 also requires a response. If the "fixed order" enables the seed (living entities) of Israel "to be" (*haya* [a nation]), then the response is on-going existence. The combination of this fixed order and the lure of God thus enables these entities to fully become themselves, and to participate in the interdependent whole as beings who continue to depend upon Others, and upon whom Others depend.

Bearing in mind this alternative ecological reading of Jer 31:35–37, I include here an eco-translation of these verses:

And so God asks:

Who reaches out and enables the sun,

Which in turn responds by pouring light abundantly upon the Earth? Who calls the moon and the stars,

whose response is made manifest in the twinkling lights of the night sky?

13. McFague, *The Body of God*, 19.

14. The "divine lure" is a phrase used by McDaniel, *Earth, Sky, Gods & Mortals*, 98. I use it interchangeably with the notion of "divine enabling/empowerment" outlined above.

And who playfully stirs up the sea so that its waves leap and roar in delight? It is the God of all existence!

If this dynamic call and response between God and Cosmos were ever to cease,

So too would every living entity on Earth come to an end.

For everything that exists is inextricably interrelated,

Says God.

As the Cosmos is unfathomably immense and is beyond human comprehension,

So the Earth itself is immeasurably vast and utterly unknowable.

Earth is mystery, and mystery necessitates reverence and awe.

It is these attitudes must form the foundation for relationality between humanity and Earth,

Concludes God.

Towards an Emerging Ecological Imaginary

Although this perspective on relationality is lamentably fleeting, it provides a significant glimpse into a symbolic order which has the capacity to contribute positively to the formation and sustenance of a contemporary ecological sensibility. The task of identifying and articulating a suitable model for the relationship between God, Earth and people is not an easy one, and this passage is by no means comprehensive in its description of the tripartite relationality. In concluding this article, however, I seek to draw together the various strands that characterize relationality in these verses, in the hope that this imagery might contribute meaningfully to an emerging ecological imaginary. Central to the depiction of relationality in Jer 31:35–37 is the image of multiple and non-hierarchical interdependent relationships among beings that exist individually as part of a vast and complex whole. In its non-hierarchical nature, this image of relationality rejects traditional dualistic stereotypes which set order against chaos and privilege the masculinized spiritual over the feminized material. Indeed, the enabling presence of the divine with[in] all bodies—from the Sun and the Sea, to the Land and its inhabitants—is a direct negation of such binary thought, affirming instead the radical integration of all.

As well as emphasizing the unity of each entity with all Others, however, the text simultaneously affirms the distinction of each entity from all Others; each individual being has its own independent value and integrity within this interdependent reality. This recognition, in turn, necessitates the acknowledgement of all beings as subjects in their own right. Within this relational context, the interaction between the vast diversity of differing subjects resembles an infinite multiplicity of I-Thou encounters, where engagement is based upon a common understanding of the autonomy, agency and inherent worth of the Other.[15]

While the brevity of this passage limits the amount of detail concerning the relational obligations within this mode of existence, the ramifications of the reality imaged in Jer 31:35–37 reverberate beyond the world of the text. More than an exercise in observation, recognition of the cosmic interdependence depicted here carries with it a strong ethical dimension. To perceive the self as one who depends upon Others and upon whom Others depend, requires broadening one's gaze beyond anthropocentric affairs to include the consideration of all living entities. It is to celebrate and enjoy the presence of otherness, while working to ensure that this otherness— this mystery—is protected. To live appropriately within this whole is thus a continuous negotiation, as individual interests are subordinated to the pragmatic imperative of interdependence and the flourishing of all.

In its cosmic perspective, the image of relationality drawn from Jer 31:35–37 does not pretend to provide solutions to the intricate and complex issues specific to the current ecological crisis. Rather, this rhetorical vision provides faith communities with a foundation for re-conceiving the relationship between God, Earth and humanity, from which these communities might address the multiplicity of issues related to this crisis. In emphasizing interdependence and the subjectivity of all, this imagery provides an alternative to the anthropocentric outlook, which is often implicit in our ideas about justice and morality. Set alongside the ever-increasing scientific discoveries that corroborate this interdependent vision, these verses have the potential to act as a powerful resource for faith communities in the ongoing endeavor to alleviate environmental degradation.

---

15. Buber, *Between Man and Man*, 1–45, suggests that this relational ontology allows for encounter that is non-appropriative yet responsive.

Bibliography

Becking, Bob. *Between Fear and Freedom: Essays on the Interpretation of Jeremiah 30–31*. Old Testament studies 51. Leiden: Brill, 2004.

Berry, Thomas. "Into the Future." In *This Sacred Earth: Religion, Nature, Environment*, edited by Roger S. Gottlieb, 410–14. New York: Routledge, 1996.

Brueggemann, Walter. *A Commentary on Jeremiah: Exile and Homecoming*. Grand Rapids: Eerdmans, 1998.

Buber, Martin. *Between Man and Man*. London: Routledge, 2002.

Lundbom, Jack R. *Jeremiah 21–36: A New Translation with Introduction and Commentary*. Anchor Bible 21B. New York: Doubleday, 2004.

Manolopoulos, Mark. *If Creation Is a Gift*. New York: State University of New York, 2009.

McDaniel, Jay B. *Earth, Sky, Gods & Mortals: Developing an Ecological Spirituality*. Mystic, CT: Twenty-Third Publications, 1990.

McFague, Sallie. *The Body of God: An Ecological Theology*. Minneapolis: Fortress, 1993.

Page, Ruth. *God and the Web of Creation*. London: SCM, 1996.

15

Christian Worship and
Human Stewardship

Mark D. Liederbach

Introduction

THE BIBLICAL ACCOUNTS OF creation found in Gen 1 and 2 contain two passages regarding the purpose and function of human beings that are vital to understand if one is to develop a proper foundation for a Christian ethic of Creation care. The first, Gen 2:15, discloses *what* God's calling and directive purpose is for his image bearers that inhabit the earth. The second, Gen 1:28 gives descriptive content to *how* God's image bearers are to function in the created order. The purpose of this paper is to develop each in turn while exploring their implications for the development of a biblical ethic of creation care.[1]

The Image Bearer's Inherent Purpose—Genesis 2:15

"Then the Lord God took the man and put him into the Garden of Eden to cultivate it and to keep it." As Gen 2:15 indicates God gave Adam a very special vocation and directive purpose as an image bearer. After God created Adam from the dust of the earth and animated him (Gen 2:7) he placed Adam into Eden in order to do something. To discover what it is he purposed

---

1. For a more developed Christological discussion of many of the themes developed in this article see Liederbach and Bible, *True North*.

for Adam to accomplish it is important to explore the meaning of the two words translated from the original Hebrew into English as "cultivate" and "keep." Contrary to what may appear to simple farming instructions in the English translations, the original Hebrew meanings of each word and the entire context of the passage point to a much richer meaning than might be apparent at first glance. Indeed, the interpretation and meaning of these words and this passage, it is safe to say, are universally recognized by those in the environmental ethics discussion as hinge points upon which much of the Christian perspective on creation care turns.

Critique of "Eco-Evangelical Orthodoxy" Translation of Genesis 2:15

One of the more prominent interpretations of these words and this verse is represented vigorously by several influential evangelical voices in the creation care debate such as Calvin DeWitt, Stephen Bouma-Prediger and Loren Wilkenson. In fact, within the realm of evangelical environmental ethics it is safe to say that their perspective has been received so favorably among "green Christians" that it can be described as the "eco-evangelical orthodox" interpretation of the passage. Understanding the key elements of this position revolves around the basic meaning of the Hebrew words *'ābad* and *shāmar*.

First of all the Hebrew word for "cultivate" is *'ābad*. In various translations of Gen 2:15 this word has been rendered as "cultivate," "tend," "till," "work," or "dress." The Hebrew word for "keep" is *shāmar*. It has been rendered in various translations as "keep," "watch over," and "safeguard." While each of these words can have a particular technical meaning, the appropriate way to render a word when seeking to translate it is to determine the best meaning as it is derived from both the context of the immediate passage and the general surrounding context of the narrative. Proper translation involves both a technically accurate term that also appropriately fits the context of the entire passage.

In his treatment of this passage, the influential zoologist and Professor of Environmental Studies Calvin DeWitt believes the most appropriate English translations for these words should be "serve and keep." As he puts it: "Genesis 2:15 conveys a marvelous teaching. Adam is expected by God to serve the garden and to keep it." His choice to interpret *'ābad* with the English word "serve" is based on his assertion that it is a "possible translation" and one that is often rendered from the same root word in the Old Testament depending on the context in which the word is found. Whether this particular context warrants the rendering of "service" he does not argue. However, having opted for this interpretation he goes on to comment that "God expected Adam and his descendants to meet the needs of the garden of creation so that it would persist and flourish . . . God also expected Adam and his descendants to keep the garden. The word for keep (*shāmar*) is sometimes translated as "guard," "safeguard," "take care of," and "look after." *Shāmar* indicates a loving, caring, sustaining kind of keeping."[2]

In a similar vein, Loren Wilkinson comments in regard to the interpretation of *ābad* and *shāmar* that "the significant thing about both words is that they describe actions undertaken not primarily for the sake of the doer, but for the sake of the object of the action: the kind of tilling which is a service of the earth. The keeping of the garden is not just for human comfort, but is a kind of preservation."[3] Thus, for Wilkinson, as for De-Witt, because the verse tells us to cultivate and keep "*it*" (i.e. the garden), he contends that the primary beneficiary of the cultivation or service (*ābad*) and keeping (*shāmar*) is to be the garden and not the man (Adam). Thus, because the immediate context of the verse is the garden, he argues that the action rendered has "it" as the primary focus. Based on this he also prefers to interpret the phrase using the possible translation of "service" toward the earth. Steven Bouma-Prediger, in *For the Beauty of the Earth*, follows suit in his treatment of Gen 2:15. In fact his rhetoric even amplifies the intensity of the significance of the point. He argues that "Genesis 2:5 speaks of humans serving the earth . . . And Genesis 2:15—the last part of which is painted on the door of every Chicago police car—defines the human calling in terms of service: We are to serve [*ābad* and protect [*shāmar*]. We are to serve and protect the garden that is creation—literally be a slave to the earth for its own good, as well as for our benefit.[4]

He reiterates this point by affirming that "Genesis 1:28 must be placed alongside Genesis 2:15, where we are told that God put the human in the garden 'to till and keep it.' To till [*ābad*] means to serve the earth for *its own sake*, and to keep [*shāmar*] means to protect the earth as one caringly guards something valuable."[5] Thus, Bouma-Prediger echoes a similar perspective to DeWitt and Wilkinson in his interpretation of *ābad* as "service" but goes further in his argument that the "service" rendered to the earth has some benefit to the human caretaker, but should primarily benefit the earth. Indeed, more than mere voluntary service, Bouma-Prediger asserts

2. DeWitt, *Earth*-Wise, 44. See also DeWitt in Gottlieb, *A Greener Faith*, 194.

3. Wilkinson, et al., *EarthKeeping in the Nineties*, 209.

4. Bouma-Prediger, *For the Beauty of the Earth*, 74.

5. Ibid, 154, my italics.

a moral imperative in which humans are meant to "slave" for the earth "for its own sake."

Each of these three approaches to understanding Gen 2:15 are correct in showing that that human concern is not central to the passage. Christian theology has been accused of making the value and purpose of created order completely subservient to human interests. In each case, these men rightly indicate that a proper reading of the text should shift the emphasis away from an anthropocentric, instrumental perspective about the purposes of creation.

While it is important to affirm this element of their interpretation, their final rendering of the passage and application of it, while technically possible, does not adequately take into context the greater picture of what is occurring in Gen 1 and 2. To put it simply, while there is an element of service that should be rendered to the earth, the text is far richer than any of these treatments allows for because of the greater context of worship in which the entire creation narrative falls.

In his *Healing the Earth* Richard A Young offers a much more in-depth study the Hebrew words *'ābad* and *shāmar* and points out that there are several common meanings the words can take on depending on the grammatical structure of the sentence and the context of the surrounding text.[6] According to Young, the most common meanings of *'ābad* in Scripture are:

1. To work, especially when there is no object (Exod 5:18).

2. To cultivate, when the object is the ground, vineyard, or the like (Gen 3:23; 4:2, 12; Deut 28:39; Prov 12:11; 28:19).

3. To work for someone either as a servant or slave (2 Sam 16:19; Exod 21:2–6).

4. To serve or worship a deity (Exod 3:12; Judg 2:11; Ps 100:2).

5. To serve in a place of worship (Num 4:37, 41).

Likewise with the Hebrew word *shāmar* Young points out that this verb also has several possible meanings that are dependent upon the general context of the passages in which they fall. These possible meanings include:

1. To watch or guard something, such as sheep (1 Sam 17:20), an entrance (1 Kgs 14:27), or a captive (1 Kgs 20:39).

2. To protect from danger (Ps 121:7; Prov 6:24).

3. To save or retain something, such as food (Gen 41:35).

---

6. Young, *Healing the Earth*, 163.

4. To do something carefully or attentively, such as observe God's laws or covenant (Exod 15:26; 19:5).[7]

Now in regard to the interpretation of these words, normally, when the ground (garden, earth) is the object of the sentence in which the verb *'abad* is found, then the meaning would best be understood as "till" or "cultivate." Thus, it is understandable, seeing as how the immediate context of Gen 2:15 involves a garden, that many English translations will render the word *'abad* as "cultivate." However, because of the larger context of the Gen 1 and 2 creation accounts, it is clear that God has an even larger agenda in mind for both Adam and the Garden. Young alludes to this larger agenda in his discussion when he points out that God's concern is with Adam functioning as a "manager to help keep order and harmony in creation" in which the service rendered was not done merely for his own sustenance but is to be *rendered unto God*.[8] Thus, Young's work is helpful in that he does not rely merely on the technical possibilities of the words at issue; rather, he appropriately seeks to place his interpretive efforts within the context of the entire Genesis narrative. And by doing so he rightly hints at the fact that the narrative context is pointing toward a much higher end than even "serving" the garden.

Clearly, there is a service being rendered by Adam as he cares for the garden. But one must be careful not to merely replace a human centered ethic with an ethic that gives final place of pre-eminence to the creation order instead of the Creator. Focusing on care for the garden "for its own sake" runs the risk of ultimately missing the powerfully motivating theocentric tenor to the entire discussion. Thus, while it is important to emphasize the idea that the created order has a God-given inherent worth, it is vital to the proper ordering and goal of both the text and the discipline of environmental ethics to recognize that the final goal or *telos* of the service rendered is not merely the flourishing of the Garden but rather the praise and glory of the One who created the Garden. God and his glory is the *telos*, not the garden.

To be fair, none of these authors ultimately takes a bio-centric position in their ethic. But at this point of exegesis their interpretive work does not adequately take into account all that is taking place in the creation narrative and thus their rendering of Gen 2:15 as "serving and protecting" the earth ultimately puts more emphasis on the creation than is necessary and less on worshipping the Creator than is warranted.[9]

7. Ibid.

8. Ibid.

9. Even with Young, however, while his final interpretive understanding of Gen

Creation as Temple

In his important work "Creation in the Image of the Glory-Spirit" Kline points out that the Gen 1 and 2 narratives are heavily laden with language picturing the created order as a temple of worship for the King of the Universe.[10] Jamieson, Fausset and Brown specifically discuss Gen 2:15 from the point of view that the Garden functioned as a sort of "whole life temple." They comment that Eden "was in fact a temple in which [Adam] worshipped God, and was daily employed in offering the sacrifices of thanksgiving and praise."[11] Greg Beale makes the same basic case that the picture of Eden described in the creation narrative has strong theological ties with the Old Testament's description of the temple as well as the idea that the whole of creation as restored by Christ is to be understood as the dwelling place or tabernacle of God.[12] Old Testament scholar Christopher Wright also concurs with this basic perspective.[13]

Building on this idea, Noel Due argues that a strong connection exists between Eden and Adam's role as the King-Priest who was designed and created to rule and shepherd all of creation. He comments that "the whole of Eden was built for worship. Adam was created to be the great leader of the creation in its glorification of God, with Eden as the garden-sanctuary of his communion with the Creator."[14] He also comments that, in interpreting the Genesis creation narratives,

> we should see humanity as being brought into, and existing in, a matrix of worship. The primal couple did not exist for themselves, or by themselves, but they existed for God, at the head of creation yet to be brought into its full glory. We see that the primal couple was given a mandate, to 'fill' the earth, and 'subdue' it and 'rule over' it (Gen. 1:26f), and a task to 'cultivate and keep' the Garden (Gen. 2:15). To engage in such tasks and to fulfill the mandate was to be their expression of worship. Their communion with God, the joy of his nearer presence, the offering of praise and adoration to him, were not to be set in some

---

2:15 does rightly suggest that the service rendered ultimately is "unto the Lord," he also ultimately under-emphasizes the larger overall context of the creation narratives and the extent to which a theocentric perspective ought to drive the interpretation and translation of Gen 2:15.

10. Kline, "Creation in the Image of the Glory-Spirit," 20–26.

11. Jamieson et al., *Commentary Critical and Explanatory.*

12. See Beale, *Temple and Church's Mission.*

13. Wright, *Mission of God,* 415.

14. Due, *Created for Worship,* 41–42.

compartmentalized fashion away from their daily activity, but the daily activity was their service to God.[15]

In light of this larger context that places the entire created order in framework of worship, it is possible—indeed preferable—to give a fuller and more proper meaning to the Hebrew words 'ābad and shāmar than merely "cultivate" and "keep" or even "serve" and "protect." Recall that Young's work, noted above, indicates that there are several possible technical meanings to these two words including "worship" and "obey." The appropriate translation, then, relies on the given context in which the word falls. Thus, it should come as no surprise—in light of the larger context of Gen 1and 2—that renowned Hebrew scholar Umberto Cassuto would make the case that while the English phrase "cultivate and keep" or even "serve and care for" may be technically accurate, the original language and context strongly suggest the idea that God placed Adam in the garden to *worship* and *obey*.[16]

Old Testament scholar John Sailhamer agrees. He points out that this important element is often lost in translation from ancient Hebrew to modern English. Many English translations, he argues, overlook the "specific purpose for God's putting man in the garden. In most [English versions] man is 'put' in the garden 'to work it and take care of it.'" Sailhamer objects, however, and argues "a more suitable translation of the Hebrew . . . would be 'to worship and obey.'" That is, when reading Gen 2:15 from the perspective of the language and the given context, the passage indicates that "Man is put in the garden to worship God and to obey him. Man's life in the garden was to be characterized by worship and obedience."[17]

To further support this idea consider that Matthews in his commentary on Gen 1–11 points out that the word 'ābad is used often for "tilling" the soil (Gen 3:23; 4:2, 12), but also describes service and worship (Exodus 3:12). The noun derivative of 'ābad ('abôdā) is often used to describe the Levitical duties in the worship of the Temple. In addition, the word shāmar describes the occupation of Abel tending to his flocks and property, but also describes protecting persons and observing "covenant stipulations." More importantly it describes the priestly duties of carrying out God's instructions and taking care of the tabernacle.[18] And as pointed out in *Theological Lexicon of the Old Testament*, the notion of shāmar meaning the keeping of commandments, statutes and instructions of God "dominates the entire semantic field in the religious realm. It appears in almost

15. Ibid.

16. Cassuto, *Commentary on the Book of Genesis*, 122.

17. Sailhamer, "Genesis," 45.

18. Matthews, *New American Commentary: Genesis 1–11:26*, 209–1 0.

all portions of the OT with widely varying expressions, grammatical constructions, and addressees . . ."[19] In other words, when in a worship or temple setting, the word *shāmar* carries with it the idea of obedient service as a spiritual service of worship.

Perhaps this is why Allen Ross comments that it is significant that these two particular words are chosen for this text. He comments:

> These two verbs are used through the Pentateuch for spiritual service. "Keep" [*shāmar*] is used for keeping the commandments and taking heed to obey God's word; "serve" [*'ābad*] describes the worship and service of the Lord, the highest privilege a person can have. Whatever activity the man was to engage in in the garden (and there is no reason to doubt that physical activity was involved), it was described in terms of spiritual service to the Lord."[20]

Thus, it is the fourth possible rendering in the above lists given by Young regarding the possible meanings of *'ābad* and *shāmar* that most fully capture the full intention of creation accounts given in Gen 1 and 2. Certainly Adam was to "cultivate and keep" the garden. And certainly Adam was to "serve and protect it." Ultimately, however, Adam's cultivation and service were to be ordered unto God as worship that he perfectly rendered in obedience. Adam was created to render this worship in fulfillment of his created nature as an image bearer and in keeping with the purpose of garden itself to serve as a temple to bring glory to God. Adam's cultivation and service would be the form and bodily practice that Adam would render as worship unto the good and wise creator of the universe.

Clearly, then, the focus of Gen 2:15 is certainly not anthropocentric, nor is it even vaguely bio-centric. It is overtly theocentric. The focus falls primarily on the Creator . . . not on his garden.

Considering the meaning and context of Gen 2:15, then, it is right and proper to conclude that in the safety of the flawless environment which God provided, Adam was created and placed in the garden to worship God and demonstrate that worship through obedience. It is the Creator who is the center point of the story, not the creation. Certainly Adam's obedience included care and proper management of the earth. Certainly it included serving it, nurturing it and helping it to flourish. Ultimately, Adam's calling and purpose was specifically to live a life of worship that ordered all his service and protection of the garden to the glory of God.

19. Jenni and Westermann, *Theological Lexicon of the Old Testament*, 3:1381–82.
20. Ross, *Creation and Blessing*, 124.

It is, then, in light of this Garden temple setting and directional order-ing of all creation care and environmental stewardship to the worship and praise of God that one can finally understand that Adam (and all humanity) was formed (caused, built or created) by God for the purpose of worship and that he—and all humanity—reach the highest possible flourishing as created image bearers when they return to God all the glory he is due in and through the way they steward God's creation (*exitus-reditus,* Rom 11:36). All service rendered in any area of life is meant to be done unto the Lord as a beautiful offering of worship and it is to be done in accordance with that basic structure of the universe perceivable via the natural and revealed law of God (1 Cor 10:31). As John Murray puts it, "the biblical ethic, as it would have been exemplified in a sinless world and as it is exemplified in redeemed humanity, knows no antithesis between duty performed in obedience to commandment and love as the fulfillment of the law."[21]

Thus, the primary motivation for creation care boils down to worship-ping and obeying in a manner that transcends mere duty-bound service for the sake of the created order. Rather, the Christian's proper motivation comes as he or she understands the context and purpose of the created or-der and experiences life's highest joys and God's fullest blessings as each image bearer rightly orders his or her practices and treatment of the created realm worshipfully toward the God who created all things.

Finally, if this interpretation and reading of Gen 2:15 is correct, then it is right to assert that this understanding totally eviscerates any notion that at its roots a truly Christian—or for that matter a rightly understood Judeo Christian—ethic is responsible for, or in any way is the driving force behind, any current ecological crises we may face.[22] While Lynn White's arguments blaming Christianity for the environmental degradations we face have been widely disseminated, his conclusions demonstrate a lack of clarity on what Christian doctrine actually teaches. This has not prevented some, however, from making claims that the teaching of the Bible in Gen 1:28 instructing Adam and Eve to "subdue" and "rule" over creation gave humans both un-limited dominion over the earth and a license for humankind to exploit the created realm in a completely utilitarian fashion. Certainly there are places and times within human history when "Christians" wrongly interpreted Scripture in regard to the purpose of the created order, and have wrongly exploited the creation to its great harm. But such a reality in practice by no means implicates that the basic teachings of Christianity actually sup-

21. Murray, *Principles of Conduct,* 37–39.

22. See, for example, White, "The Historical Roots of Our Ecologic Crisis," a now widely disseminated article that asserted Christianity was to blame for the current and ongoing ecological crisis.

port such a position or that this was the normative practice.[23] Indeed, to the degree any blame falls on Christianity it should not be on the Christian teachings *per se* but either on persons wrongly acting in the name of Christianity or on wrongly interpreted Christian doctrine. An exploration of the Gen 1:28 text helps demonstrate why this is so.[24]

Genesis 1:28—Subdue and Rule: The Image Bearer's Principled Instructions for Worshipful Obedience

"And God blessed them: and God said to them, 'Be fruitful and multiply, and fill the earth, and subdue it; and rule over the fish of the sea and over the birds of the sky, and over every living thing that moves on the earth'" (Gen 1:28 NASB).

Two Key Words—Subdue and Rule

Regardless of whether the claims made against Christianity by White have substance or not, there can be no doubt that Gen 1:28 gives to humanity a form of *headship* over the rest of creation. The words "subdue" and "rule" make that clear. Once again, an in-depth examination of the meaning of these words and their context in Gen 1 and 2 proves helpful.

First, the word "subdue" in the Hebrew is *kābash*. This word appears in the Old Testament 15 different times in various contexts. Its root meanings relates to treading something down. In its various contexts it can mean:

1. to conquer an enemy (Num 32:22, 29; 2 Sam 8:11; Zech 9:15).

2. to bring conquered people under military control (Josh 18:1).

3. to bring people into subjection (1 Chron 22:18; 2 Chron 28:10).

4. to bring into slavery (Neh 5:5; Jer 34:11, 16).

5. to tread our sins under foot (Mic 7:19).

6. to molest the queen (Esth 7:8).

As Young points out the image often depicted in *kābash* "is that of a conqueror putting his foot on the neck of a conquered enemy (see Josh 10:24)."[25] He goes on to point out that "when used of the earth [*kābash*]

---

23. Bouma-Prediger, *For the Beauty of the Earth*, 74.

24. Schaeffer and Middlemann, *Pollution and the Death of Man*, 59.

25. Young, *Healing the Earth*, 161–62.

denotes exercising "some form of control or power over nature." The object of *kābash* is the earth, which must be understood as all creation, not simply the physical earth, for the following thought expands it to include living creatures.[26]

The other word in question is "rule" which is a translation of the Hebrew word *rādāh* which is also frequently translated (in the KJV for example) as "have dominion." This word appears over 20 times in the Old Testament and its root meaning implies the trampling down of something and is often used to show the rule or dominion of a leader over a nation or group of people. In its various contexts it can mean:

1. divine rule over the earth (Ps 72:8, 110:2)

2. Israel ruling over her oppressors (Isa 4 1:2)

3. nations ruling over Israel (Lev 26:17; Neh 9:28)

4. one nation ruling another (Ezek 29:15)

5. leaders ruling the people (2 Chron 8:10).[27]

This word does not necessarily imply the same strength of rule or submission that *kābash* does. In fact, in several places in the Old Testament God implores his people not to "rule" (*rādāh*) harshly or unjustly (Lev 25:43–53; Ezek 34:1–6). Young points out that "when used in reference to creation, [*rādāh*] would convey the idea of ruling or governing the natural order. The idea conveyed by *rādāh* is simply to exercise one's right of rule or authority over another. There is no connotation in the word itself of being harsh or ruthless."[28]

Genesis 1:28 in the Context of Theocentric Worship

At this point, in order to determine the proper meaning and usage of these terms in the Gen 1:28 context, it is wise once again to consider several overriding themes present in the creation narratives. First, from the very first words of the biblical text "in the beginning God . . ." we discover a point often overlooked when considering the creation accounts: God reveals himself not only as the key player in the discussion but the subject of the discussion. That is, while the things God creates are amazing, it is God himself as the creator that is the central point of the text and the ultimate and primary

26. Ibid.

27. Ibid, 162.

28. Ibid.

subject of the story.[29] Second, this God who is the strong, loving, and careful artisan behind this wondrously created world repeatedly expressed his pleasure with the created realm by indicated that what he saw was "good." Third, Gen 1:26–27 depicts God intentionally creating human beings as image bearers who in their very essence, then, should not be understood some type of post enlightenment autonomous self-maximizers but rather as worshippers created to "image" God as they lived in his world. And finally, in exploring the meaning of Gen 2:15 it was discovered that the created purpose of God's image bearers was to return unto God the glory he as creator alone is due through worshipful and obedience.

From this context, then, one can begin to understand that while the words *kābash* ("subdue") and *rādāh* ("rule") are muscular words of strength and purpose, their objective should not be understood to imply harsh brutality and unlimited tyranny over the earth. Rather, as God's image bearers are instructed to subdue and rule the created order they are meant to do so as his representatives. Their rule is to be loving, graceful, careful, and purposeful as God is loving, graceful, careful and purposeful. The strength of their leadership and shaping efforts, then, was meant to be in conformity with the nature of how God created them to be: worshippers who through their joyful obedience would seek to shape the creation in a manner that would increasingly bring glory to their Maker. Ronald Manahan captures the essence of this idea when he writes: "These are certainly forceful terms, but neither by itself necessarily pictures harshness. This element must be supplied by context. These terms are ones of action, *doing* as a consequence of what humans are (image-bearers). The action is formative and shaping, but always as a consequence of what humans are."[30]

One may stop for a moment and wonder why (if the world was without sin or blemish) would the first couple be given the command to "subdue" and "rule" the created order at all. After all, wasn't the garden already "perfect"? To answer this question one need merely consider the different possible meanings of the word "perfect." Perfection can be used to indicate "without blemish" and it can also be used to indicate "completeness" or "totality." It would seem, then, that in regard to the created order, God did indeed create a world "without blemish" (i.e. perfect, sinless), but that he also created it with room for improvement as Adam and Eve grew in their knowledge and experience of God and his created realm. It seems God made both them and the garden with a capacity for expansion and improvement towards a fulfillment of its created potential.

29. For further development of this idea Liederbach and Bible, *True North*, 31–51.

30. Manahan, "Christ as the Second Adam," 51.

The implications of this calling and purpose are rich and worth considering deeply. For if God's image bearers could be restored to such a calling and vision the implications for creation care would be enormous. Instead of a harsh domination of the created order, Christians steeped in biblical doctrine would understand that bringing the raw potential of God's created realm does not require exploitation but rather a careful revealing and enhancement of the inherent beauty and value present in the world through loving work and labor rightly ordered to God as worship. This idea is captured beautifully by Tolkien in his classic *The Lord of the Rings* when through the mouth of Gimli the dwarf he describes how beauty can be revealed through loving *kābash* and *rādāh*.

> Strange are the ways of men, Legolas! Here they have one of the marvels of the Northern World, and what do they say of it? Caves, they say! Caves! . . . No dwarf could be unmoved by such loveliness . . . We would tend these glades of flowering stone, not quarry them. With cautious skill, tap by tap—a small chip of rock and no more, perhaps, in a whole anxious day—so we could work, and as the years went by, we should open up new ways, and display far chambers that are still dark, glimpsed only as a void beyond fissures in the rock. And lights, Legolas! We should make lights . . . and when we wished we would drive away the night that has lain there since the hills were made; and when we desired rest, we would let the night return."[31]

Through this character's awe-filled and respectful joy over the wonders of the Glittering Caves at Helm's Deep, Tolkien captures much of the attitude and motivation that should drive image bearers given the freedom to co-create with God in this wondrous world. With cautious skill, tap by tap, humans working to open up the vast wonders of the created world might gradually yet stunningly enhance the beauty that is there and adorn it with still more beauty that they create.

With this idea in mind, then, it is possible to now identify why the critique of Christianity offered by Lynn White is so wrong. The biblical text clearly does not give humans some type of unlimited dominion in which they have absolute rights to do with creation whatever they please. Rather, as unstained image bearers their worshipful work would always be aligned to loving will of God and the maximizing of God's glory in the created realm. Working in light of the Gen 1:28 instructions to subdue and rule they would have been in complete congruence with the eternal law by which God created both them and the universe. Thus, to interpret Gen 1:28 as some type

---

31 Tolkien, *Lord of the Rings: The Two Towers*, 166.

of "cultural mandate" or "dominion mandate" in which fallen sinners can do whatever they please would be a complete misunderstanding of the text and context. Indeed, "approval for the exercise of absolute or unlimited power is alien to Gen 1 and to the Old Testament as a whole."[32]

Instead, given the context of sinless worshippers asked to subdue and rule, the text should be understood to mean that while God did indeed give them freedom, that freedom to act was given as a freedom meant to be aligned in complete harmony with God's divine intent, heart and will. Their relationship with the rest of the creation order would not have been understood as "an alien duty stemming from a hard command, that is, as a joyless obligation."[33] Rather, they would have acted in respect that involved both wonder and delight. As Vern Poythress puts it, "The 'dominion' of Genesis 1:28 is thus to be understood as a thoughtful, caring dominion, a dominion expressing God's goodness and care, and not a heartless, brutal, crushing dominion. Genesis 1–2 repudiates the sinful perversion of dominion into destructive exploitation."[34] In the history of the church "dominion was taken for granted, but it was usually the dominion of benevolence, not exploitation, and it was assumed that this benevolence was the normative state of Eden."[35]

This is why even Richard Young is wrong on this point when he properly argues against Gen 1:28 being used as an unlimited dominion and cultural mandate but then suggests that it is best understood as an "ecological mandate" and that "God's concern when He finished creation was not our impacting society with theistic values, but taking care of what He had just finished making. This was *preeminent on God's mind*."[36] No—Gen 1:28 is emphatically not an ecological mandate. It is a *worship mandate!* The preeminent thing on God's mind was that all of creation—both human and nonhuman—would reach the heights of their existence by worshipping him and therein finding joys unimaginable. Would that mean they would rightly care for his planet? Certainly. Was caring for the planet his ultimate concern? Certainly not. The primary calling and task of the human being is not care for the garden but to worship the Creator of the garden.

32. Nash, *Loving Nature,* 104.

33. Santmire, *Brother Earth,* 86.

34. Poythress, *Redeeming Science,* 150.

35. Nash, *Loving Nature,* 103.

36. Young, 160–61, my italics.

Conclusion

In light of these truths, then, it is proper to conclude that while interpreting Gen 2:15 does include working for, tilling, caring for and guarding the garden, there is a far more beautiful context that drives us to understand that Adam's primary job description was to be the lead worshipper for the entire created realm! In addition, it is also proper to assert, in diametrical opposition to the accusations made by those who would lay blame for the world's ecological problems at the feet of Christianity, that the solution to any environmental crisis comes not in dismissing Christianity and the dominion mandate but in rightly understanding Gen 1:28 as a worship mandate and fully owning it as the most promising way forward!

In the final analysis, worshipful obedience that subdues and rules the created order to the Glory of God is clearly meant to indicate that in the fullness of their nature as image bearers, Adam and Eve (and their descendants) were given a mandate as benevolent rulers to work hard with great joy at the prospect of rendering to God a continuous, eternal act of worship in a way that loved, cared for, shaped and served the created realm. That is what they were created for, that is what the garden was created for, and that is how they *and it* would have fulfilled the ultimate purpose each was created for—the maximization of the Glory of God.

Bibliography

Beale, G. K. *The Temple and the Church's Mission: A Biblical Theology of the Dwelling Place of God*. Downers Grove, IL: InterVarsity, 2004.

Bouma-Prediger, Steven. *For the Beauty of the Earth*. Grand Rapids: Baker, 2002.

Cassuto, Umberto. *A Commentary on the Book of Genesis*. Translated by Israel Abrahams. Jerusalem: Magnes, 1978.

DeWitt, Calvin B. *Earth-Wise: A Biblical Response to Environmental Issues*. 2nd ed. Grand Rapids: Faith Alive, 2005.

Due, Noel. *Created for Worship: From Genesis to Revelation to You*. Fern, Scotland: Christian Focus, 2005.

Gottlieb, Roger S. *A Greener Faith*. Oxford: Oxford University Press, 2006.

Jamieson, Robert, et al. *Commentary Critical and Explanatory on the Whole Bible*. Oak Harbor: Logos Research Systems, 1998.

Jenni, Ernst, and Claus Westermann, eds. *Theological Lexicon of the Old Testament*. Translated by Mark E. Biddle. Peabody, MA: Hendrickson, 1994.

Kline, Meredith G. "Creation in the Image of the Glory-Spirit." *Westminster Theological Journal* 39 (1977) 250–72.

———. *Images of the Spirit*. Grand Rapids: Baker, 1980.

Liederbach, Mark, and Seth Bible. *True North: Christ, the Gospel and Creation Care*. Nashville: B & H Academic, 2012.

Manahan, Ronald. "Christ as the Second Adam." In *The Environment and the Christian*, edited by Calvin B. DeWitt, 45–56. Grand Rapids: Baker, 1991.

Matthews, Kenneth A. *The New American Commentary: Genesis 1–11:26*. Nashville: Broadman & Holman, 1996.

Murray, John. *Principles of Conduct*. Grand Rapid: Eerdmans, 1957.

Nash, James A. *Loving Nature: Ecological Integrity and Christian Responsibility*. Nashville: Abingdon, 1991.

Poythress, Vern S. *Redeeming Science: A God-Centered Approach*. Wheaton, IL: Crossway, 2006.

Ross, Allen P. *Creation and Blessing: A Guide to the Study and Exposition of Genesis*. Grand Rapids: Baker, 1996.

Sailhamer, John H. "Genesis." In *The Expositor's Bible Commentary* vol. 2, *Genesis, Exodus, Leviticus, Numbers*, edited by Walter C. Kaiser and Bruce K. Waltke. Grand Rapids: Regency, 1990.

Santmire, H. Paul. *Brother Earth: Nature, God and Ecology in Time of Crisis*. New York: Nelson, 1970.

Schaeffer, Francis, and Udo Middlemann. *Pollution and the Death of Man*. Wheaton, IL: Crossway, 1970.

Tolkien, J. R. R. *The Lord of the Rings: The Two Towers*. New York: Ballantine, 2012.

White, Lynn. "The Historical Roots of Our Ecologic Crisis." *Science* 155, no. 3767 (1967) 1203–7.

Wilkinson, Loren, et al. *EarthKeeping in the Nineties: Stewardship of Creation*. Grand Rapids: Eerdmans, 1991.

Wright, Christopher J. H. *The Mission of God*. Downers Grove: IVP Academic, 2006.

Young, Richard A. *Healing the Earth: A Theocentric Perspective on Environmental Problems*. Nashville: Broadman & Holman, 1994.

16

Reading the Magnificat in a Time of Crisis

Taking and Giving Life

Anne Elvey

Introduction

THE ANTHROPOCENE IS A name for the age in which we are living, a time in which human activity is having effects on a geological and global scale.[1] For around fifty years, probably longer, what we have been facing has been described as a crisis, an ecological crisis, and we have heard and been distressed by talk of environmental destruction and ecocide.[2] Such is the critical time in which we live, where on average the climate is warming and will continue to do so, where we are in the sixth major extinction period, where there are unimaginable losses of biodiversity and suitable habitats, both human and other-than-human, where overpopulation and overconsumption have become jointly problematic, where our children and grandchildren and their children and their children's children will likely bear the cost, where we have made some responses in tackling pollution, in conservation, and in divestment from fossil fuels, where there is much more to be done. How might a song such as the Magnificat, sung or recited

---

1. See Chakrabarty, "Climate of History."

2. At least since Lynn White's oft cited 1967 article this has been described as an ecological crisis: White, "Historical Roots of Our Ecological Crisis."

daily in monasteries and convents, churches and private homes, be prayed effectively in this time?

I will take what might seem a strange route to address this question. My path takes me through a brief survey of the way the Magnificat has been referenced especially in creative writing in the press in Australia in the first half of the twentieth century, to a particular focus on a story entitled "Magnificat" by Australian writer H. (Henrietta) Drake-Brockman (1901–1968).[3] The story appeared in *The West Australian* in January 1939.[4] Written as the Second World War approached, Drake-Brockman's short story "Magnificat" raised serious questions concerning giving and taking life, with direct reference to Mary's song in the Gospel of Luke. I will draw some threads of interpretation from Drake-Brockman's story before turning to the Gospel of Luke and asking about the threads of death and life in the Magnificat. Finally, I will suggest one way in which the widely-used song-poem-prayer that is the Magnificat might suggest prayers for our time.

The Magnificat in Australia

As part of both the biblical and liturgical tradition of Christianity and the European cultural tradition of choral composition and performance, the Magnificat came to Australia with British colonization. In addition to the many references to nineteenth- and twentieth-century performances of the Magnificat, Handel's or Bach's for example, the Magnificat is mentioned in the daily press as early as 1860, in an article in *The Argus* entitled "Church of England Mission to the Aborigine," where Mr. Goodwin reports on his visit to "the Native Training Institution at Poonindie, which lies 10 miles to the north of the town of Port Lincoln:" ". . . The Rev. O. Hammond read service, the whole congregation joining in the responses, in a devout and intelligent manner . . . reading in audible yet subdued voice the alternate verses of the psalms, the 'Magnificat' and 'Deus Misereatur' . . ."[5] In 1875, *The Argus'* "special correspondent" reports on "A Visit to the Melanesian Mission Station," where "The congregation led by the Rev. Mr. Brooke at the

---

3. The Benedictus and Nunc Dimittis, also prayed daily, appear in the Australian press, in various forms, with the Nunc Dimittis occasioning creative writing, but mostly with reference to a final farewell in the face of age or approaching death, and not with quite the variety of reference that the Magnificat seems to occasion.

4. Drake-Brockmann, "Magnificat."

5. Goodwin, "Church of England Mission to the Aborigine."

harmonium, chanted the *Magnificat*, the *Nunc Dimitis*, and the psalms, in excellent style."[6]

In the twentieth century, across the country, creative writings themed on the Magnificat were published from time to time. Arthur Symons' 1909 "Magnificat" in the Adelaide *Quiz*, "A satirical, social and sporting journal," praises God for the speaker's erotic love of a woman.[7] A more pious version appears in an article on The Magnificat in 1915 in the *Prahran Chronicle*, shifting the subject of the song to its traditional speaker Mary, so that "Daily at the vesper hour, / Mary's name is praised," and she is "Great in her magnificence."[8] The biblical Magnificat is printed in full in the *Newcastle Morning Herald and Miners' Advocate* on Christmas Day 1915 alongside other Christian religious material.[9] In January 1917, *The Register*, Adelaide, publishes Frederic Warner's poem "Earth's Magnificat" which lists what the speaker cannot know compared with the little he does, for example:

> I may not know the story of the earth
>
> The sea with all its secrets, wide and deep
>
> I may not know what is beyond death's sleep
>
> or all the strange sweet mystery of birth

But he praises nonetheless:

> Although my mind may question this or that,
>
> I gladly join in earth's magnificat.[10]

This is Job joined with Luke's Mary, but with the focus shifted to Earth as prompt for and agent of praise. Only at the close does the speaker turn explicitly toward the divine: "And at the feet of God adoring fall."[11] Clearly, the verse does not match the quality of the poetics of either Job or the Magnificat, but it suggests an interesting shift of emphasis, one which has resonance with Lola Gornall's sonnet, "Magnificat," published in *The Australian Worker*, Sydney, 1919. Here the speaker's (seaside?) garden is locus of the sacred:

---

6. Special Correspondent, "Visit to the Melanesian Mission Station."

7. Symons, "Magnificat." See, also, "SA Newspapers."

8. From "The Parish Supplement."

9. "Religious Topics."

10. Warner, "Earth's Magnificat."

11. Ibid.

The sea's High Mass, the Psalms the wind forsook.

The rosary of Morn, the fugue of Night,

The holy vespers that the flowers keep . . .

I need no priest to pray with lowered eyes

For me: God feels the thrill of my delight . . .

and in the final line God looks on her with evident fondness.[12]

A sermon by Rev. J. H. Jowett, D.D., entitled "Life's Magnificat" and published in both *The Maitland Daily Mercury* and *The Maitland Weekly Mercury* in 1920 refers to Ps 70:4, but implicitly also to Luke's Magnificat, and focuses on a kind of joy such that for the psalmists: "God's statutes have become their songs," and "by God's grace our hearts can sing the Magnificat through everything."[13] This seems to me a good way of describing song in relation to country, such that for traditional owners the laws of country are their song. Can the statutes of Earth or, if one prefers, the statutes of a godly Creation become our song?

In 1926, the *Freeman's Journal* (Sydney) presents a more traditional verse entitled "Magnificat" by Charles O'Donnell, C.S.C, which narrates Mary's visit to Elizabeth.[14] While "rivers" are "not so strong and sweet" as Mary, nonetheless the song allows the Earth and its weather, sun and moon, to interact as agents with the travelling woman, leading to the intimacy of the two cousins and the telling lines toward the end: "And then the traveler, full of grace, / Sang, or her heart had died." Amidst the piety and sentimentality of the verse O'Donnell picks up something true about the song, the way it stands on the side of life at a critical point where an unnamed (in his verse) oppression might occasion despair and where human life and action is always more-than-human. This more-than-human agency[15] also appears in an unattributed verse "Wind and Wave" published in 1933 on the "Matrons and Maids" page of the *Catholic Freeman's Journal* (Sydney), formerly the *Freeman's Journal*, where the wind seems to sing "Mary's deathless hymn" and the waves murmur "Our Lady's Rosary."[16]

12. Gornall, "Magnificat."

13. Jowett, "Life's Magnificat."

14. O'Donnell, "Magnificat."

15. On more-than-human and material agency, see, for example, Bennett, *Vibrant Matter*; Knappett and Malafouris, *Material Agency*; Elvey, *Matter of the Text*.

16. "Wind and Wave."

What these examples suggest is not only that the Magnificat, recited or sung daily, captured the imaginations of settler Australians as an important part of their colonial and religious heritage, but that it formed a kind of template for exploring experiences of the sacred sometimes in a more-than-human frame. The instances also pick up on the issues of death and life central to the Lukan Magnificat, and the way the song itself, in its performance, can be empowering for life. In this tradition, H. Drake-Brockman's short story "Magnificat" poignantly juxtaposes the song with the horror of war.

H. Drake-Brockman's "Magnificat"

Henrietta Drake-Brockman's husband Geoffrey, born in 1885, was a civil engineer. Part of the Drake-Brockman family, descendants of Geoffrey's great grandfather William Locke Brockman's nephew James Groves, were Western Australian establishment and held property, kept Aboriginal people parochially, and featured contentiously in Sally Morgan's *My Place*. Geoffrey Drake-Brockman had fought in World War I. Henrietta was born in 1901 and married Geoffrey in 1921. Her two children were born around 1924 and 1927, so by the time she is writing "Magnificat" she is herself a mother of growing children.[17] Drake-Brockman's "Magnificat" appears in January 1939 on the same page of *The West Australian* as a reprint of an article by Winston Churchill, P.C., M.P., "Dangers in Eastern Europe: Poland and the Balkans," where he writes "All Eastern Europe spends the Christmas in deep fear. Against whom will the next blow be directed?"[18] Beside the threat of Nazism and Churchill's hope that Eastern European states will unite against it, and in so doing engage the support of Western democracies, Drake-Brockman tells a story of a mother and son whose apartment is bombed in an air strike. The precise location remains unspecified. While likely Czechoslovakia, Poland, or the Balkans is meant, there is a universal theme to the mother-son narrative. A woman rouses herself after the terror of a bombing and thinking her son is dead finds him still breathing but with his legs severed. She decides to spare first herself, and incidentally her son, the pain of wakening as he bleeds to death, and uses a cushion to smoother him. While she hopes to avoid the look he will give her—charging her with

---

17. Cowan, "Drake-Brockman, Henrietta Frances (1901–1968)." For Judith Drake-Brockman's "take" on the "Morgan controversy," see Drake-Brockman, "Sally Morgan Controversy." Some family tree information was derived from the open access part of http://www.brockman.net.au/. For a different understand of the Drake-Brockman–Sally Morgan conflict, see Probyn-Rapsey, "Kin-fused Reconciliation."

18. Churchill, "Dangers in Eastern Europe."

the betrayal that war is of the life that she gave in his birth—in death his open eyes seem nonetheless to accuse her. The repetitions, short sentences, exclamations, and ellipses work to heighten the drama. The descriptions of her bodily experience, the vivid colors, the trembling of her hand, together situate the experience of the violence of war as embodied—a sensory corporeal experience in which sensation is saturated. The references to birth at this moment of dying evoke the life-death nexus, and place it at the cusp of the maternal. The coda after the asterisks shifts the focus to a bomber, someone's equally celebrated son, returning to base, satisfied with his work: "Every bomb a bull's-eye. Those new carriers worked like a dream." The story becomes at one level a protest at the impending war, or at least at the inevitability of the harm it will occasion, a harm which undoes a basic trust not only between mother and child, but between creator and creation.

The story is titled "Magnificat" and perhaps this is in part to evoke the religious heritage of the European woman who several times exclaims "Mother of God!" At first when the son, whom she had thought dead is alive (surely an echo of the joy and perhaps also the compassion of the father in the parable of the lost/prodigal son in Luke 15), the woman prays the opening line of the Magnificat. Later when she recalls the child's birth and her participation in the wondrous life-giving of creation, she prays this line: *Behold, from henceforth all generations shall call me blessed.* As I have argued elsewhere and will suggest below, these generations open to the multiple more than human genealogies of creation.[19] In the deliberate reference to the Magnificat, Drake-Brockman's narrative opens a space for interpretative conversation between the story and the song, through: 1) the strong maternal thematic which to some extent gets backgrounded (as does the Earth) in Luke's song (in favor of human issues of justice and liberation, and a male genealogy); 2) the function of both story and song as protest; and 3) the implication that the Magnificat like the story stands in sight of the cross.[20]

Reading the Magnificat in Luke: A Conversation

I will take up those three threads of the maternal, protest, and the cross for the beginnings of an interpretative conversation with the Magnificat in Luke's gospel.

19. Elvey, "Hermeneutics of Retrieval."

20. A similar link is made in a verse published in 1941. O'Leary, "Magnificat—Nunc Dimittis."

1. Recovering the Maternal and the Earth
at the Nexus of Life and Death

The maternal, in particular the body in pregnancy, and the Earth, as I have shown previously, share a quality of gift-life givenness, a material givenness, that is necessary for human and other forms of mammalian life.[21] This quality of givenness is in tension with the kinds of hyperseparations, or dualisms, of which Val Plumwood is rightly critical: self-other; heaven-earth; spirit-matter; mind-body; master-slave. The last of these supposed oppositions is at issue in the world of Lukan reversals of rich-poor and oppressor-oppressed, where good news means liberation and forgiveness of the kind of debt that keeps people in slavery not only to sin, but also—and it can be argued primarily—materially to unjust economic, social, and political systems.[22] At the same time, these issues of death and life, are embedded in what Michael Trainor identifies as the underlying biblical story of creation embedded in the infancy narratives of Luke.[23] This creation and birth story for Luke stands in tension with the Roman imperial story (2:1–7)[24] and offers a different kind of peace on and for—and we might want to add in cooperation with—Earth (2:14). The visiting angels bringing a message of peace from the skies (also part of the cosmos in which Earth is itself embedded) are also part of creation for the first century CE writer of Luke. In the Magnificat the issues of life and death are evident not only in the tropes of power and wealth, sustenance and satiation (1:51–53), but also in the divine mercy—both toward the humble or humiliated woman (1:48, 50) and through the covenant with the ancestors toward the people of Israel (1:54–55). This mercy is expressed in Luke in what Brendan Byrne describes as the hospitality of God, evident in the tropes of forgiveness and compassion, the latter of which carries also the thread of the maternal.[25]

---

21. Elvey, "The Material Given;" *Ecological Feminist Reading of the Gospel of Luke*.

22. Plumwood, *Feminism and the Mastery of Nature*; Elvey, "Can There Be a Forgiveness That Makes a Difference Ecologically?"

23. Trainor, *About Earth's Child*, esp. 64–90.

24. Reid, "Overture to the Gospel of Luke," 429. There is a growing literature on Luke's attitude to the Roman Empire; see my brief discussion in Elvey, "Rethinking Neighbour Love," 64–67.

25. Byrne, *Hospitality of God*; Elvey, *Ecological Feminist Reading of the Gospel of Luke*, 225.

2. Stories and Songs of Protest

Earlier I noted, however, that despite the song's being sung by a woman—and I accept Mary rather than Elizabeth, as the Lukan singer[26]—unlike the visitation episode in which it is set, the song appears to make little direct reference to the maternal. Instead, it seems at one level to re-inscribe dualisms of rich and poor, power and weakness, oppressed and oppressor, through the (in some cases) violent reversal of these (1:51). While at one point the song refers to generations generically (1:50), later the reference is to the male ancestral line of Abraham and his sons (1:55). Nonetheless, the reference recalls the covenant with the people (1:55) and the reversals signal that, as several scholars—including Warren Carter and Barbara Reid—have argued, the song is a song of protest.[27]

In allowing an interpretative conversation between Drake-Brockman's story and Luke's Magnificat we might note on the one hand the way the story sets up the shock of the mother's mercy killing of her child as a protest against the death-dealing of war, however just or otherwise, and the Lukan song sets up the shock of violent reversals as a protest against the underlying oppression they symbolize. On the other hand, there is a stark difference: Drake-Brockman's story can also be read as a protest against the failures of the God of the song at the point where, in war, creation (human and we can add other-than-human) seems to be betrayed by the creator, as death overtakes life. In Mary's song God's promise is spoken as life-giving protest against death-dealing oppression.

3. Standing in Sight of the Cross

Drake-Brockman's story with its focus on a mother witnessing (and hastening) the dying of her son moves us from the infancy narratives, in which the Magnificat is situated in Luke, to something like the crucifixion narrative. The image of the Pieta (albeit with a young rather than an adult child) comes to mind. The link between birth narrative and cross is one that appears in

26. The reference to Hannah's song, recalling her barrenness, and in particular the humiliation of the speaker have raised the question whether Elizabeth might have been the speaker of the song, but the reference to humiliation accompanies the speaker's self-description as *doulé* (1:48) echoing Mary's self-description in 1:38. Moreover, the Greek textual tradition supports the acceptance of Mary as speaker. See further, Bovon, *Luke 1*, 60. On translating *tapeinó sin* as "humiliation," see Fitzmyer, *Gospel according to Luke I–IX*, 367, and the discussion in Schaberg, *Illegitimacy of Jesus*, 97–98.

27. Reid, "Overture to the Gospel of Luke;" Reid, "Women Prophets of God's Alternative Reign"; Carter, "Singing in the Reign."

Matt 1–2, especially in the warning of the magi, the slaughter of the children, and the flight to Egypt (Matt 2:1–18), but also in Mary's encounter with Simeon in Luke (2:33–35). In the birth of the child is the shadow of his death. Both women, the mother in Drake-Brockman's "Magnificat" and Mary in Luke's Gospel, will outlive their sons.

In our contemporary context, as Norman Habel has long reminded us, when we face our contemporary ecological crisis, we stand in sight of the cross, with and as part of a crucified Earth, witness to the scorched places human activity has created or decreated.[28] What might be called the contemporary "war" on creation is at this nexus where creation seems to have been betrayed by the creator, because of one part of creation: humankind, and more particularly a large subgroup of humankind that are consciously and unconsciously wreaking havoc, not unlike the bomber.

In our traditions, religious and cultural, the Magnificat, a Lukan song with deep roots in the Jewish scriptures—for example, 1 Sam 2:1–10; and other women's songs, Exod 15:19–20; Judg 5:1–31; Jdt 16:1–17, and Psalms—offers the possibility of celebrating life and protesting damage. The song is open, then, to the way the gift-like givenness of creation unsettles the death-dealing of oppressive structures based in self-other, master-slave, rich-poor, and culture-nature dualisms.

Praying the Magnificat in a Time of Ecological Crisis

How might praying the Magnificat as part of the hours, or at Evensong, or as a Second Testament psalm, or as a song of protest, inform a culture of care for creation?

The cadences of the Magnificat in any good English translation are such that it is well nigh impossible to write a "Magnificat" that is anywhere near as potent. But just as the song has offered a model for early settler Australians to shape their experiences, it may suggest contemporary prayers to us. In the following, in the form of a prayer rather than a poem, I take up three aspects: generations, mercy and reversal, noting nonetheless that reversal can be problematic in that it can simply reinstate the power relations reversed.

> Our souls and our spirits celebrate
>
> Earth enlarges
>
> We breathe Earth's breath

28. Habel, "Crucified Land;" Habel, *Rainbow of Mysteries*, 214–19.

God has seen the mountaintop removed
and the valley filled with tailings

God knows the shame of kin torn from Country
and has looked on the coral in its reef

On this basis we are called fortunate
and God, holy
whose mercy is from generation to generation

for air and oceans, mercy
for dying species, mercy
for inundated islands, mercy
for displaced islanders, mercy
for asylum seekers, mercy
for our children and grandchildren, mercy
for all species now and to come, mercy

God has scattered the proud in the thoughts of their hearts

God has brought down coal magnates
and renewed despoiled habitats

God has sustained endangered species
and summoned to account the shareholders

God has slowed the thundering roadtrain and
from the pouch of the prone roo has lifted the joey

God has shaken the foundations of our comfort
and crawled into the burrow of the endling[29]

29. An endling is the last surviving individual of a species.

We barely believe this to be true

because God does not do this alone—

reminding us of the promise

Earth is waiting for us to remember

Earth is waiting for us to abide

It is by Earth's covenant we are bound with God

and our descendants forever

Bibliography

Bennett, Jane. *Vibrant Matter: A Political Ecology of Things.* Durham: Duke University Press, 2010.

Bovon, François. *Luke 1: A Commentary on the Gospel of Luke 1:1—9:50.* Translated by Christine M. Thomas. *Hermeneia 63A,* edited by Helmut Koester. Accordance electronic ed. Minneapolis: Fortress, 2002.

Byrne, Brendan. *The Hospitality of God: A Reading of Luke's Gospel.* Strathfield: St Pauls, 2000.

Chakrabarty, Dipesh. "The Climate of History: Four Theses." *Critical Inquiry* 35 (2009) 197–222.

Churchill, Winston, P.C, M.P. "Dangers in Eastern Europe: Poland and the Balkans." *The West Australian* (Saturday 7 January 1939) 5.

Cowan, Peter. "Drake-Brockman, Henrietta Frances (1901–1968)." *Australian Dictionary of Biography.* http://adb.anu.edu.au/biography/drake-brockman-henrietta-frances-10683.

Drake-Brockmann, H. (Henrietta). "Magnificat." *The West Australian* (Perth, Saturday 7 January 1939) 5.

Drake-Brockman, Judith. "The Sally Morgan Controversy." http://www.brockman.net.au/morgan.html.

Carter, Warren. "Singing in the Reign: Performing Luke's Songs and Negotiating the Roman Empire (Luke 1–2)." In *Luke-Acts and Empire: Essays in Honor of Robert L. Brawley,* edited by David Rhoads et al., 23–43. Ebook. Princeton Theological Monograph Series 151. Eugene: Pickwick, 2011.

Elvey, Anne. "Can There Be a Forgiveness That Makes a Difference Ecologically? An Eco-Materialist Account of Forgiveness as Freedom (*áphesis*) in the Gospel of Luke." *Pacifica: Australasian Theological Studies* 22 (2009) 148–70.

———. "A Hermeneutics of Retrieval: Breath and Earth Voice in the Magnificat—Does Earth Care for the Poor?" Paper given in the Ecological Hermeneutics Section of the Society of Biblical Literature, Baltimore, November 2013.

———. "The Material Given: Bodies, Pregnant Bodies and Earth." *Australian Feminist Studies* 18 (2003) 199–209.

———. *The Matter of the Text: Material Engagements between Luke and the Five Senses.* The Bible in the Modern World 37. Sheffield: Sheffield Phoenix, 2011.

———. "Rethinking Neighbour Love: A Conversation between Political Theology and Ecological Ethics." In *Where the Wild Ox Roams: Biblical Essays in Honour of Norman C. Habel*, edited by Alan H. Cadwallader and Peter L. Trudinger, 58–75. Sheffield: Sheffield Phoenix, 2013.

Fitzmyer, Joseph A. *The Gospel according to Luke I–IX: Introduction, Translation, and Notes.* Anchor Bible 28. New York: Doubleday, 1981.

Goodwin, Mr. "Church of England Mission to the Aborigine." *The Argus* (Melbourne, Monday 23 January 1860) 5.

Gornall, Lola. "Magnificat." *The Australian Worker* (Sydney, Thursday 20 March 1919) 13.

Habel, Norman. "The Crucified Land: Towards Our Reconciliation with the Earth." *Colloquium: The Australian and New Zealand Theological Review* 28.2 (1996) 3–18.

———. *Rainbow of Mysteries: Meeting the Sacred in Nature.* Ebook. Kelowna: CopperHouse, 2012.

Jowett, Rev. J. H., D. D. "Life's Magnificat." *The Maitland Daily Mercury* (Thursday 22 July 1920) 2. Also appears in *The Maitland Weekly Mercury* (Saturday 24 July 1920) 5.

Knappett, Carl, and Lambros Malafouris, eds. *Material Agency: Toward a Non-Anthropocentric Approach.* New York: Springer, 2008.

Morgan, Sally. *My Place.* Fremantle: Fremantle Arts Centre, 1987.

O'Donnell, Charles, C.S.C. "Magnificat." *Freeman's Journal* (Sydney, Thursday 4 March 1926) 31.

O'Leary, Isabel. "Magnificat—Nunc Dimittis." *The Catholic Press* (Sydney, Thursday 28 August 1941) 10.

"The Parish Supplement." Reprinted in *Prahran Chronicle* (Saturday 18 September 1915) 4.

Plumwood, Val. *Feminism and the Mastery of Nature.* Edited by Teresa Brennan. Feminism for Today. London: Routledge, 1993.

Probyn-Rapsey, Fiona. "Kin-fused Reconciliation: Bringing Them Home, Bringing Us Home." *Australian Humanities Review* 42 (August–September 2007). http://www.australianhumanitiesreview.org/archive/Issue-August-September-2007/Probyn.html.

Reid, Barbara E. "An Overture to the Gospel of Luke." *Currents in Theology and Mission* 39 (2012) 428–34.

———. "Women Prophets of God's Alternative Reign." In *Luke–Acts and Empire: Essays in Honor of Robert L. Brawley*, edited by David Rhoads et al., 44–59. Ebook, Princeton Theological Monograph Series 151. Eugene, OR: Pickwick, 2011.

"Religious Topics." *Newcastle Morning Herald and Miners' Advocate* (Saturday 25 December 1915) 14.

"SA Newspapers: Comic Papers." South Australia Memory. State Library of South Australia. http://www.samemory.sa.gov.au/site/page.cfm?u=1471.

Schaberg, Jane. *The Illegitimacy of Jesus: A Feminist Theological Interpretation of the Infancy Narratives.* New York: Crossroad, 1990.

Special Correspondent. "A Visit to the Melanesian Mission Station." *The Argus* (Melbourne, Saturday 13 February 1875) 9.

Symons, Arthur. "Magnificat." *Quiz* (Adelaide, Friday 23 April 1909) 2.

Trainor, Michael. *About Earth's Child: An Ecological Listening to the Gospel of Luke.* Earth Bible Commentary Series 2. Sheffield: Sheffield Phoenix, 2012.

Warner, Frederic. "Earth's Magnificat." *The Register* (Adelaide, Saturday 6 January 1917) 4.

White, Lynn. "The Historical Roots of Our Ecological Crisis." In *This Sacred Earth: Religion, Nature, Environment,* edited by Roger S. Gottlieb, 184–93. New York: Routledge, 1996 [1967].

"Wind and Wave." *Catholic Freeman's Journal* (Sydney, Thursday 5 October 1933) 3.

EPILOGUE

A Spirituality of the Earth

Heather Eaton

I COME FROM CANADA. IT is a vast land of Great Lakes, coasts, mountains, prairies, forests, and tundra. The seasons are pronounced, with hot summers and cold winters, often with excessive snow. The natural world is a prominent feature of daily life. The many Indigenous nations, the first peoples on this land, understand the natural world to be infused with spirit, sacred presence, and spiritual wisdom. Today most other Canadians do not consider, or experience, the natural world to be related to their spiritual concerns. The theme of this book is *Rediscovering the Spiritual in God's Creation*. What will assist this process? How can we retrieve a spiritual attentiveness to the natural world? How can we learn from Geswanouth Slahoot, known as Chief Dan George, former chief of the Tsleil-Waututh Nation, a Salish band on Vancouver Island, Canada?

> *The beauty of the trees,*
> *the softness of the air,*
> *the fragrance of the grass speak to me,*
> *and my heart soars.*
>
> —Chief Dan George

". . . ask the animals, and they will teach you, or the birds of the air, and they will tell you; or speak to the Earth, and it will teach you, or let the fish of the sea inform you. Which of all these does not know that the hand of God has done this?" (Job 12:7–9).

The cosmos, the Earth, the natural world have been at the basis of many, if not most, spiritual traditions. Religious language, from all traditions, is

229

infused with images of nature. The most primal spiritual insights, that nature and sacred are connected, are found in Aboriginal cultures, as well as in Hindu, Buddhist, Jain, Zoroastrian, Daoist, Confucian, Jewish, Christian, Islam and Baha'i traditions. Poets, who allow the natural world to penetrate their senses, exalt the depths of the "nature." The term "creation" has had several meanings over time, and often not referring to the natural world.

Creation in the Christian Traditions

What forms and informs the views and meanings given to creation involves myriad blending of science, scriptures, doctrines, beliefs, imagination and desires. Interpretations of "creation" are affected by the metaphysics, anthropology, theodicy and ontologies of their time. Core beliefs about creation have repercussions for interpretations of God, nature, and the role of humans within the scheme of things. These beliefs and interpretations are central aspects of the Christian theological scaffold. Major interpretive shifts, such as if all of creation manifests Divine presence, or none of it does, effect virtually all key theological tenets such as anthropology, sin, salvation and teleology.[1]

There is a long trajectory of doctrinal and theological discussions, over centuries, about creation. Most of this focuses on why and how God created the world. The classic Christian doctrine of creation is that of *creatio ex nihilo*: God freely created everything in form and being out of absolutely nothing. There are countless debates about eternity and temporality, of divine and natural law, natural and supernatural, *Imago Dei*, the fall, salvation, divine action, providence, and a host of other topics.[2] Speculative, philosophical approaches have governed these inquiries.

Gradually the meaning of creation was transformed into how to relate to existence. In general terms, this included an existential angst or ambiguity towards human life and towards the exigencies of negotiating with the natural world. Over time the doctrine of creation became ensnared with the doctrine of the fall. While having several variations, notions of the fall incorporated a pervasive attitude that creation is not as God intended it. This, of course, is not God's fault. It is due to the influence of evil, and the

1. Eaton, "Creation," 56–66.

2. Topics of God's freedom, kenosis, nothingness, formlessness, matter and substance, being and non-being, primordial nature, why something out of nothing, why something at all . . . omnipotence, omniscience, Trinitarian theology, the ontological orientation towards evil or goodness . . . and dozens more have preoccupied innumerable theological themes for centuries.

choices and actions of creatures with freedom. Creation is damaged, typically blamed on human disobedience, freedom, or willful ignorance. Some thought that the whole of creation has fallen, and is corrupt. This theological view of creation is structured within a firm natural and supernatural divide. The dominant Christian position is that the fall irreparably harmed both human relations with God and the character of the creation. Suffering and mortality, for humans, are the consequences. Creation became the context for the human drama of salvation. Humans need to be saved to a better, different or other world/realm of existence.

Within this interpretation, the image of the divine is obscured or imperceptible in creation. Salvation customarily means to be saved from this corrupt creation. Humans will be saved from this creation to a transhistorical reality in which they will be redeemed, healed and (re)united with God in an "afterlife." This has led to strong otherworldly theologies and expectations, where life on Earth is regarded as a diminished and provisional form of existence. Eternity trumps temporality. It is important to grasp that in this view, life and existence as we know them are inadequate or flawed and thus unacceptable. This, concisely stated, is the dominant stance within most Christian theologies, past and present.

There is a second, less known, historical current of thought about the nature of creation. This approach here is mainly about creation as the phenomenological order: the universe, galaxies, Earth and the natural world. This stream of thought about creation has taken the cosmos and the natural world to be a place of divine revelation: as primary, secondary or as parallel to the customary Christian notions of revelation. Influential thinkers such as Hildegard of Bingen and Thomas Aquinas studied cosmological parameters and integrated these in to their theological frameworks. They learned the best science of their day. Still others, known for their "creation spirituality," such as Meister Eckhart, Francis of Assisi and Julian of Norwich attended to the natural world, and its spiritual revelations. A mutual influence between natural sciences and spirituality was fundamental. For example, for Thomas Aquinas, errors of reasoning about the natural world led directly to errors concerning the divine world. There is an equally long history of these views of creation, albeit often peripheral to the prevailing beliefs.

Over time, Christian worldviews developed an intensely anthropocentric worldview. Traditional Christian ideas separated the natural world from spiritual imagery and religious experiences. The spiritual emphasis on human distinctiveness from and superiority to the natural world fostered a tenacious anthropocentrism that was built into theological scaffolds, and infused Christian cultures. Fall-redemption theologies overtook Christian cultures and religious imagination. The Christian tradition constantly tries to "lift" humanity above the Earth and the limits it represents. The natural world, if not corrupt, disappeared as a theological reference or source of revelation. It has no inherent, spiritual or sacred presence. The fallout is attitudes and actions that continually break with the integrity of the natural world.

Euro-western cultures live within a worldview established on an alienation of humans from the Earth. The operative Christian worldview, with its emphasis that human origin and destiny are elsewhere, is a profoundly human-centered ideology. Ecotheologians constantly address this pervasive anthropocentrism, the Christian emphasis on humanity's transcendence over the natural world, and the thrust to desacralize it.[3]

The foremost concern for the redemptive process has concealed the realization that the disintegration of the natural world is also the destruction of the primordial manifestation of the divine. Disregarding the primordial, vital and profound relationships between the spiritual and creation—spirit and nature—as well as the intellectual alliances between science—especially evolution—and theology, has caused an absence of concern for the natural world. As a result there is a diminished Christian awareness of a sacred indwelling presence in the natural world, or creation. Some would argue that this is one of the central causes of the ecological crisis, and the excessive domination and exploitation of the Earth.

Over the past twenty years, "creation" has come to mean the 13.8 billion year process of the universe, from the original fireball to the present.[4] Countless theologians have learned what cosmological and evolutionary sciences explain about "creation." Creation stories have been exhumed and studied, with myriad debates about Genesis versus science, narratives versus metanarratives, faith versus scientific data, and justice versus earth-based spiritualties. Although theologies of creation are increasing, few theologians study evolution in depth. Taking evolution seriously dislocates all the topics of this essay: creation, God, humanity and the natural world. Consideration of evolution invites attentiveness to processes of emergence, complexity, diversity, patterns, ingenuity and inter-relations. Evolution exposes an absolute dependence on the natural world. We, in fact, are not the reference point.

Many today are trying to retrieve, renew or arouse a connection between spirit and nature. Ecotheology has expanded over the past thirty years exponentially. It is encouraging that these transformations are occurring.

3. Pearson, "On Being Public," 51.

4. From Pierre Teilhard de Chardin and Alfred North Whitehead to the present, many seek an integration of cosmological and earth sciences with theology. Current conversations exist in all Christian traditions, among many people.

Ecotheology, now an independent field, crosses into systematics, ethics, history, biblical studies, liturgy, and spirituality, and spans the diversity of Christianities. Methodologies are multiple. Ecotheology has become a comprehensive reform of Christianity, as well as a new expression.[5] My focus here, also with the ecological crisis in mind, is on reconnecting nature to spirit, human to nature, and understanding the continuity between spirit, nature and humanity.

Humans, Nature and Spirit: Four Configurations

Our experiences, conceptualizations of, and behaviors towards the natural world are interrelated. There are several configurations of this triad. For example, many consider that the natural world is not related to the sacred, or involved in salvation history. The natural world is simply the backdrop for the human drama. In this view, only humans are in the image and likeness of God. Spirit and nature are unrelated. We might see nature as a threat or as a set of resources for our use. Either way, watersheds can be drained, animals displaced and hunted for sport, species can be genetically modified or driven to extinction, and these will not be spiritual issues. Perhaps we need to be better stewards of this creation, and be attentive to an equal distribution of the resources of the natural world. However, creation itself is not part of the image of God, or spiritually relevant, in this view.

For those who connect spirit and nature, there are three distinct configurations. One is metaphoric. To speak of God is to use metaphors, and nature is one set of metaphors. God is like the wind, a mother eagle, a rock, a dove, still waters, fire, or a gentle breeze of the evening. Here, the natural world teaches us about God: we can discern something of the spirit of God because this is God's creation, thus reveals God's ways. In this way, nature points to something about God.

Another way is to experience nature and spirit as ontologically intermingled. Nature is animated with spirit and is alive with sacred presence: a form of Christian animism. Throughout history there are countless forms of animism where nature is perceived to be filled with distinct spirits, or inspirited with living, sacred power. Places (groves, mountains, rivers, caves) and life forms are modes of divine presence. Here creation reveals the divine because nature is infused, enlivened or permeated with sacred presence. This bond between nature and spirit can be either pantheism, or panentheism: the latter understanding God to be within and beyond the world, both

5. See Conradie, "Contemporary Challenges to Christian Ecotheology."

immanent and transcendent. In this understanding the natural world can be in the image and likeness of God. Nature does not simply point to a way to understand God; it reveals God.

A final way of connecting spirit and nature considers spirituality to be an integral dimension of the cosmos, Earth, nature and us. This involves seeing ourselves as embedded in the natural world, part of an Earth community. We are nature. We are nature reflecting on itself, we are nature with a concept of nature (Susan Griffin[6]). Other expressions are that humans are living matter (Vladimir Vernadsky), or walking talking minerals (Margulis and Sagan[7]), or the Earth walking. Some have described humanity as the self-consciousness element of Earth's crust, or the Earth reflecting back on itself.[8]

To take seriously that we are of the Earth or a living dimension of the Earth is an immense challenge to the customary Christian worldview. It pushes us not only to *rediscover* the spirit in nature, but also to grapple with *who we are* in the scheme of creation, this biosphere or Earth community. In this configuration, we cannot understand who we are outside of the Earth community.

In order to heal the split between spirit and nature, we need to re-examine the meaning of creation. From my stance, there is no "creation" other than the one in which we inhabit. It extends to the boundaries of the universe, although the immediate vicinity is the Earth. And creation, this planet, is entering an ecological crisis with unprecedented causes and proportions. Therefore to address the theme of creation means to learn about this Earth, through the natural sciences. It means learning something about the natural world: the biosphere, evolution, and Earth dynamics.

As far as we know, creation begins 13.8 billion years ago. To grasp the complexity and resourcefulness of creation is to understand, even minimally, the processes and patterns of the universe, including the formation of galaxies, solar systems, and our blue/green planet. Earth, 4.5 billion years, is the only planet we know that has spawned life. To discern the spiritual in creation is to know something about the biosphere: this sphere of life, and its evolution, diversity, density, emergent processes, and interconnections. Understanding evolution is key to perceiving anew the spiritual in creation, with a restored integration of science and spirituality.

6. Griffin, *Woman and Nature.*

7. Margulis and Sagan, *Dazzle Gradually*, 49.

8. Berry, *Dream of the Earth*, 198.

Revolution of Evolution

What is Evolution? Evolution is not merely an idea, a theory or a concept, but is the name of a process of nature (Ernst Mayr).

Evolution describes the processes of the natural world, from the origins of life to the present. It addresses the dynamics between a common genetic base of life and the mechanisms of population change over generations: or descent with modification. While seemingly simple, contemporary notions of evolution refer to a multidisciplinary synthesis, consensus or mosaic, building on but far beyond Darwin or neo-Darwinian notions of natural selection.[9] The term evolution represents the combination and assimilation of immense quantities of data from geology and plate tectonics to particular amino acid reactions in biochemistry, coming from dozens of disciplines. The overwhelming agreement is that evolution is not a hypothesis: it is the developing descriptions of the dynamic and organic processes of life on Earth.[10] Evolution indicates that processes of nature are living and dynamic, not orderly or mechanistic, neither random nor determined. It is patterned but not predictable.

Earth has generated several periods of life expansion and complexifications, interspersed with four or five mass extinctions. The last massive extinction was sixty-five million years ago, with the demise of the impressive dinosaurs. Evolutionary processes generated life again, but the recovery of biodiversity was chaotic.[11] Millions of years were needed to regenerate and innovate pathways for the emergence of life and the egression of our era, the Cenozoic: the age of birds, fish, flowers and mammals. This era has generated the greatest diversity of life, most complex interactions.

Mammals thrived, developing hooves or pads, composite vision, placenta, grinding teeth, herbivore and carnivore digestive tracts, and forms of consciousness. Many animals developed relationship structures and/or bonding patterns: pods, herds, packs, flocks, colonies, hives, prides, gaggles. Diversity and complexity are characteristics of the Cenozoic. From mammals emerged multiple species of primates. From twenty-three million years ago there is evidence of the first hominids, evolved from bonobos

9. For a detailed explanation of the multiple meanings of evolution see Meyer and Keas, "The Meanings of Evolution."

10. There are intense debates concerning which are the primary evolutionary mechanisms—for instance, concerning the role of behavioral changes or genetic mutations, and whether evolution is merely *matter in motion* or if change occurs from multiple pressures and innovations. I am presenting evolution using recent interpretations suggesting that the processes are dynamic, organic, intricate, interrelated, and composite.

11. See Wilf, et al., "Decoupled Plant and Insect Diversity."

and chimpanzees (98.77 percent of DNA base pairs are identical between humans and chimpanzees). This animal was bipedal four million years ago, with a shift from *homo erectus* to *homo sapiens* four to three hundred thousand years ago. Here is a creature with technological savvy, greater memory, elaborate brain functions, symbolic representation, culture, language and self-consciousness. We too are emergent from and part of evolutionary development processes of the Cenozoic era of Earth. All our attributes and sensibilities have evolved from Earth processes.

What is known now about evolution can induce a revolution of awareness of what is meant by "creation;" that is, the history of the biosphere, of human emergence from and embeddedness in processes of the natural world, and of the elaborate life generating capacity of the Earth community. To take evolution seriously is to change reference points. It means genuinely situating ourselves within, not apart from or as the final note of, a compelling, ever-changing symphony of life. Evolution provides us with a time line, of histories that do not involve us, of our kinship with other animals, and of seeing our radical dependency on innumerable organisms for basic survival. Evolution bends the mind, expands the horizon, and reverses the reference points. Earth is not our context: it is our source.[12] Evolution beckons us to become scientifically literate, and to situate ourselves in a larger physical and spirituality reality, in a larger horizon of meaning. This change in reference points opens the doors to considering a spirituality abiding in and emanating from creation.

We begin to see ourselves as more than living "with nature," or succumbing to the forces of nature. We are nature, and are one of the forces of nature. We emerged from, are embedded in and surrounded by immense life-projects. We are the only species to develop a particular conscious awareness of the emergent process whence we came. My purpose here is to accentuate the depth of continuity between the Earth processes and ourselves. This does not override differentiations, or ignore the innumerable distinctions between nature and culture, the social constructions of nature, or that our lives are replete with mediated experiences. We need to recognize that we live on a thin layer of culture over a vast expanse of nature.

To persistently speak of humans and "the environment" is ridiculous in the face of interrelated planetary dynamics, evolutionary processes, and emergent complexities. To presume sharp demarcations between humans and "nature" is the norm. Herein lies one of the axial lines within the operative religious imagination that hampers awareness that spirituality is

---

12. This awareness permeates the work of Thomas Berry, but at a cosmic level. My comment is adapted from Haught, *Deeper than Darwin*.

intrinsic to the natural world. Increasingly it is recognized that we know very little of the deep realities of the Earth, and its 4.4-billion-year geo-genesis. Consideration of evolution invites attentiveness to processes of emergence, complexity, diversity, patterns, ingenuity and interrelations. Theories of emergent complexity, ingenuity, entanglement, relationality and new materialism have developed from the scientific explorations into countless interconnected systems and relations intertwined throughout the biosphere.

When evolution is the starting point for a reflection on rediscovering the spiritual in creation, then spirituality is situated in much larger process-es. Furthermore, an evolutionary perspective requires that we think more about the nature of religion, of religious consciousness, and what experi-ences and knowledge are represented by spiritual sensibilities.

The Natural World is Revelatory

Relationships between religious/spiritual experiences and the natural world are fundamental to most religions and many cultures. They are powerful, animating, orienting experiences. Wonder and awe are classical responses to spiritual awakenings and attentiveness to the natural world. Religious texts, poets, mystics and nature writers are replete with expressions of wonder and awe that blend nature and spirit. The natural world has been a primary source of spiritual insight, guidance and inspiration for millennia.

When we learn something of evolution, these same sensibilities are engaged. How can we not marvel? Evolution tells tales beyond our wildest fantasies: sea creatures as large as elephants become a type of amphibian, then wolf-like, and then return to the sea as a mammal: the contemporary whales.[13] To understand, even minimally, the immense and elaborate plan-etary hydrologic cycle is stunning and breathtaking. What little we know of Earth's intricacies dazzles the human imagination. From the genetic and mi-crobiotic aspects to the dinosaurs, the processes and life forms are incred-ible. If we attend, even momentarily, to the elegance of birds, the ingenuity of insect communication, and the emotions of mammals, how is it possible not to be thrilled and inspired by the creativity, diversity, power and beauty?

Furthermore, we are within this evolutionary process. In our totality we are of the Earth. We are Earthlings. The Earth is our origin, our nourish-ment, and our guide. Human life, in all its complexity and diversity, is best understood in continuity with the processes and dynamics of the universe, within the evolutionary activities of Earth. This means that our spirituality

13. See Gingerich, et al., "Origin of Whales."

itself is Earth-derived. Phrased differently, if humans have developed a sensibility we call spiritual, it is because it developed within the planetary processes, perhaps intensified with self and symbolic consciousness.

Evolution can open up the possibility of profound spiritual experiences. We are moved, like Teilhard de Chardin, to claim we live in a divine milieu and that matter, spirit and life are intertwined in a sacred process. We can "see" a deeper reality: one that kindles the religious imagination, awakens us to the Earth, and ignites a fire to sustain life. Evolution can open awareness or consciousness to an Earth mysticism: a blend of the best of science and religion. A renewed form of Earth mysticism is required to counter ecological and evolutionary ruin. It is needed to provide sufficient psychic energy to attend to the tasks of this era, and to avoid a crippling despair. To have a religious experience of the Earth is not new, but is indispensable today. Evolution awakens the religious imagination, beyond belief.

Evolution and Christian Perspectives

To accept this view changes a great deal as to how to do theology in the face of the ecological crisis. While religion/theology and science are experiencing a renewed dialogue, and ecotheology is growing, few delve in depth into studies of evolution. It should equally be noted that evolution has not been integrated into Euro-western worldviews. Thus, for many Christians, integrating evolution, or even considering it, is not self evident, or even relevant. Science and faith are NOMA—non-overlapping magisteria—as described by Stephen Jay Gould.

For those who engage Christianity with evolution, there are several intellectual forms.[14] I will present two ways of uniting evolution and Christianity, each with distinct starting points, presuppositions, theological foundations, and spiritual priorities. Both approaches can utilize the rich themes within the Christian tradition. The difference rests on what is primary and secondary, and how one goes about rediscovering the spiritual in creation.

In the first, the natural world is valued spiritually and ethically because Christianity affirms this to be true. Christianity is viewed as a decisive and ultimate framework, and thus evolution is integrated into a Christian horizon and worldview. The natural world would be deemed as spiritual in

---

14. In this chapter I am not discussing creationism, which in all its forms is a doctrinaire, ideological, unscientific, and anti-intellectual worldview. Intelligent design is significantly more complex, diverse, and intellectually compelling than creationism. My proposition does not accept the teleology of ID and conflicts with creationism. See Eaton, "Revolution of Evolution."

so far as the Christian tradition can either integrate the natural world into a fall-redemption theology, or strengthen the creation-based spiritualities mentioned earlier. Theologies of "Intelligent Design" are a good example of this engagement. New interpretations of Christianity are coming forth, suggesting that the natural world is part of a creation that is good, evolving, and in process. Other efforts, such as those of the World Council of Churches on Justice Peace and Integrity of Creation would be an example of an anthropocentric orientation, yet accepting human dependence on the natural world. Together these efforts position evolution within various Christian frameworks.

The second form is where the spiritual dimension of the natural world is foundational and intrinsic. It is a dimension woven into the fabric of the universe. The Christian traditions, along with all religious and spiritual traditions, are expressions of, and responsive to, this spiritual dimension. My view is that we need to situate Christianity, indeed all religious traditions, into a much larger human history, which is further nested into the Cenozoic era, and into Earth history. If one considers that a spiritual dimension of the natural world is inherent, then the natural world is a starting point for comprehending spiritual sensibilities. This means that neither the bible nor the tradition are appropriate starting points for perceiving, let alone retrieving, a spirituality in creation. Dogmas, doctrine, church fathers and mothers are not the key interlocutors. Fall-redemption salvation theologies are not the ultimate frameworks. Christianity, or any religion, is not the central revelation. Humanity is not the principal reference point. The issue is about starting points: if we have spiritual sensibilities it is because they are embedded in and developed from Earth's processes.

We would need to accept the edict that the Earth is primary and that humans are derivative, as comments Thomas Berry. This means we must understand something about evolution to understand anything about this spirit-infused world. We must have theories about religions that consider their emergence in the planetary history, and within hominid development. Religions would be understood as part of the evolution of symbolic consciousness. In this vein, religions can be appreciated as diverse, profound expressions, or languages, about the depth, breadth, complexity and boundaries of existence. They are experiential in essence, and revelatory about intense encounters with the exigencies and myriad dimensions of life, experienced and expressed in highly symbolic language. They bond human communities and assist in forging intimate relations with the broader Earth community. Religious ideas link humans to the larger matrix of indeterminacy and mystery from which life arises, unfolds, and flourishes.

Earth is not our context; it is our birthplace, affirming that humanity belongs here, in the natural world, embedded in creation. Humanity, along with the entire natural world, is an emergent process of a spectacularly creative and ingenious evolutionary reality. Evolution strengthens rather than diminishes the importance of religious consciousness, but requires concentrated theological rethinking.[15]

A Spiritual Vision

To rediscover the spiritual in creation means to rethink creation. It is no longer intelligent to speak of creation without learning about evolution. However, in general theology has not taken evolution seriously, on the terms of evolution. There is a generation of ecotheologians who have ventured far into an evolutionary, ecological frame of reference. In recent history there is Sallie McFague, John Haught, Rosemary Radford Ruether, Anne Primavasi, Ian Barbour, Wentzel van Huyssteen, and most notably Thomas Berry. These theologians have influenced countless more to deeply rethink anew the relationship between spirituality and creation. There is a direct relationship between the topic of spirituality, theology, the natural world and the increasing ecological crisis. The retrieval of nature to the Christian horizon is occurring, due to intense ecotheology efforts over the past thirty years. However, the integration of evolution has not yet transpired in any extensive or effective manner. In fact, Haught argues that much of the reluctance of Christian theology to address ecological issues in depth stems from a prior reluctance to think about evolution.

What I am presenting here in discussing spirituality and creation is not a spirituality that is directed toward a spiritual appreciation of the Earth. Nor is it enlarging our spirituality to incorporate Earth. Nor is it to increase our metaphors for God to include nature. I am suggesting that whatever we call spirituality is essentially an active process, and an embedded dimension of all reality: an entanglement of immanence and transcendence, animating Earth and developed in at least human species. This is the starting point to perceive the breadth and depth of what spirituality in creation can mean. This position is within the trajectory of Hildegard of Bingen, Teilhard de Chardin, Thomas Berry and others who immersed themselves in discerning the spiritual in creation, informed by an intellectual breadth and interior depth that rarely exists today.

---

15. See Eaton, "Revolution of Evolution."

Rediscovering the Spiritual in Creation:
New Meaning to Salvation and Spirituality

For Teilhard de Chardin, creation is ongoing, as are revelation and salvation. These are intertwined processes of increasing concentration and intensity, embedded in evolutionary progressions of increasing complexity that thicken the nature of all reality. This means that at a foundational level, there is continuity, mutual entanglement and co-evolution among matter, spirit, consciousness, self-consciousness and interiority. Spirituality is an integral aspect within the larger contexts of creative dynamics of evolutionary processes. Salvation is an activity within creation. There is no salvation as a deliverance from the created and creative order.

Christian theology in its operative forms is ill equipped to move to such an evolutionary paradigm. The fall-redemption scaffold is unable to incorporate these views. They require a new theological scaffold. Why such a bold claim? I offer two reasons.

The first is that religions cannot be the starting point for a reflection on spirituality in nature. It needs to be within an evolutionary process. To accept a spiritual awareness is to consider its developmental origins, prior to and within the evolution of hominids. This requires an understanding of the emergence of symbolic consciousness, out of which a responsive spiritual sensibility emerges.[16] These sensibilities are later expressed in religious imagery and language. It should also be noted that this symbolic, metaphoric and imaginative mode of being is the *modus operandi* of humans. A symbolic consciousness is the way humans process and navigate the world. It is not through or with symbols or images that we think and comprehend. It is within symbols. Religions are symbolic languages that engender symbolic representations of the world. Part of religious worldviews is the intricate dance between spirituality, interiority, life-experiences and the natural world.

For this to occur, Christian theology needs to know itself as a symbolic and mythic language, and grapple directly with the realms of the imagination, the experiential bases, and the trans-rational, aesthetic, and emotional expressions. Christian efforts need to not only engage in interreligious

---

16. This understanding of symbolic consciousness comes from several sources: the biological anthropologist Terrence Deacon in *The Symbolic Species*; John W. Dixon, a theologian who studied the symbolic dimension of religions consciousness, especially the emergence of Neolithic awareness, in *Images of Truth*; theologian Wentzel van Huyssteen and the Gifford lecture series, *Alone in the World?*; anthropologist David Lewis-Williams in *The Mind in the Cave*; Stanley Greenspan and Stuart Shanker in *First Idea*; and anthropologist John E. Pfeiffer in *The Creative Explosion*.

dialogue, but also interpret themselves within a plurality of religions. Yet, the lack of knowledge about the plethora of historical and current religions in Christian context is appalling. Christian imperialism and certitude continue to operate. Normative meanings of doctrines, revelations and beliefs, and biblical interpretations have led to fundamentalism ubiquitous across Christian theologies. Due to this, Christianity is rarely interpreted with respect to theories of religion, contextual and cultural processes, or even within the breadth of plurality among Christianities.

The second reason is the persistent, yet intellectually feeble, promise of a better world elsewhere. How are the concepts of the fall, sin and redemption meaningful and intelligible today? Do we still believe that humans are ontologically superior to the rest of the Earth community? That we must be saved from nature? That our true destiny is elsewhere? Few tackle these questions with the depth and new thinking they deserve, at least not publicly.

Ivone Gebara offers a valuable assessment. At the basis of domination is a flight from life's provisos: vulnerability, finitude and mortality. The primal sin is negating these conditions of life, resulting in escapist spiritualities, a refusal to accept the sufferings and limits of life, and a fall into domination—of land, animals and peoples.[17] This flight has created distortions throughout theological systems. For Gebara, our salvation is found in returning to our embodied selves, refusing escapism and domination, and embracing with joy and sorrow the genuine limitations, richness and struggles of life in community and of human solidarity with all life. Death is an inherent part of the human, indeed all, reality, not that from which we are to be saved. Gebara suggests an understanding of sin, redemption, revelation, creation, nature, humanity and the divine that could provide a new scaffold for theology.

From a different viewpoint, these Christian cultural promises of a superior world permeate the psychic orientation and expectations in Euro-western contexts. As Christianity ebbs from cultural power, the commitments to a different, better world do not diminish. Once again belief about afterlife is often a refusal to accept the conditions and limits of life, an emphasis and praxis to "improve the world." Most of Christian theology is submerged in these same waters.

I think that fall-redemption theologies, and the customary beliefs about a post-death resurrection and afterlife, need to be reinterpreted in order to sharpen our appreciation for existence as given. It could heighten our awareness of an indwelling spirit or sacred presence—one in which we live and have our being. Perhaps that would be enough salvation for a lifetime.

17. Cited in Ruether, "Ecofeminism," 105.

In order to rediscover the spiritual in creation, we need to understand how it was lost. A way forward is to situate religious consciousness within the processes of the universe and earth, not the reverse. The most appropriate notion of creation is to know what we can know of the origins and development of the universe. Specifically, Earth processes are the source out of which our spiritual sensibilities and we emerged and flourished, and it is a primary reference point. Perhaps a new revelatory experience is taking place, an experience wherein human consciousness awakens to the grandeur and sacred quality of the Earth process.

We need a spiritual vision that teaches us how to be present to the Earth, on Earth's terms. Spiritualities come from the realm of insights rather than data. Spiritualities are teachers of consciousness.[18] Spirituality is like breathing, as intimate and as vital as breath. It is about desire, a zest for life, and the ability to feel awe and wonder. Spirituality is the capacity to experience reverence in the face of the immensity and elegance of existence. Developing a spiritual consciousness is often described as moving from death to life, from sleep to consciousness, from illusion to enlightenment, from confinement to liberation, or from confusion to clarity.

A spiritual vision adequate for our ecological era requires an awakening to the Earth. For this to occur we need the best of Earth sciences. Authentic respect for the natural world informs a depth of vision that leads to a most profound religious response. If we contemplate the elegance of the Earth, and the fact that we emerged from and are animated by these great processes, we are inspired and energized. Such reflection informs and sustains a vision—a place from which to think and act. Such awareness leads to a profound spiritual and ethical awakening, and insightful political actions. To see and know the Earth as such requires a new way of perceiving.

Conclusion

A great deal is at stake in this exploration of a spirituality in creation. To consider the level of ecological ruin currently occurring on Earth is devastating. That we, with our religious certainties, images of progress, and appetites for domination are destroying the extraordinary life communities—of which we know almost nothing—is a moral and ecological sin of unspeakable proportions. This is also a spiritual depravity.

As Norman Habel has written, "to violate the Earth is to tear God's masks, to scar God's physical face, to desecrate God's earthly dwelling."[19]

18. Eaton, "Responding to Climate Change."

19. See Habel, "Key Ecojustice Principles."

Thomas Berry writes: "The natural world is the larger sacred community to which we belong. To become alienated from this community is to become destitute in all that makes us human. To damage this community is to diminish our own existence."[20] A diminished Earth will dull our spiritual sensitivities and awareness. Our horizons will shrink; inner lives wither, and spirituality will expire. Berry continues: "So integral is our inner world with the outer world that if this outer world is damaged, then the inner life of our souls is diminished proportionately."[21]

We need a spiritual awakening. This creation based theological orientation does not respond directly to all our religious concerns. It does not address oppression, structural violence, and the interlocking mechanisms of domination. It addresses inspiration. What will inspire, inspirit us to reawaken to the natural world? We need to be bold, to claim, with confidence, a spirituality in creation. If we don't the loss will be unthinkable.

Bibliography

Berry, Thomas. *The Christian Future and the Fate of Earth*, edited by Mary Evelyn Tucker and John Grim. Maryknoll, NY: Orbis, 2009.

———. *The Dream of the Earth*, San Francisco: Sierra Club, 1988.

Conradie, Ernst M. "Contemporary Challenges to Christian Ecotheology: Some Reflections on the State of the Debate after Five Decades." Paper delivered at the Ecumenical Institute of Bossey, Switzerland, May 2013.

Cousins, Elwert. "Convergence of Cultures and Religions in Light of the Evolution of Consciousness." *Zygon* 34 (1998) 209–19.

Deacon, Terrence, *The Symbolic Species: The Co-Evolution of Language and the Brain*. New York: Norton, 1998.

Dixon, John W., Jr. *Images of Truth: Religion and the Art of Seeing*. Ventures in Religion 3. Atlanta: Scholars, 1996.

Eaton, Heather. "Creation: God, Humans and the Natural World." *Concilium* 4 (2012) 56–66.

———. "An Ecological Imaginary: Evolution and Religion in an Ecological Era." In *Ecological Awareness: Exploring Religion, Ethics and Aesthetics*, edited by Sigurd Bergmann and Heather Eaton, 7–23. Studies in Religion and the Environment/ Studien zur Religion und Umwelt 3. Berlin: LIT Verlag, 2011.

———. "Forces of Nature: Aesthetics and Ethics." In *Aesth/Ethics in Environmental Change: Hiking through the Arts, Ecology, Religion and Ethics of the Environment*, edited by Sigurd Bergmann et al., 109–26. Studies in Religion and the Environment/ Studien zur Religion und Umwelt 7. Berlin: LIT Verlag 2013.

———. "Insights from Evolution, Cosmology and Earth Sciences." In *ECOTHEE: Ecological Theology and Environmental Ethics*, edited by Lucas Andrianos et al., 407–26. Kolympari: Orthodox Academy of Crete, 2009.

20. Berry, *Dream of the Earth*, 81.

21. Berry, *The Christian Future*, 60.

———. "Responding to Climate Change: Reflections on Scientific Realities, Spiritual Imperatives." *The Ecumenist* 45 (2008) 1–4.

———. "The Revolution of Evolution." *Worldviews: Environment, Culture, Religion* 111 (2007) 6–31.

———. "Subjectivity and Suffering: Transgenic Animals, Christianity, and the Need to Re-evaluate." *Worldviews: Global Religions, Culture and Ecology* 141 (2010) 26–57.

Eldredge, N., and S. J. Gould. "Punctuated Equilibria: An Alternative to Phyletic Gradualism." In *Models in Paleobiology*, edited by Thomas J. M. Schopf, 82–115. San Francisco: Freeman Cooper, 1972.

Gingerich, Philip D., et al. "Origin of Whales from Early Artiodactyls: Hands and Feet of Eocene Protocetidae from Pakistan." *Science* 293 (2001) 2239-42.

Goodenough, Ursula. *The Sacred Depths of Nature*. New York: Oxford University Press, 2000.

Gould, Stephen Jay. *The Structure of Evolutionary Theory*. Cambridge, MA: Belknap, 2002.

Greenspan, Stanley I., and Stuart G. Shanker. *The First Idea: How Symbols, Language, and Intelligence Evolved from Our Primate Ancestors to Modern Humans*. Cambridge, MA: De Capo, 2004.

Gregerson, Neils H., ed. *From Complexity to Life: On the Emergence of Life and Meaning*. Oxford: Oxford University Press, 2005.

Griffin, Susan. *Woman and Nature: The Roaring Inside Her*. New York: Harper Colophon, 1980.

Habel, Norman. "Key Ecojustice Principles: A *Theologia Crucis* Perspective." *Ecotheology* 5–6 (1998) 114-25.

Harding, Stephen. *Animate Earth: Science, Intuition and Gaia*. White River Junction, VT: Chelsea Green, 2006.

Haught, John. *Deeper than Darwin: The Prospect for Religion in the Age of Evolution*. Boulder: Westview, 2003.

———. *The Promise of Nature: Ecology and Cosmic Purpose*. New York: Paulist, 1993.

Kauffmann, Stuart A. *Reinventing the Sacred: A New View of Science, Reason and Religion*. New York: Perseus, 2008.

Lewis-Williams, David. *The Mind in the Cave, Consciousness and the Origins of Art*. New York: Thames & Hudson, 2002.

Margulis, Lynn, and Dorion Sagan. *Dazzle Gradually: Reflections on the Nature of Nature*. White River Junction, VT: Chelsea Green, 2007.

Mayr, Ernst. *What Evolution Is*. New York: Basic, 2001.

Meyer, S.C., and M.N. Keas. "The Meanings of Evolution." In *Darwinism, Design and Public Education*, edited by John Angus Campbell and Stephen C. Meyer, 135–56. East Lansing: Michigan State University Press, 2003.

Pearson, C. "On Being Public about Ecotheology." *Ecotheology* 6.1–2 (2001) 42–59.

Pfeiffer, John E., *The Creative Explosion: An Inquiry into the Origins of Art and Religion*. New York: Horizon, 1986.

Ruether, Rosemary Radford. "Ecofeminism: The Challenge to Theology." In *Christianity and Ecology: Seeking the Well-Being of Earth and Humans*, edited by Dieter T. Hessel and Rosemary Radford Ruether, 113–26. Cambridge: Harvard University Press, 2000.

Taylor, Charles. *Modern Social Imaginaries*. Durham: Duke University Press, 2004.

van Huyssteen, J. Wentzel. *Alone in the World? Science and Theology on Human Uniqueness.* Gifford Lectures 2004. Grand Rapids: Eerdmans, 2004.

Voland, Eckart, and Karl Grammer, eds. *Evolutionary Aesthetics.* New York: Springer, 2003.

Wilf, Peter, et al. "Decoupled Plant and Insect Diversity after the End-Cretaceous Extinction." *Science* 313 (2006) 1112–15.

www.ingramcontent.com/pod-product-compliance
Lightning Source LLC
Chambersburg PA
CBHW071849270326
41929CB00013B/2161